Affective Economies, Neoliberalism, and Governmentality

Advanced capitalism is characterised by a level of symbolic production that not only results in a dematerialisation of labour, but also increasingly relies on highly emotional components, ranging from consumption desire to workforce management. Feelings as varied as love, anger, and desire are integral to neoliberal processes, though not in unproblematic and monolithic ways. Whereas some accounts decry capitalism's hold on the emotional realm, as the commodified search for soul mates through online dating sites or Starbucks' promotion of fair-trade coffee suggest, others counter that emotions represent a privileged site of resistance to market rationality. Relying on different case studies ranging from drone strikes, the 2008 economic crisis in Ireland, and marriage migration management, this volume builds on this productive tension between subjection and resistance through the lenses of the concept of governmentality. Developed by Michel Foucault, governmentality sheds light on the ways in which economic and political life are now being managed through logics of security and economic calculations. This volume explores how individuals might become emotionally attached to regimes of power that are detrimental to them, how neoliberal processes are concomitant with the valorisation of certain emotional dispositions, and how affective economies might provide a site of resistance.

This book was originally published as a special issue of *Global Society*.

Anne-Marie D'Aoust is an Assistant Professor in the Department of Political Science at the Université du Québec à Montréal. Her research focuses on the connections between love, governmentality, and security practices. Her recent publications appeared in *International Political Sociology* and *Disciplining the Transnational Mobility of People* (Palgrave Macmillan, 2013).

Affective Economies, Neoliberalism, and Governmentality

Edited by
Anne-Marie D'Aoust

Routledge
Taylor & Francis Group
LONDON AND NEW YORK

First published 2015 by Routledge

2 Park Square, Milton Park, Abingdon, Oxon OX14 4RN
711 Third Avenue, New York, NY 10017, USA

Routledge is an imprint of the Taylor & Francis Group, an informa business

First issued in paperback 2017

British Library Cataloguing in Publication Data
A catalogue record for this book is available from the British Library

ISBN 13: 978-1-138-84394-3 (hbk)
ISBN 13: 978-1-138-05800-2 (pbk)

Typeset in Palatino
by RefineCatch Limited, Bungay, Suffolk

Contents

Citation Information

The chapters in this book were originally published in the *Global Society*, volume 28, issue 3 (July 2014). When citing this material, please use the original page numbering for each article, as follows:

Chapter 1
Ties that Bind? Engaging Emotions, Governmentality and Neoliberalism: Introduction to the Special Issue
Anne-Marie D'Aoust
Global Society, volume 28, issue 3 (July 2014) pp. 267–276

Chapter 2
Parrhēsia Today: Drone Strikes, Fearless Speech and the Contentious Politics of Security
William Walters
Global Society, volume 28, issue 3 (July 2014) pp. 277–299

Chapter 3
The Capitalisation of 'Excess Life' through Life Insurance
Luis Lobo-Guerrero
Global Society, volume 28, issue 3 (July 2014) pp. 300–316

Chapter 4
Love as Project of (Im)Mobility: Love, Sovereignty and Governmentality in Marriage Migration Management Practices
Anne-Marie D'Aoust
Global Society, volume 28, issue 3 (July 2014) pp. 317–335

Chapter 5
No Good Deed Goes Unrewarded: The Values/Virtues of Transnational Volunteerism in Neoliberal Capital
Wanda Vrasti and Jean Michel Montsion
Global Society, volume 28, issue 3 (July 2014) pp. 336–355

Chapter 6

"Retail Therapy in the Dragon's Den": Neoliberalism and Affective Labour in the Popular Culture of Ireland's Financial Crisis
Nicholas J. Kiersey
Global Society, volume 28, issue 3 (July 2014) pp. 356–374

Chapter 7

Affective Economies in the Governance of Trafficking and Sex Work in Vietnam
Nadine Voelkner
Global Society, volume 28, issue 3 (July 2014) pp. 375–390

Please direct any queries you may have about the citations to clsuk.permissions@cengage.com

Ties that Bind? Engaging Emotions, Governmentality and Neoliberalism: Introduction

ANNE-MARIE D'AOUST

This introduction to the special issue on "Emotions, Governmentality and Neoliberalism" situates the theme inside the recent International Relations literature devoted to emotions and affect. This literature misses an engagement with governmentality, notably because Michel Foucault's prime concern with practical rationalities, such as "the conduct of conduct" in the case of governmentality, led to an assumption that these were devoid of emotional dimensions. Paying attention to governmentality allows us to examine how emotions and rationality actually intermingle, notably by putting the body at the centre of analysis in ways that do not make it the locus of a pre-social "affect." All six contributions to the special issue are then individually discussed around the three key dimensions they all seek to address and emphasise: (1) the ways in which emotions partake in relations of power, sometimes to the point where individuals can become emotionally attached to regimes of power that hurt them; (2) the ways in which neoliberal processes are concomitant with the enclosure and valorisation of certain subjective/emotional dispositions; and, finally (3) the ways in which emotions can challenge or exceed existing relations of power.

Despite the fact that we are far from being able to identify an emotional or affective turn in International Relations (IR), there has been a renewed interest in the subject in recent years, to the point that "articles on the topic are increasingly less likely to begin by noting that the study of emotions is a recent occurrence in IR and there is more work to be done."[1] Indeed, most conventional works that consider emotions as a key variable in explaining state behaviour[2] or even geopolitics[3] now coexist

1. B. Sasley, "Emotions in International Relations", *E-International Relations*, 12 June 2013, available: <http://www.e-ir.info/2013/06/12/emotions-in-international-relations/> (accessed 17 September 2013).

2. N.C. Crawford, "The Passion of World Politics: Propositions on Emotion and Emotional Relationships", *International Security*, Vol. 24, No. 4 (2000), pp. 116–156; J. Mercer, "Human Nature and the First Image: Emotion and International Politics", *Journal of International Relations and Development*, Vol. 9, No. 3 (2006), pp. 288–303; B.E. Sasley, "Theorizing State Emotions", *International Studies Review*, Vol. 13, No. 3 (2011), pp. 452–476.

3. Dominic Moisi, *The Geopolitics of Emotions: How Cultures of Fear, Humiliation and Hope Are Reshaping the World* (London: Bodley Head, 2009).

alongside more critical scholarship—ranging from constructivist[4] to feminist,[5] poststructuralist[6] and postcolonial works[7]—that examine how emotions come about and imbue political life. Parallel to this renewed engagement with emotions, scholars began to address the issue of affect and its relevance in world politics.[8] Affect is here seen as preceding cognition, as being experienced as a physical intensity. This double engagement certainly reflects the difference that many scholars make between the two terms, following the famous distinction proposed by cultural scholar Brian Massumi:

> An emotion is a subjective content, the socio-linguistic fixing of the quality of an experience which is from that point onward defined as personal. Emotion is qualified intensity, the conventional, consensual point of insertion of intensity into semantically and semiotically formed progressions, into narrativizable action-reaction circuits, into function and meaning. *It is intensity owned and recognized.* It is crucial to theorize the difference between affect and emotion. If some have the impression that it has waned, it is because affect is unqualified. As such, it is not ownable or recognizable, and is thus resistant to critique.[9]

This flourishing scholarship is certainly not limited to IR. In fact, several scholars have pointed to an emotional or an affective turn in disciplines as varied as sociology, geography and anthropology, if not the whole of social sciences. While several factors can explain this renewed engagement, Ruth Leys draws our attention to the fact that it appears to be closely tied to broader epistemological anxieties, along with a sense that our world has been increasingly falling into the grip of (global) governmentality.[10] Governmentality, as Michel Foucault explained, refers to the conduct of conduct, to "the ensemble formed by institutions, procedures, analyses and reflections, calculation, and tactics that allow

---

4. B.J. Steele, *Ontological Security in International Relations: Self-Identity and the IR State* (London and New York: Routledge, 2008); Janice Bialley Mattern, "Emotional Practices in World Politics", in E. Adler and V. Pouliot (eds.), *The Practice Turn in International Relations* (Cambridge: Cambridge University Press, 2008), pp. 63–86.

5. Rachel Pain, "Globalized Fear? Toward an Emotional Geopolitics", *Progress in Human Geography*, Vol. 33, No. 4 (2009), pp. 466–486; R. Soreanu, "Feminist Scholarship in International Relations and the Politics of Disciplinary Emotion", *Millennium—Journal of International Studies*, Vol. 37, No. 1 (2008), pp. 123–151; M. Zalewski, "Theorizing Emotion: Affective Borders in *Homeland*", *Critical Studies on Security*, Vol. 1, No. 1 (2013), pp. 133–135.

6. R. Bleiker, "The Aesthetic Turn in International Political Theory", *Millennium: Journal of International Studies*, Vol. 30, No. 3 (2001), pp. 509–533; R. Bleiker and E. Hutchison, "Fear No More: Emotions and World Politics", *Review of International Studies*, Vol. 34, Supp. S1 (2008), pp. 115–135.

7. L.H.M. Ling, *Postcolonial International Relations: Conquest and Desire between Asia and the West* (London: Palgrave Macmillan, 2002).

8. A.G. Ross, *Mixed Emotions: Beyond Fear and Hatred in International Conflicts* (Chicago, IL: University of Chicago Press, 2013).

9. B. Massumi, "The Autonomy of Affect", *Cultural Critique*, Vol. 31 (1995), p. 88. My emphasis.

10. For different takes on the "global" nature of governmentality, see W. Larner and W. Walters (eds.), *Global Governmentality: Governing International Spaces* (London and New York: Routledge, 2004); M. Doucet and M. de Larrinaga (eds.), *Security and Global Governmentality: Globalization, Governance and the State* (Abingdon and New York: Routledge, 2008); N. Kiersey, "World State or Global Governmentality? Constitutive Power and Resistance in a Post-Imperial World", *Global Change, Peace and Security*, Vol. 20, No. 3 (2008), pp. 357–374; J. Joseph, "Poverty Reduction and the New Global Governmentality", *Alternatives: Global, Local, Political*, Vol. 35, No 1 (2010), pp. 29–51.

the exercise of this very specific, albeit very complex, power that has the population as its target, political economy as its major form of knowledge and apparatuses of security as its essential technical instrument."[11]

This understanding of the rationalisation of life, argues Leys, leads contemporary scholars to carefully characterise emotions and affect as non-rationality, thus in effect reproducing the very dichotomy between emotion and rationality they sought to question in the first place. From Nigel Thrift to William Connelly and Brian Massumi, she claims that what

> motivates these scholars is the desire to contest a certain account of how, in their view, political argument and rationality have been thought to operate. These theorists are gripped by the notion that most philosophers and critics in the past (Kantians, neo-Kantians, Habermasians) have overvalued the role of reason and rationality in politics, ethics, and aesthetics, with the result that they have given too flat or "unlayered" or disembodied an account of the ways in which people actually form their political opinions and judgments.[12]

But Foucault's prime concern with practical rationalities, such as "the conduct of conduct" in the case of governmentality, does not mean that they are devoid of emotional dimensions. Advanced capitalism, for instance, is characterised by a level of symbolic production that not only results in a dematerialisation of labour, but also increasingly relies on highly emotional components, ranging from consumption desire to workforce management. Feelings as varied as love, anxiety, anger and desire are integral to neoliberal processes, though not in unproblematic and monolithic ways.[13] Whereas some accounts decry capitalism's hold on the emotional realm, as the commodified search for soul mates through the use of online dating sites or Starbucks' promotion of fair trade coffee appear to suggest, others counter that emotions in fact might represent the privileged site of resistance to market rationality. Again, such binary perspectives, as human geographer Nancy Ettlinger critically points out, often reflect an ontological discursive commitment to consider emotions as either integral to capitalism or as belonging to a sphere of resistance distinct from it.[14]

Governmentality and Emotions

Paying attention to governmentality allows us to examine how emotions and rationality actually intermingle, notably by putting the body at the centre of analysis in ways that do not make it the locus of a pre-social "affect." In fact, we need to be wary of drawing too sharp a distinction between emotions and affect. Keeping this distinction implicitly reproduces an assumption that "a model of human subjectivity exists, one that pits the self against social norms and 'true feeling' against convention, thus reproducing the divide between experience and expression

11. M. Foucault, *Security, Territory, Population: Lectures at the Collège de France, 1977–1978*, trans. G. Burchell (Basingstoke: Palgrave Macmillan, 2007), p. 108.

12. R. Leys, "The Turn to Affect: A Critique", *Critical Inquiry*, Vol. 37, No. 3 (2011), p. 436.

13. For an overview, see W. Vrasti, "'Caring Capitalism' and the Duplicity of Critique", *Theory and Event*, Vol. 14, No. 4 (2011), <http://muse.jhu.edu/journals/theory_and_event/toc/tae.14.4.html>.

14. N. Ettlinger, "Whose Capitalism? Mean Discourse and/or Actions of the Heart", *Emotion, Space and Society*, Vol. 2, No. 1 (2009), pp. 92–107.

(ruled by norms or 'discourse')."[15] In other words, to paraphrase Scheer, insisting on the distinction between affect and emotions leads to an unintended understanding that expressions of emotions is the proper domain of social scientific studies, leaving "the body" as a proper stable and ahistorical site of affect that needs to be understood through the "natural sciences," such as neurosciences.

Whereas Foucault himself did not engage much with emotions, his thorough engagement with the body entails that they do have a bearing on the ways in which we should conceive of governmentality and its workings. Emotions can certainly be seen as yet another instrumental way through which practical rationalities can be enacted or as an effect of specific power/knowledge relations subjected to historical and social variations. Understood in this way, emotions are usually only noted in passing in works relying on governmentality as a key framework as either technologies of government "imbued with aspirations for the shaping of conduct in the hope of producing certain desired effects,"[16] or as socially conditioned desired states (of happiness, wisdom, etc.) individually attainable through technologies of the self.[17] While relevant, these readings tend to overemphasise the rationality of emotional expression, deployment and management. Even more, they often neglect the important role of emotional excess in management practices, as well as the discrepancy between actual emotional practices and discourses of emotional management.[18]

As Monique Scheer insists, we need to forego a linear understanding of emotions whereby they are seen as triggered responses to an event or a situation: "The claim that emotions 'happen to' the subject splits mind from body, locating the subject in the mind. On this reading, the emotions are viewed as outside the subject and thus acquire a sort of autonomy."[19] Emotions are not free-floating forces, but they are also not something "we" possess:

> Emotions are not a property—that is, something that I or we have. Rather, the surface of bodies "surfaces" as an effect of the impressions left by others. Emotions produce the very surfaces and boundaries by which specific kinds of objects can be delineated. In this respect the objects of emotions "circulate". As they move through the circulations of objects such objects become "sticky" or saturated with effect, as sites of personal and social tension or contestation, as emotions are "made". Emotions are thus a form of world-making, which allow us

15. M. Scheer, "Are Emotions a Kind of Practice (And Is That What Makes Them Have a History)? A Bourdieusian Approach to Understanding Emotion", *History and Theory*, Vol. 51, No. 2 (2012), p. 196.

16. N. Rose, *Powers of Freedom: Reframing Political Thought* (New York: Cambridge University Press, 1999), p. 52.

17. As Foucault explained, technologies of the self "permit individuals to effect, by their own means, or with the help of others a certain number of operations on their own bodies, and souls, thoughts, conduct and way of being so as to transform themselves, in order to attain a certain state of happiness, purity, wisdom, perfection or immortality." M. Foucault, "Technologies of the Self", in L.H. Martin, H. Gutman and P.H. Hutton (eds.), *Technologies of the Self: A Seminar with Michel Foucault* (Amherst: University of Massachusetts Press, 1988), p. 18.

18. But for a different take on governmentality and love as a specific emotion, see A.M. D'Aoust, "In the Name of Love: Marriage Migration, Governmentality and Technologies of Love", *International Political Sociology*, Vol. 7, No. 3 (2013), pp. 258–274.

19. Scheer, *op. cit.*, pp. 206–207.

to address the question of how subjects come to embody both meaning and belonging.[20]

Not only are emotions central to subjectification and meaning-making, but they also cannot be dissociated from the materiality of bodies, whose very signification or "readability" hangs on emotional meaning. Because bodies are always situated, sexualised and racialised, they do not feel the same way—to ourselves, but also to others. For instance, specific emotions give a certain materiality to some bodies and not others, as Judith Butler's reflections on which bodies are grievable or not in war made clear.[21] Therefore, emotions cannot be uncoupled from relations of power that characterise and permeate the social field.

As John Protevi and others have argued, the body is central to Foucault's work, be it as an object of knowledge, a target of power or a matter of concern in technologies of the self.[22] It is precisely because emotions are central to the intelligibility of bodies, and vice versa, that they should be seen as central to the very phenomenon of the art of governing Foucault was concerned with. Therefore, when engaging with key notions such as governmentality, we need to keep in mind that emotions like happiness or self-esteem are not *simply* a by-product or consequence of subjectification processes. The latter "also operate at the level of affect, through the material production of specific modes of experience."[23]

Neoliberalism as a Regime of Emotional Governance

Despite not sharing a commitment to a singular theorisation of emotions here, all contributors nonetheless take seriously Sara Ahmed's insight that emotions should be understood as economic in themselves, as they circulate between individual and collective subjects to create, secure and challenge specific bodies and social hierarchies.[24]

As a result, whereas contributors like William Walters or Anne-Marie D'Aoust engage in discussions about the signification of specific emotions such as courage or love, others like Nicholas Kiersey or Nadine Voelkner prefer to speak of affective economies or even of emotional states, as does Luis Lobo-Guerrero.

Still, each contribution acknowledges the different dimensions and tensions inherent to discussions about such complex and loaded notions as "governmentality," "emotions" and "neoliberalism." Three dimensions especially stand out for all contributors. Each seeks to address and emphasise: (1) the ways in which emotions partake in relations of power, sometimes to the point where individuals can become emotionally attached to regimes of power that disadvantage or even hurt them; (2) the ways in which neoliberal processes are concomitant with the

20. K. Fierke, *Political Self-Sacrifice: Agency, Body and Emotion in International Relations* (Cambridge: Cambridge University Press, 2013), p. 93.

21. See J. Butler, *Precarious Life: The Powers of Mourning and Violence* (London and New York: Verso, 2004); and J. Butler, *Frames of War: When is Life Grievable?* (London and New York: Verso, 2009).

22. J. Protevi, "Body", in L. Lawlor and J. Nale (eds.), *The Cambridge Foucault Lexicon* (Cambridge: Cambridge University Press, forthcoming).

23. L. Dawney, "The Interruption: Investigating Subjectification and Affect", *Environment and Planning D: Society and Space*, Vol. 31, No. 4 (2013), p. 632.

24. See S. Ahmed, *The Cultural Politics of Emotions* (New York: Routledge, 2004); and S. Ahmed, "Affective Economies", *Social Text*, Vol. 22, No. 2 (2004), pp. 117–139.

enclosure and valorisation of certain subjective/emotional dispositions; and, finally, (3) the ways in which emotions can challenge or exceed existing relations of power.

Whereas the contributors to this special issue all examine connections between emotions, governmentality and neoliberalism, they do not understand the implications of this specific node in the same way, nor do they take their analyses in the same direction. Such variation in their theoretical inclinations and lines of inquiry is not fortuitous. For one thing, they reflect the richness of current governmentality studies, characterised by a refusal to see governmentality as being a fully formed theoretical edifice that only calls for testing or deployment in different settings. In that sense, all the authors here use Foucault's insights on governmentality as a springboard to inquiry, rather than a carefully established map to be followed.

However, and perhaps more importantly, these different trajectories reflect different contemporary ways of taking up Foucault's ambitious challenge to simultaneously take down, through his reflections on governmentality, "two 'cold monsters' at the same time: the economy and the state."[25] Ute Tellmann points out that Foucault's own project ends up being more successful at undoing "the cold monster of the state" than providing a careful analytics "of the malleable forms of temporality, spatiality and valuation inherent in the economic."[26] She insists that, when engaging with governmentality, we should pay as much attention to making "visible the market's own 'machine of seeing'"[27] as to questioning how the political ends up being conceived of as a form of economic ordering.

Nicholas Kiersey, Wanda Vrasti and Jean Michel Montsion (this issue) take this injunction seriously, and point to the fact that the market's own "machine of seeing" is inextricably linked to a machine of feeling as well. All three locate their intervention in an attempt to reconcile Foucault's notions of governmentality with Marxist criticisms of neoliberalism.[28] Here, their engagement with neoliberalism is not limited to a way of doing things in a maximised economy; it also encompasses an economic-political understanding of the term that reflects a specific development in the capitalist system. Neoliberalism monetises forms of sociality, communication, language and affect which were there all along; it uses these to reproduce its logic and produce value. From there, they ask to what extent these modes of subjectivity challenge or strengthen neoliberal economic practices. How do affective economies participate in the consolidation of various apparatuses of security? What are the sociological and political processes sustaining this new form of political economy? If neoliberalism directly taps into emotional realms such as care and compassion, what forms can resistance or emancipatory practices take, and how can they be envisioned?

---

25. U. Tellmann, "Foucault and the Invisible Economy", *Foucault Studies*, No. 6 (2009), p. 6.

26. *Ibid.*

27. *Ibid.*, p. 14 and p. 22.

28. On such attempts, see notably T. Lemke, "Foucault, Governmentality, and Critique", *Rethinking Marxism: A Journal of Economics, Culture and Society*, Vol. 14, No. 3 (2002), pp. 49–64; C. Barnett, "The Consolations of 'Neoliberalism'", *Geoforum*, Vol. 36, No. 1 (2005), pp. 7–12; J. Weidner, "Governmentality, Capitalism, and Subjectivity", *Global Society*, Vol. 23, No. 4 (2009), pp. 387–411; S. Legrand, "Le marxisme oublié de Foucault", *Actuel Marx*, No. 36 (2004), pp. 27–43; and J. Joseph, *The Social in the Global: Social Theory, Governmentality and Global Politics* (Cambridge: Cambridge University Press, 2012).

Neoliberalism, argues Graham Burchell, concerns people *"at the very heart of themselves by making its rationality the condition of their active freedom."*[29] Contesting and resisting regimes of power thus becomes even more difficult when we link them to our own sense of freedom and well-being, both emotional and physical. Through the examination of two different instances of transnational voluntarism, Vrasti and Montsion convincingly show us that emotional and capital flows are in fact aligned, and that voluntarism, far from being a selfless virtue, is congruent with neoliberalism's double injunction of market rationality and social responsibility. The idea that emotions are central to the reproduction of labour inside capitalism is not new in itself. Some authors have pointed out that Marx acknowledges emotions, notably in the *Economic and Philosophic Manuscripts of 1844*, and that "[e]motionality, including alienation, estrangement, and disenchantment with the world, translates into the economic practices that reduce individuals to being defined in monetary, labour-value terms."[30] But Vrasti and Montsion make the case that it is the *intensity* and visibility (this issue) of this reproductive process that has changed, and that needs to be addressed. Drawing from the experiences of Chinese international students volunteering in Canada, and Western students volunteering in Ghana, Vrasti and Montsion's ethnographic accounts show that voluntarism is more than personal emotional fulfilment. It is first and foremost a way to acquire much-needed emotional competencies to succeed inside global capitalism. "Being a volunteer," they insist, "is not just about feeling responsible (read: "giving back") to the community so much as about becoming a subject responsible for its own skills and assets" (this issue). In an ironic twist, voluntarism might thus not help to change the world as we know it, and challenge different relations of power, as much as help sustain social relations in ways that are congruent with the ethos of neoliberal capital.

If Vrasti and Montsion explore how a specific emotional economy might help to sustain neoliberal regimes of power and make them work on a daily basis, Kiersey, for his part, demonstrates how this emotional economy is central when such regimes come into crisis. Turning his attention to popular culture and reinvestment strategies in Ireland following the 2008 economic crisis, Kiersey details how strategies of keeping the Irish economy afloat are explicitly built on a self-conscious turn towards affective labour and affective subjectivation, the cornerstone of which remains "the ability to make people like *you* as much as, if not more than, the product you are trying to sell" (this issue). Popular Irish TV shows such as *Retail Therapy* and *Dragon's Den* are exemplary of this shift. Building on the work of autonomist Marxists and scholars of governmentality, Kiersey's piece highlights how changes in capitalism are concomitant with technologies of the self, as successful entrepreneurs depicted and praised in *Dragon's Den* and *Retail Therapy* display appropriate affective dispositions towards clients, the goods they produce, but also the national economic market. Building on

29. G. Burchell, "Liberal Government and Techniques of the Self", in A. Barry, T. Osborne and N. Rose (eds.), *Foucault and Political Reason: Liberalism, Neo-Liberalism and Rationalities of Government* (Chicago, IL: University of Chicago Press, 1996), p. 30. Emphasis in original.

30. N.K. Denzin, *On Understanding Emotion* (New Brunswick, NJ: Transaction Publishers, 2009 [1984]), 2nd edition, p. 32. For a recent re-reading of Marx's work attuned to the role of emotions in his theory of human nature, see L. Frank Weyher, "Re-reading Sociology via the Emotions: Karl Marx's Theory of Human Nature and Estrangement", *Sociological Perspectives*, Vol. 55, No. 2 (2012), pp. 341–362.

Foucault's concept of governmentality and Michael Hardt and Antonio Negri's discussions of affective labour, Kiersey invites us to reconsider how power relations play out in an economy characterised by the hegemony of immaterial and emotional labour: "By virtue of the way capitalism extracts surplus today, through the production of knowledge, desires and affects, the question of power is not simply a question of the production of this or that type of subjectivity, but rather a question of the real and intense ways in which the 'commanding heights' of the economy have become immanent through the hegemony of immaterial labour" (this issue).

Vrasti and Montsion and Kiersey's contributions highlight the development of a specific affective economy integral to social relations required by neoliberalism, envisioned as both an ideological and an economic framework. Through their respective case studies, they illustrate how this affective economy becomes a central feature of neoliberalism understood as governmentality: an art of governing.[31] Here, neoliberalism is first and foremost understood as practices, as a mode of rationalisation that produces regimes of truth. To understand how emotions become entangled in neoliberal projects and rationalities, we must turn to specific policy projects and examine how they mobilise emotions to achieve certain ends.

Nadine Voelkner's study of anti-trafficking policies in the Hau Giang province in Vietnam presents a case of the governmentalisation of shame, as women and children identified in villages at risk of trafficking become targeted as a population requiring intervention on the part of the government, the community and non-governmental organisations (NGOs). These women become equated with victims of trafficking, as both are said to result in unruly migration flows stemming from years of neoliberal economic policies and discourses of proper femininity and risk. This governmentalisation of shame also enables the government to reinvigorate a discourse on socialism and good citizenship. This renewed nationalism is specifically tied to the female body, argues Voelkner, and develops in reaction to neoliberal policies: "Vietnamese gender presents a subject through which the government and society are constituting traditions of the national Self in the face of capitalist integration" (this issue). Discourses of respectability and shame fuelled by NGOs such as the International Labour Organization (ILO) create new forms of governance where the state's ideal of femininity becomes channelled at the commune level, where NGOs train women to be good, risk-conscious, self-governing moral subjects. The state's activities become more concerned with "a probalistic ethos of riskiness" characteristic of liberal governmentality.[32]

Accounting for Contestations, Resistance and Excess

Such accounts of emotional attachment to regimes of power, along with the increasingly complex techniques of government deployed in the name of security, appear to open the window to a bleak horizon with limited possibilities of resistance and contestation. Granting that Foucault's work has first and foremost been

31. For a short overview of the distinction between neoliberal policy, ideology and governmentality, see W. Larner, "Neo-Liberalism: Policy, Ideology, Governmentality", *Studies in Political Economy*, Vol. 63 (2000), pp. 5–25.

32. W. Walters, *Governmentality: Critical Encounters* (New York: Routledge, 2012), p. 35.

espoused by scholars keen to examine the intricacies of power and securitisation processes, William Walters nevertheless insists that it has more to offer to the study of contentious politics than is currently acknowledged. Openness to resistance and contestation is thus central to Walters', Lobo-Guerrero's and D'Aoust's engagement with neoliberalism and governmentality. Foucault's concept of *parrhēsia*, Walters suggests, might help us to recast the centrality of emotions like courage in contestation practices of securitisation processes taking place inside neoliberal governance. Through a detailed analysis of the photojournalism of Noor Behram, who documented drones strikes in Pakistan, Walters examines how understanding the workings of "parrhesiastic exposure" can help us obtain a better analysis of contestation and subversion of power. Emotionality, far from being ancillary to such exposure from courageous lone individuals entangled in complex networks, is central to them, both in its unfolding and success: "Because they speak *frankly* and *courageously*, their words *might strike a chord* with the sovereign or with the demos. As a consequence, there is always *the hope* in *parrhēsia* that this frank speech will have a positive impact on the affairs of the community, and their act will be met with a certain respect rather than punishment" (this issue; emphasis added).

Foucault speaks of *parrhēsia* as "an attitude, a manner of being," and talks of "parrhesiastic games." While he casts parrhesiastic acts as games, such a presentation is clearly meant to emphasise the importance of the relations between actors involved in them, rather than their playfulness and their emotional, imaginative dimensions. Yet, if we follow Luis Lobo-Guerrero, both might end up being most central to the risk assessment practices of life insurance, along with their contestation. Life insurance and its promises, argues Lobo-Guerrero, are far from innocent practices: "They are entrenched within political imaginaries of protection, imaginaries that entail institutionalised ways of understanding what it means to promote and safeguard a way of life. They are embedded within a very particular capitalist appreciation of economics in which insurance operates as a technology of financial reparation by means of creating markets of security" (this issue). Life insurance creates value on previously dreaded events, and creates a moral economy where individuals adjust their conduct in an economy of security where practices aimed at rendering life safe are valued and encouraged. But rather than simply detailing how life insurance partakes in governmentality, Lobo-Guerrero wonders what gets sacrificed by insurers in the process of ascribing "value" to life, and how this excess of valuing process can be seen as a source of resistance inside governmentality. The excess to this valuing process, he suggests, defies the imaginative capacities of insurers, the ones that precisely make life meaningful as capital. Turning to *Code 46*, a science-fiction movie where insurance has taken over, Lobo-Guerrero details how the excess that challenges the security and risk-free existence of the insured life has a deep emotional quality to it, as a drive that "represents a space of freedom, a space of wild uncertainty, of passionate existence where anything is possible, where anything could potentially be achieved, where the magical stands a chance" (this issue). This passionate call for hope has some Deleuzian echoes to it, and speaks to affect as a life-force, a possibility.

Investigating the role of love in relation to governmentality, D'Aoust suggests that while love should be accounted for in the governmentality of marriage migrants in Europe, it cannot be seen as simply being yet another domain colonised by the cold forces of neoliberal rationality. She makes the case for understanding love as both an object of governmental calculations in projects of immobility, and a movement that participates in projects of mobility. "Love," she explains, "is movement—an idea translated in the very idea of emotional transports. . . . [W]hen it comes to marriage migration and family reunification more generally, love becomes transport, a way of travelling: love moves people across borders" (this issue). In that sense, it partakes in, while also challenging, orderly and rationalised circulation. Through an examination of different migration management practices, D'Aoust rejects an essentialist ontological understanding of love, favouring instead the idea of love as a technology. Looking at the different ways in which technologies of love are being used and deployed to contain and discipline marriage migrants, she draws attention to the excess that such uses entail, and which should be accounted for if we want to understand potential forms of resistance against this affective governance. "Technologies of love," she reminds us, "are no different from other technological artiefacts: the movement they bring about and try to foster, the relations they establish, do not always work as anticipated" (this issue). Such excess is important to account for, as it testifies to the fact that emotional governance is never complete. It allows for new forms of unanticipated openness and possible forms of resistance inside the rationalised framework of border management.

Whereas all contributors' initial empirical work has led them to consider the connections between emotions, governmentality and neoliberalism, their respective insights certainly do not exhaust all possible configurations and entanglements of emotions and rationality in the conduct of conduct. A deep concern for thinking critically about the present, and for resisting the thwarting of our political imagination when faced with governmental processes, unquestionably animated all contributors. In that sense, they are still struggling with the same epistemological concerns that gave the initial impulse to the affect literature: how can we understand emotions in relation to rationality, if we admit that both are intermingled,[33] and how do we resist the over-rationalisation of life? It may well be, therefore, that, more than an embrace of an "emotional turn" in IR, it is an embrace of the complexities of a politics of hope that we should strive for.

About the Author

Anne-Marie D'Aoust is Assistant Professor in the Department of Political Science at the Université du Québec à Montréal. Her recent publications on marriage migration have appeared in *International Political Sociology* and in Martin Geiger and Antoine Pécoud's *Disciplining the Transnational Mobility of People* (Palgrave Macmillan, 2013). Her other projects include issues of language and the sociology of the discipline of IR, and an investigation of "Security and Its Publics," carried out in collaboration with William Walters.

33. See for instance M.T. Pham, "Emotion and Rationality: A Critical Review and Interpretation of Empirical Evidence", *Review of General Psychology*, Vol. 11, No. 2 (2007), pp. 155–178.

Parrhēsia Today: Drone Strikes, Fearless Speech and the Contentious Politics of Security

WILLIAM WALTERS

Foucault is more often used to theorise political logics of securitisation than to understand the contestation of security policies. Yet Foucault's work offers a wealth of conceptual tools and ideas pertinent to the study of the contentious politics of security. In his lectures on parrhēsia *in Ancient Greece, Foucault explored the practice whereby individuals choose at great risk to confront rulers or publics with uncomfortable truths. This article argues that a refashioned concept of* parrhēsia *can illuminate certain elements of the contentious politics of security today. The article develops this claim through an examination of the photojournalism of Noor Behram, a man who has spent four years photographing and exposing US drone strikes in the region of Waziristan in Pakistan. The article analyses Behram's activity in terms of parrhesiastic exposure, a concept that is intended to capture aspects of the changed circumstances under which fearless speech can be exercised in mass-mediated, globalised societies. The article concludes by observing how further engagement with* parrhēsia *might contribute to our understanding of political action, the relationship between emotions and political struggle, and the politics of secrecy.*

Foucault and the Contentious Politics of Security

In a recent examination of the relevance of Foucault's idea of counter-conduct for understanding the politics of protest, Carl Death observes that, for all the discussion of power and resistance associated with Foucault's thought, "the direct influence of Foucault's work on contemporary social movement studies is more limited than one might expect."[1] This he ascribes in part to an assumption on the part of many scholars that Foucault had "more to say about regimes of power than he did about forms of resistance or alternative politics."[2]

*For their critical comments on previous versions of this article I am grateful to Peter Adey, Anne-Marie D'Aoust, Danielle Leduc, Anelynda Mielke and Muhammad Ali Nasir. Julia Calvert provided invaluable editorial assistance. The criticisms of two anonymous reviewers helped me sharpen the argument significantly. Interviews during June and July 2012 with the Bureau of Investigative Journalism, Reprieve, Shahzad Akbar and Edmund Clark deepened my understanding of the drone war issue in Pakistan and Noor Behram's critical practice. Funding for this research was generously provided by the Social Science and Humanities Research Council of Canada (grant # 410-2010-1884).

1. Carl Death, "Counter-Conducts: A Foucauldian Analytics of Protest", *Social Movement Studies*, Vol. 9, No. 3 (2010), p. 236.

2. *Ibid.* Death mentions J. Simons' *Foucault and the Political* (London: Routledge, 1995), p. 82, as illustrative in this respect.

I suspect a similar assumption is also at work in critical security studies. Foucault's explorations of governmentality, disciplinary and bio-power, his methodological reflections on genealogy and microphysics, and conceptual themes like *dispositif* and panopticism have made a very significant impression on studies of securitisation. More often than not, however, Foucault is called upon to theorise techniques of control and strategies of power. When it comes to analysing the politics of security, notwithstanding certain notable exceptions,[3] far less attention has been paid to his writings on a range of topics that we might group under the broad heading of logics of contestation. This would include Foucault's thematisation of counter-conducts,[4] his outline of an analytics of struggle,[5] or the various reflections on revolt, refusal and the responsibilities and rights of the governed that are scattered across his interviews and which sometimes arise in the context of Foucault's own engagement in specific conflicts.[6] When scholars have sought tools and guidelines for theorising the contentious politics of security, they have usually looked elsewhere—to the areas of postcolonial theory, theories of enactment and performativity, sociological studies of fields and bureaucratic struggles, and philosophies of action and interruption.[7] Foucault is of course indirectly present in many of these debates via the influential place he has within, say, Butler's thinking on performativity or Rancière's work on politics. But I argue that Foucault's writings also offer a great deal that might be *directly* relevant to the study of contestations of security. Granted, it is indeed the case that, for all his insistence on the inseparability of power and resistance, when it comes to his major works—the monographs on madness, punishment, illness and sexuality, and the lectures on government—it is the schemes, tactics and dreams of experts and authorities that take centre stage in his explorations. However, this should not mean that we cannot push Foucault's thoughts on contestation, and more importantly the kind of ethos of inquiry he brings to political analysis, much further than we have to date.

A key lesson we learn from Foucault on power is the need to break regimes down. Instead of positing big systems of power, after Foucault we begin to see power in terms of its polymorphous character and changing forms. However, this variegated landscape of power is less evident when we turn to the analysis of contestations of security. There, it seems, our thinking is still blunted by some rather lumpy and undifferentiated categories like "resistance." When it comes to thinking on the contentious politics of security, the richness of the analytics of power stands in sharp contrast to the thin and rather impoverished analytics of contestation that are at our disposal.[8]

---

3. For example, see L. Amoore, "'There is No Great Refusal': The Ambivalent Politics of Resistance", in Marieke de Goede (ed.), *International Political Economy and Postructural Politics* (New York: Palgrave Macmillan, 2006); on "psy disciplines" and the contestation of military authority, see Alison Howell, *Madness in International Relations* (Abingdon/New York: Routledge, 2011).

4. Michel Foucault, *Security, Territory, Population: Lectures at the Collège de France, 1977–78* (New York: Palgrave Macmillan, 2007).

5. For example, Michel Foucault, "The Subject and Power", in J. Faubion (ed.), *Michel Foucault. Power* (New York: New Press, 2000).

6. Michel Foucault, "Useless to Revolt?", in Faubion, *op. cit.*

7. I borrow the idea of contentious politics from social movement theory where it organises the study of a broad range of disruptive political claims-making activities; see Charles Tilly and Sidney Tarrow, *Contentious Politics* (Boulder, CO: Paradigm Publishers, 2007).

8. See Death, *op. cit.*

It is with the aim of beginning to redress this imbalance that I take up Foucault's discussion of *parrhēsia*[9] in this paper. *Parrhēsia* is a political and ethical practice that Foucault traces back to Ancient Greece. Foucault interprets *parrhēsia* as "fearless speech," "free-spokenness (*franc-parler*),"[10] "the act of truth"[11] and one among several "modalities of truth telling."[12] In its political version, *parrhēsia* is exemplified by the citizen who speaks critically in front of a tyrant or an assembly, voicing a truth he or she feels needs to be heard, and risking the wrath of the sovereign or people in doing so. *Parrhēsia* is therefore an act: it is not just a matter of *what* is said but the fact that an individual "binds" themselves then and there to that truth, assuming ownership of their words.[13] But *parrhēsia* is also for Foucault a game.[14] The parrhesiast is prepared to risk much in voicing an uncomfortable truth. At the same time they hope that, precisely because they speak frankly and courageously, their words might strike a chord with the sovereign or with the demos. As a consequence, there is always the hope in *parrhēsia* that this frank speech will have a positive impact on the affairs of the community, and their act will be met with a certain respect rather than punishment.

In this article I argue that the idea of *parrhēsia* can contribute to a more nuanced and variegated understanding of contestation within the field of security today. There are at least three ways in which *parrhēsia* can be useful:

1. *Parrhēsia* can sensitise us to the impact that *individual* (or, more accurately, *individualised*) actions and the mobilisation of personal, embodied, experienced truths can make on the politics of security. The analysis of *parrhēsia* can compensate for the tendency to analyse resistance mainly at the level of the activity of groups, or to associate transformation only with the pressure of faceless social forces. It can thus contribute to a growing interest among scholars in the difference made by *acts*.[15]
2. *Parrhēsia* alerts us to the place of courage and personal commitment in politics. Hence it might contribute to an expansion of our understanding of the force of emotions and affects in effecting political change.
3. *Parrhēsia* addresses situations where speaking out is dangerous. Few things are more dangerous in our societies than speaking out and disclosing certain truths pertaining to the *arcana imperii*, the secrets of the state. *Parrhēsia* can therefore be a useful tool to expand understanding of the politics and modalities of secrecy and disclosure, an aspect of security studies that surely merits further theoretical reflection.[16]

9. There is some variation in the transliteration of this word. In the social science literature it appears as parresia, parrēsia and parrhēsia. I adopt the latter and for reasons of consistency have changed certain quotations, indicating this with square brackets.

10. Michel Foucault, *The Courage of Truth (The Government of Self and Others II): Lectures at the Collège de France, 1983–1984* (New York: Palgrave Macmillan, 2011), p. 2.

11. *Ibid.*, p. 11.

12. *Ibid.*, p. 2.

13. Michel Foucault, *The Government of Self and Others: Lectures at the Collège de France, 1982–1983* (New York: Palgrave Macmillan, 2010), p. 65.

14. For example, Michel Foucault, *Fearless Speech*, ed. J. Pearson (New York: Semiotext(e), 2001), pp. 16–17.

15. Jef Huysmans, "What's in an Act? On Security Speech Acts and Little Security Nothings", *Security Dialogue*, Vol. 42, No. 4–5 (2011); Engin Isin and Greg Neilson (eds.), *Acts of Citizenship* (London: Zed Books, 2008), pp. 371–383.

16. Peter Galison, "Removing Knowledge", in B. Latour and P. Weibel (eds.), *Making Things Public: Atmospheres of Democracy* (Cambridge, MA: MIT Press, 2005); Eva Horn, "Logics of Political

In making this argument for the relevance of Foucault's investigation of *parrhēsia* to the study of the contentious politics of security, it is necessary to offer a caveat. It is certainly not my intention to cast Foucault as a kind of philosophical Home Depot—all your conceptual tools conveniently gathered under one roof! I mentioned above that a range of theories and authors have been utilised by scholars interested in theorising contestation within security fields. This theoretical pluralism is a positive feature of the literature, and definitely not something I wish to criticise. My point is a different one. Echoing Death's point about social movement studies,[17] or Ferguson's recent argument about governmentalities of the left,[18] it is that Foucault has more to offer the study of the contentious politics of security than has hitherto been acknowledged. This is the argument I seek to develop by means of a discussion of *parrhēsia*.

My argument proceeds in three sections. First, I briefly introduce Foucault's writing on *parrhēsia*. Then, I consider the question of *parrhēsia today*: is it valid and useful to use this concept in the analysis of contemporary issues? *Parrhēsia* is a useful concept, I argue, but should not be projected onto contemporary situations without qualification. Our world is not that of Ancient Greece. For example, how do the forms of publicity, the forms of sovereignty, the forms of communication and representation that distinguish modern societies affect the ways in which an individual might speak out critically against authorities today? In the final section I connect this discussion of *parrhēsia* to a particular incident. I examine the recent case of Noor Behram, a man who has spoken out in the context of the USA's use of armed drones in Pakistan to target suspected militants in its global war on terror. Behram is a resident of Waziristan, the region of Pakistan where drone strikes have been especially intense. For many years he made it his mission to photograph each strike, documenting extensive civilian casualties that had not been acknowledged by western media or governments. At considerable risk he claims to be placing a truth about the nature of drone warfare before a western public. Building on this case I develop a concept of *parrhesiastic exposure*. This is intended to capture certain transformations within this mode of truth telling. Finally, in my conclusion I relate this discussion of *parrhēsia* back to debates in critical security studies, highlighting its relevance for our understanding of the politics of individual action, courage and emotions and, albeit very briefly, the politics of secrecy.

Foucault on *Parrhēsia*

Towards the end of 1983 Foucault delivered a series of six lectures at Berkeley. The theme was "discourse and truth."[19] Concluding these lectures, Foucault explained that he sought to engage "not . . . with the problem of truth, but with the problem

Secrecy", *Theory, Culture & Society*, Vol. 28, No. 2 (2011), pp. 103–122; Joseph Masco, "Lie Detectors: On Secrets and Hypersecurity in Los Alamos", *Public Culture*, Vol. 14, No. 3 (2002), pp. 441–467.

17. Death, *op. cit.*

18. James Ferguson, "Toward a Left Art of Government: From 'Foucauldian Critique' to Foucauldian Politics", *History of the Human Sciences*, Vol. 24, No. 4 (2011), pp. 61–68.

19. In this article I read the Berkeley lectures (published from tape-recordings as Foucault, *Fearless Speech, op. cit.*) in conjunction with the final two lecture series Foucault delivered at the Collège de France, both of which orbit around the problem of *parrhēsia*. These are Foucault, *The Government of Self and Others, op. cit.* and Foucault, *The Courage of Truth, op. cit.*

of the truth-teller, or of truth-telling as an activity."[20] The lectures centre upon a particular mode of truth telling called *parrhēsia* that Foucault locates in Ancient Greece. *Parrhēsia* makes it first appearance in Greek literature "in Euripides [c.484–407 BC], and occurs throughout the ancient Greek world of letters from the end of the Fifth Century BC."[21]

Parrhēsia is one of several "modalities of truth-telling." The others that Foucault mentions are prophecy (where a person speaks not "in his own name" but typically "transmits the word of God"), the wisdom of the sage, and *tekhnē* (the "know how" or expertise of doctors and other technicians).[22] One reason he looks to Antiquity to study truth telling is that it enables him to "separate out" these different modalities. "Because, in Antiquity, they are fairly clearly distinguished and embodied."[23] In his studies of governmentality, Foucault had emphasised the necessity of moving to the "outside" of the state by investigating the rationalities and practices through which it is constituted.[24] Part of making that move involved identifying archaic forms like *polizei* that—because they are quite alien to us today—foster a kind of reflexivity about our own logics of rule. With *parrhēsia* he seems to apply a similar kind of historical method to the practice of truth telling.

But there are significant differences in Foucault's method as well. Foucault notes that *parrhēsia* is a "spidery kind of notion."[25] Unlike some of the other archaic concepts that Foucault reintroduces into the present, it does not reside at the centre of its own dedicated body of literature. Unlike, say, *Polizeiwissenschaft*, there are very few great treatises or compendia devoted to the understanding and exercise of *parrhēsia*. "It is a notion which is used and referred to, but it is not considered directly or thematized as such."[26] With *parrhēsia* Foucault is following fine trails, tracking this practice as it scuttles nimbly across discursive surfaces, appearing in historical encounters, now disappearing, then reappearing. "It is a theme which runs from one system to another, from one doctrine to another, so that it is quite difficult to define its meaning precisely or identify its precise system."[27] Like a spider web, there is a centre but it is not fully fixed.

So what is *parrhēsia?* In introducing these lectures Foucault offers the following summary of this complex term.

> [*Parrhēsia*] is a verbal activity in which a speaker expresses his personal relationship to truth, and risks his life because he recognizes truth-telling as a duty to improve or help other people (as well as himself). In [*parrhēsia*], the speaker uses his freedom and chooses frankness instead of persuasion, truth instead of falsehood or silence, the risk of death

---

20. Foucault, *Fearless Speech, op. cit.*, p. 169.
21. *Ibid.*, p. 11.
22. Foucault, *The Courage of Truth, op. cit.*, pp. 15–31.
23. *Ibid.*, p. 26.
24. Michel Foucault, *The Birth of Biopolitics: Lectures at the Collège de France 1978–1979* (New York: Palgrave Macmillan, 2008), p. 78.
25. Foucault, *The Government of Self and Others, op. cit.*, p. 45.
26. *Ibid.*
27. *Ibid.*

> instead of life and security, criticism instead of flattery, and moral duty instead of self-interest and moral apathy.[28]

In one of the more illuminating commentaries and uses of Foucault's discussion of *parrhēsia*, Jonathan Simon clarifies some of its features. *Parrhēsia* is speech, but a particular kind of speech. It is not to be confused with the pursuit of truth by means of "reasoned argument," nor does it entail "the manipulation of less reflective instincts (as philosophy or rhetoric might)." Instead, *parrhēsia* refers to a truth that "comes uniquely from her self and her experience and is directed critically at a listener whose power places the speaker in potential danger."[29]

> In the classic Athenian mode, a parrhesiastic speaker confronted a god, a sovereign, or the assembled citizenry through a direct revelation of experienced truth. As such, [*parrhēsia*] is dangerous speech, raising the possibility that those with power will retaliate against the speaker as much as the possibility that the holder of power will be shamed or otherwise moved to redress the wrong. Because of its risk, [*parrhēsia*] was not a form of self-interest or therapy. Rather, it was a recognition of a duty to another or to society as a whole.[30]

Parrhēsia is not a static practice but is capable of taking several forms. We can read Foucault's project as providing elements in a *history* of *parrhēsia*. "His main point," according to Martin Jay, "is that it migrated from a public concept as a guide to good citizenship in Athenian democracy into a more personal quality, a way to fashion a good life."[31] In the former case, there is a "political *parrhēsia*":[32] an individual addresses the sovereign or people frankly and critically about the follies of government. Foucault juxtaposes this with "*parrhēsia* in the field of ethics":[33] an individual offers frank criticism to a friend or confidant. They value that relationship and that person so highly they are prepared to risk that same relationship in the hope that their words will produce a positive effect in their interlocutor.

In a way that is consistent with a great deal of his writing on relations of power and truth, Foucault likens *parrhēsia* to a game. This is because it entails a set of moves and countermoves, risks and interactions. What is it that grounds the truth claims of the parrhesiast? What is the basis on which their words might carry weight? It is not the appeal to the accumulated knowledge of a profession that the technician mobilises. Nor is it like the word of God that the prophet transmits. Instead, it is a sense that the parrhesiast is a person of conviction and courage, who speaks of something they know from personal experience. But note it is their precise context that gives their words a certain force: because their words are very likely to be unpopular, there is little they have to gain personally from uttering

28. Foucault, *Fearless Speech, op. cit.*, pp. 19–20, quoted in Jonathan Simon, "Parrhesiastic Accountability: Investigatory Commissions and Executive Power in an Age of Terror", *Yale Law Journal*, Vol. 114 (2005) p. 1422.

29. Simon, "Parrhesiastic Accountability", *op. cit.*, p. 1422.

30. *Ibid.*

31. Martin Jay, "Visual Parrhēsia? Foucault and the Truth of the Gaze", in M. Jay (ed.), *Essays from the Edge: Parerga and Paralipomena* (Charlottesville, VA: University of Virginia Press, 2011), p. 83.

32. Foucault, *The Courage of Truth, op. cit.*, p. 73.

33. *Ibid.*

them. They are to be taken seriously precisely because they freely risk so much in order to speak. "If there is a kind of 'proof' of the sincerity of the *parrhesiastes*, it is his *courage*. The fact that a speaker says something dangerous—different from what the majority believes—is a strong indication that he is a *parrhesiastes*."[34]

Parrhēsia Today?

Does *parrhēsia* exist today? More appropriately, can we relate this notion of *parrhēsia*, drawn as it is from Antiquity, to contemporary experiences of political rule and its contestation? Can the idea of *parrhēsia* advance our understanding of the contentious politics of security? I think the answer to these questions is yes, but it is a qualified one.

Understood as a subject of philosophical reflection and problematisation, *parrhēsia* went into decline in Greece during the fourth century BC. It barely registers in modern theories of government.[35] Foucault observes that where the "parrhesiastic modality" does appear it is only as something "grafted on or underpinned" by one of the other modes of truth telling he compares it with.[36] Hence, revolutionary discourse, which Foucault regards as a modern form of prophetic truth telling, can play a parrhesiastic role when it undertakes a critique of society. And the discourse of scientists, the modality of *tekhnē*, can have a parrhesiastic function when it challenges prevalent "prejudices," "dominant institutions" and "current ways of doing things."[37] More than that, Foucault gives us little indication about what *parrhēsia* might mean today, or where we might find it.

According to Simon one of the most visible ways in which *parrhēsia* occurs today is in connection with the political activity of victims. "Today, victims have emerged as perhaps the most important source of [*parrhēsia*]. By reproducing the violent emotions they have experienced, victims who choose to speak parrhesiastically can destabilize political and legal authority."[38] Speaking of the United States, he notes that for more than two decades this parrhesiastic force has been directed against the criminal justice system, with victims of violent crime speaking out "against the courts, parole boards, and other decisionmakers whose management of dangerous criminals has failed them."[39]

However, this political energy that some victims can stir up when they speak out can operate in other forums and issue areas. Observers of politics have noted the way in which official public inquiries are often convened in the expectation that they will contain or even depoliticise controversies.[40] But Simon notes that with the 9/11 Commission this was not the case, whatever the original intentions of the Bush administration. In this particular case there were the communities who, constituting themselves as the 9/11 families, brought a form of truth and a political energy to the Commission that was different.[41] "The Commission's

34. Foucault, *Fearless Speech*, *op. cit.*, p. 15. His italics.
35. Simon, "Parrhesiastic Accountability", *op. cit.*
36. Foucault, *The Courage of Truth*, *op. cit.*, p. 30.
37. *Ibid.*
38. Simon, "Parrhesiastic Accountability", *op. cit.*, p. 1422.
39. *Ibid.*
40. Andrew Barry, "The Anti-Political Economy", *Economy and Society*, Vol. 31, No. 2 (2002), pp. 75–94.
41. As one anonymous reviewer pointed out, the case of the victims/families could be compared with individuals who protest wars as parents of (dead) soldiers. For example, see Tina Managhan, "Grieving Dead Soldiers, Disavowing Loss: Cindy Sheehan and the Im/possibility of the American

relationship with the victims transformed it from an institution anchored completely in the analytics of truth to one infused with parrhesiastic truth."[42] As a result, where the Commission might have been expected to do little more than cover up for the errors of the government, it became capable of bringing a certain measure of accountability to bear upon an executive branch that had, under the guise of national emergency, largely escaped scrutiny.

Another area where we might glimpse *parrhēsia* today is in the disclosure of the whistleblower.[43] When in 1984 Mordecai Vananu revealed details of Israel's secret nuclear weapons programme to London's *The Sunday Times*, he demonstrated that if the rise of the nuclear state would call forth what Masco has termed a secret governmentality on a truly massive scale,[44] such a regime would soon engender its own forms of counter-conduct. This secret governmentality would prove to be susceptible to the episodic acts of disclosure on the part of scientists, technicians and military personnel who, under various circumstances, felt compelled to speak out. The fact that Vananu was snatched from Rome, drugged and transported to Israel, tried behind closed doors and then sentenced to 24 years imprisonment illustrates amply the kind of risks associated with this modern form of *parrhēsia*. The fact that Vananu was a junior technician working within the nuclear complex, that he revealed *technical* details, suggests that what we are seeing in this case is some combination of *parrhēsia* and *tekhnē*.

In suggesting that Vananu exemplifies the whistleblower as parrhesiast I do beg an important question. The fact that Vananu was considered by many as a traitor (especially in Israel) yet elsewhere celebrated by the anti-nuclear movement and repeatedly nominated for the Nobel Peace Prize suggests there will nearly always be heated questions of identity at play.[45] When individuals speak out on controversial issues they invariably attract smear campaigns and accusations about their true motivations. Is the revelation of state secrets motivated purely by conscience or is the truth teller driven by less noble considerations? Are they seeking financial reward? Do they bear allegiance to another state? These doubts prompt us to ask certain questions as scholars. Does a public have to recognise their act as courageous, as truthful for it to count as *parrhēsia*? If their speech does *not* provoke self-questioning on the part of a sovereign or a public, is it still *parrhēsia*? *Which* public needs to listen, and over what time scale do we judge the impact of their speech? These are difficult questions, and the ambiguity they suggest may be enough for the more positivist-minded analyst to conclude that *parrhēsia* is too fuzzy and hence "inoperable" as a concept for examining contestation in the field of security governance. Notwithstanding these reservations, I think we can say that by its very nature *parrhēsia* is always going to be an essentially contested activity. The very recognition of an act *as parrhēsia*—rather than heresy or treason—is a political act. For this reason

---

Antiwar Movement", *Geopolitics*, Vol. 16, No. 2 (2011), pp. 438–466. The fact that they speak as fathers, and especially mothers, suggests in turn a whole dimension of gender that could be brought into the study of *parrhēsia*.

42. Simon, "Parrhesiastic Accountability", *op. cit.*, p. 1423.

43. Wim Vandekerckhove and Suzan Langenberg, "Can We Organize Courage? Implications of Foucault's Parrhēsia", *Electronic Journal of Business Ethics and Organization Studies*, Vol. 17 (2012), pp. 35–44.

44. See Masco, *op. cit.*

45. "Vananu: Traitor or Prisoner of Conscience", *Sydney Morning Herald*, 22 April 2004, available: <http://www.smh.com.au/articles/2004/04/21/1082530235940.html> (accessed 11 July 2013).

parrhēsia is as much a matter of social *interaction* as it is a matter of individual *action*.[46]

Thus far I have given two examples that do bear strong resemblances to the kinds of truth telling that, Foucault tells us, ancient societies recognised as *parrhēsia*. But to satisfactorily address the question of *parrhēsia* today—or more specifically, what *parrhēsia* is today—it is not sufficient to merely identify contemporary expressions. To proceed along that path is to repeat the move of many scholars who, having read Foucault's writing on panopticism, or more lately neoliberalism, applied these concepts rather directly to the present, and found panopticism and neoliberalism lurking everywhere! This move leads invariably to overgeneralisation and a loss of specificity and historicity in our understanding of power relations. Concepts that Foucault fashioned with a certain "proximity to concrete situations,"[47] concepts forged through encounters with particular knowledges and designed to express singular constellations of rationality and practice, become generalised in a way that effaces rather than enhances our capacity to discern change. Rather than treat *parrhēsia* as a unity, a name for a thing existing in the world, it is better to see it as an analytic, or following Deleuze, in terms of "lines of [continuous] variation."[48] If absolutely nothing about the world is fixed, if "variations are all that exist,"[49] then our task is a different one. We need to engage *parrhēsia* at the level of its "grafts" (Foucault), or what I have elsewhere called critical encounters.[50]

One way to tackle this theme of variation is by considering what we might call the *mediation* of *parrhēsia*. The parrhesiastic speech that Foucault reconstructs from the Ancient world is always specifically located speech. It happens in particular places and social contexts: in the agora before an assembly of citizens, in the court before a king, or, removed from public view, in the ear of the tyrannical prince. It seems that for *parrhēsia* to happen, all the players in the parrhesiastic game have to be physically present at the same time. It is "the great scene of the man standing up to the tyrant and telling the truth before the eyes and ears of the whole court."[51]

With contemporary forms of *parrhēsia* it is rarely the case that fearless speech is performed and experienced in this way. Certainly there can be the frank statement uttered before a commission or inquiry. Recall the words of Richard Clarke when he began his testimony to the 9/11 Commission: "Your government failed you, those entrusted with protecting you failed you, and I failed you."[52] And such words are all the more powerful for being spoken unexpectedly before an assembled audience. But if such acts of frank speech attain a certain power today to unsettle, enrage or shame an audience, it is not only or even primarily on the scale of those physically present at the moment of utterance. Concomitant

---

46. Vandekerckhove and Langenberg, *op. cit.*, pp. 35–36.

47. Paul Rabinow, *Anthropos Today: Reflections on Modern Equipment* (Princeton, NJ: Princeton University Press, 2003), p. 3.

48. Gilles Deleuze, "What is a Dispositif?", in T.J. Armstrong (ed.), *Michel Foucault, Philosopher* (New York: Routledge, 1992), p. 166.

49. Paul Veyne, *Foucault, His Thought, His Character* (Malden, MA: Polity, 2010), p. 10.

50. William Walters, *Governmentality: Critical Encouters* (Abingdon/New York: Routledge, 2012).

51. Foucault, *The Government of Self and Others, op. cit.*, p. 65.

52. As quoted in CBS News, "Your Government Failed You", 11 February 2009, available: <http://www.cbsnews.com/2100-224_162-608526.html> (accessed 11 July 2013).

with the rise of the modern public sphere, that particular "social space mediated by the reflexive circulation of discourse,"[53] the coordinates of parrhesiastic activity have changed significantly. With the rise of "mediated visibility,"[54] we speak, hear and see in the midst of distributed technological assemblages that far exceed the boundaries of the agora, the court or even the nation. If it is true that parrhesiastic activity is by definition never reducible to the action of its subject but dependent upon a certain risky interaction with others, then it is also true that under conditions of extensive technological and communicative mediation, the geographical and temporal scales on which this interaction can occur have been stretched considerably.

New forms of mediation and the way in which they change the time and place of *parrhēsia* provoke a further question. Is it still *parrhēsia* if an angry crowd cannot immediately stone you, or the king cast you into prison? Is it still *parrhēsia* if a vast ocean separates you from the addressees of your frank criticism? Here I think we need to recognise that it is not just the power and the scale of communication that have been vastly extended. The technologies of violence and intimidation by which the affronted sovereign can respond to the parrhesiast have also changed dramatically since Ancient Greece. Targeted assassination by drone or commando elite are only the most recent techniques available to the vengeful sovereign. What the long history of spies, assassins and, more recently, the networking of national intelligence agencies confirm—and what Mordecai Vananu discovered to his great personal cost—is that to speak out is sometimes to risk everything, no matter where you go on earth.

In this section I have asked some questions about *parrhēsia* today. One preliminary conclusion we can draw is that there is a relationship between the possibility and effectiveness of *parrhēsia* and the scales on which communicative and political power operate. But these are by no means the only lines of variation we should consider. In his careful reading of the Ancient Greeks, Foucault also discerns a relationship between *parrhēsia* and the political character of rule. For the Ancient Greeks, "democracy is not the privileged site of *parrhēsia* , but the place in which *parrhēsia* is most difficult to practice."[55] In part this is because in a democracy, where the freedom to speak is widely distributed, it becomes harder to discern frank and courageous speech amidst "the hubbub of all the orators arguing with each other and trying to seduce the people."[56] I will return to the question of the relationship of *parrhēsia* to forms of political government in my conclusion.

But more immediately, another variable we should consider is the expressive forms of *parrhēsia*. In Foucault's explorations, *parrhēsia* is nearly always a *verbal* activity. One of the points I develop in the short case that follows is that verbal activity does not exhaust the possible forms of fearless "speech." In confronting a public with uncomfortable truths today, it is more likely that the truth teller will—if they are to engage an audience and hold its attention—need to employ some combination of words, images and sounds.[57] This is especially the case

53. Michael Warner, *Publics and Counterpublics* (New York: Zone, 2005), p. 90.

54. John Thompson, "The New Visibility", *Theory, Culture & Society*, Vol. 22, No. 6 (2005), pp. 31–52.

55. Foucault, *The Courage of Truth*, *op. cit.*, p. 57.

56. *Ibid.*, p. 37.

57. Michael C. Williams, "Words, Images, Enemies: Securitization and International Politics", *International Studies Quarterly*, Vol. 47, No. 4 (2003), pp. 511–531.

whenever *parrhēsia* is combined with other modes of truth telling, such as the *tekhnē* of documentary and photography. In such situations *parrhēsia* resembles the situations that Rancière describes as *demonstration*: its mode is simultaneously "argumentative and poetic,"[58] that is, a matter of building argument "and opening up the world where argument can be received and have an impact."[59] Fearless speech under contemporary conditions is compelled to negotiate between two poles. It has to retain a commitment to frankness and clarity in order to convey its critical point. But it must also utilise expressive forms that garner attention within a public space where attention is in short supply.

To summarise, Foucault's exploration of *parrhēsia* does provide us with a valuable analytical tool to illuminate certain forms of truth telling and their place within contentious politics today. However, use of the concept has to be sensitive to the very different circumstances under which individuals and groups speak out. Among other things it needs to take account of the changing topographies of the public sphere, the expanded reach of technologies of violence and retribution, and new expressive forms and modes of communication. Given these changes, perhaps it makes sense to view *parrhēsia* less as a pure form, and more as an adjective that might qualify particular practices and experiences. This, at least, is the direction Simon takes when he speaks of parrhesiastic accountability, and the line I pursue in the remainder of this article where I consider the practice and condition of parrhesiastic exposure.

Parrhesiastic Exposure: Noor Behram's Documentation of the Covert Drone War in Waziristan

Since at least June 2004 the US government has been using armed unmanned aerial vehicles (UAVs or "drones") to conduct hundreds of missile strikes in northwest Pakistan.[60] The use of drones to carry out so-called "targeted assassinations" against suspected terrorists marks a new and dramatic turn in US counterterrorism policy. Data collected by investigative journalists seeking to expose this otherwise largely secret war reveal that the advent of the Obama presidency saw a marked escalation in the use of drones, both in northwest Pakistan and increasingly in other regions.[61] The Bush presidency approach to counterterrorism was associated in the public eye at least with wars in Iraq and Afghanistan conducted in the name of counterterrorism and "regime change," with the secretive programme of extraordinary rendition, with techniques of interrogation and torture such as waterboarding, and with the detention facilities of Abu Ghraib and

58. Jacques Rancière, *Disagreement: Politics and Philosophy* (Minneapolis: University of Minnesota Press, 1999), p. 59.

59. *Ibid.*, p. 56.

60. International Human Rights and Conflict Resolution Clinic (Stanford Law School) and Global Justice Clinic (NYU Law School), *Living Under Drones: Death, Injury, and Trauma to Civilians from US Drone Practices in Pakistan* (September 2012); The Bureau of Investigative Journalism (TBIJ), "Secret Documents Show Brennan's 'No Civilian Drone Deaths' Claim Was False", 11 April 2013, available: <http://www.thebureauinvestigates.com/2013/04/11/secret-us-documents-show-brennans-no-civilian-drone-deaths-claim-was-false/> (accessed 11 July 2013); Ian Shaw and Majed Akhter, "The Unbearable Humanness of Drone Warfare in Fata, Pakistan", *Antipode*, Vol. 44, No. 2 (2012), pp. 1490–1509.

61. TBIJ, *op. cit.*

Guantanamo. By contrast, the Obama approach is increasingly identified with such practices as the policy of targeted assassination, the "kill list" and the Hellfire missile dispatched by the Predator and Reaper drones.[62]

For many years the USA's use of drones in Pakistan's Federally Administered Tribal Areas (FATA), the area where most of the strikes have taken place, went largely unreported in western media. "For years, the government would neither confirm nor deny the existence of the strikes, and only began to outline the practices and legal justifications following significant pressure from domestic and international civil society."[63] It is only very recently that a more detailed picture of this covert drone war is emerging. One of its most controversial features is the issue of civilian casualties. For example, in June 2011, John Brennan (at the time Obama's chief counterterrorism adviser) went on record claiming there had been no civilian casualties for "almost a year." Yet evidence is fast being accumulated that tells a different story.[64]

Scholarship on drone war has escalated almost in proportion to the use of drones as a new weapon of counterterrorism and surveillance tool. For example, scholars have begun to assess what the drone means in terms of new kinds of scopic regime, surveillance practice and security scape,[65] and how its potential for killing by remote control might shape the future of war and peace.[66]

What has been less examined, and what interests me here, are the practices by which drone warfare has been constituted as an object of public knowledge in the first place. What practices have individuated a set of events *as* "covert drone war," and disclosed these events before a public? How has the campaign being waged in North Waziristan become not just a front line in the global war on terror, but also a key site in the contentious politics of security? To answer these questions we could of course examine the work of investigative journalists and human rights campaigners who have sought to uncover the covert drone war. We might also consider the networks of communication and intra-elite negotiations in Washington and other capitals, the practice of leaking to shape and control the way in which knowledge of this programme has been brought into the public realm. But while these are important lines to follow, I want to pursue a different angle in the remainder of this article. I want to ask how one tells the truth about the covert war on terror, and what it costs to tell that truth. What role does the courageous activity and speech of particular individuals and not just organisations play in making this war more visible to a public?

To answer these questions I propose to link the previous discussion of contemporary *parrhēsia* to one particular case: the photojournalism of Noor Behram.

In July 2011 several international newspapers and websites carried stories about a man who had made it his mission to bear witness to the impact of the war on

---

62. Jo Becker and Scott Shane, "Secret 'Kill List' Proves a Test of Obama's Principles and Will", *New York Times*, 29 May 2012, available: <http://www.nytimes.com/2012/05/29/world/obamas-leadership-in-war-on-al-qaeda.html?_r=2&pagewanted=all&> (accessed 15 July 2013).

63. *Living under Drones*, *op. cit.*

64. TBIJ, *op. cit.*

65. Tyler Wall and Torin Monahan, "Surveillance and Violence from Afar: The Politics of Drones and Liminal Security-Scapes", *Theoretical Criminology*, Vol. 15, No. 3 (2011), pp. 239–254.

66. Frank Sauer and Niklas Schörnig, "Killer Drones: The 'Silver Bullet' of Democratic Warfare?", *Security Dialogue*, Vol. 43, No. 4 (2012), pp. 363–380.

terror, and of drone war in particular, on his home region.[67] They told the story of Noor Behram, a resident of Waziristan and journalist, who had spent the past four years documenting the "collateral damage" of US drone strikes in this "tribal area," "interviewing survivors of drone attacks, shooting video footage and close-up stills of the damage."[68] *Spiegel Online* reports that between 2007 and 2011, and working independently from his employer, Al Jazeera, Behram visited 70 sites and witnessed 600 corpses.[69] Taking photographs under such circumstances was not easy. "He had to ask permission ... from clan elders and Taliban commanders. He had to convince them he was not a spy, not one of the people who pass on coordinates for possible drone strikes to the CIA."[70]

> Behram's work appears *to reveal the truth* about the US drone campaign in Pakistan's tribal region—that far more civilians are being killed than Americans or Pakistanis will admit. His images cannot be independently verified but are backed up by credible documentation. It also raises questions about the ethics of this new video-game warfare. How likely is it that a "reachback operator" sitting at a video screen 7,500 miles away at the CIA headquarters in Langley, Virginia, will hit the right target in the middle of the night?[71]

Behram's work was displayed at an art event in Lahore in the autumn of 2011. British press coverage of Behram's work was sparked by its prominent inclusion in a multimedia exhibit at London's Beaconsfield gallery entitled "Gaming in Waziristan." Here his photos and videos were shown alongside some other artistic explorations of drone warfare and surveillance. In the US major media outlets had, until very recently, been quite circumspect in their reporting of drone strikes. Nevertheless, Behram's photographs were the subject of a major article in *Wired*'s online Danger Room blog, which announced them as "rare photos from a war zone most Americans never see."[72] As *Wired* put it, despite reservations due to the questions "anonymous US officials" had raised about Behram's collaborators, "after careful consideration, we chose to publish some

---

67. Hasnain Kazim, "Drone War in Pakistan: Photos from the Ground Show Civilian Casualties", *Spiegel Online International*, 18 July 2011, available: <http://www.spiegel.de/international/world/drone-war-in-pakistan-photos-from-the-ground-show-civilian-casualties-a-775131.html>; Jemima Khan, "Under Fire from Afar: Harrowing Exhibition Reveals Damage Done by Drones in Pakistan", *The Independent*, 29 July 2011, available: <http://www.independent.co.uk/news/world/asia/under-fire-from-afar-harrowing-exhibition-reveals-damage-done-by-drones-in-pakistan-2327832.html?action=Gallery&ino=3>; Saeed Shah and Peter Beaumont, "US Drone Strikes in Pakistan Claiming Many Civilian Victims, Says Campaigner", *The Guardian*, 17 July 2011, available: <http://www.guardian.co.uk/world/2011/jul/17/us-drone-strikes-pakistan-waziristan> (all accessed 15 July 2013).

68. Jemima Khan, *op. cit.*

69. Kazim, *op. cit.*

70. *Ibid.*

71. Jemima Khan, *op. cit.* My italics.

72. Spencer Ackerman, "Rare Photographs Show Ground Zero of the Drone War", *Wired*, 12 December 2012, available: <http://www.wired.com/dangerroom/2011/12/photos-pakistan-drone-war/?utm_source=Contextly&utm_medium=RelatedLinks&utm_campaign=Previous&pid=999&viewall=true> (accessed 11 July 2013).

of these images because of the inherent journalistic value in depicting a largely unseen battlefield."[73]

In *Wired*, a selection of Behram's photographs document a series of drone strikes. A place name and a date is given for each photo. Behram's recollection of the scene accompanies each image: particular smells, stories, characters are attached to pictures that testify to incidents of loss, horror and destruction.

For example, one image is entitled "Dande Darpa Khel, August 21, 2009." It shows three young children standing in a field of debris. A fire is glimpsed in the background, suggesting the missile attack was very recent. The two older children stare straight at the camera, the youngest, in the middle, turns her head to look at her sister. Apparently in shock, all three hold up pieces of their neighbour's house, clutching it "as if the rubble could comfort them." "The stench that Behram smelled when he arrived at Dande Darpa Khel came from the charred bodies of Bismullah Khan and his wife. Near the bombed-out remains of their house, Behram found the Khan's three living children." According to Behram, "These kids had no idea where their parents were. They didn't know their parents were killed."[74]

On first inspection Behram's activity possesses many of the hallmarks and characteristics that Foucault identifies as *parrhēsia*. Consider it first as a form of truth telling. Faced with the covert war and the secrecy of the US and Pakistani governments, a number of groups are doing the essential work of reporting the as-yet-unreported. They are making visible the toll that the drone campaign is taking in terms of civilian deaths, damage to communities, and social and psychological harm. Such data are now being gathered in the form familiar to modern social research: reports, graphs, statistics, often accompanied by testimonies gathered from witnesses and survivors.[75]

Behram's reporting is, in contrast, much more situated, personal and embodied. His disclosure is an act in its own right, a relatively undetached account of what he saw and felt as he arrived at each scene. Behram is a subject in this war: he speaks in part as a resident living in its midst. One photo is entitled "Above Noor Behram's Home in North Waziristan, Dec. 12, 2010" and reveals a grainy image of a drone hovering against a grey sky. Bird-like because of its altitude, the drone is circling above his house.

Second, and perhaps more specifically, Behram is taking great risks to tell this truth about the drone war. Some of this danger is hinted at in his own words.[76] He tells of local communities who are hostile to the presence of media, whom they do not trust and sometimes blame. Hence, in one case he took a quick picture of the destruction of a house then decided to leave the scene "in order to defuse hostility."[77] Another risk, perhaps far more serious, is the threat of himself being killed in a drone strike.[78] There are grounds to believe the US has

73. *Ibid.* As one of Behram's allies explained to me in an interview (London, 4 July 2012), this exhibition was a matter of bringing truths about the activities in FATA to bear upon mainstream Pakistani society. FATA was not only remote to the west, but to metropolitan Pakistan as well.

74. *Ibid.*

75. For example, see TBIJ, *op. cit.*; *Living under Drones*, *op. cit.*

76. Kazim, *op. cit.*

77. Ackerman, *op. cit.*

78. Kazim, *op. cit.*

made the follow-up strike one of its practices. Funeral goers and rescuers, it seems, are sometimes considered legitimate targets.[79]

But above and beyond these dangers lies the possibility of being deliberately targeted and assassinated for speaking out. Here we should recall the fate of Hayatullah Khan, a journalist whose past work included freelancing for PBS's *Frontline*. Khan reported the death of an alleged Al Qaeda figure named Hamza Rabia and four others in December 2005 in the town of Miran Shah. Khan's story and pictures of shrapnel indicated the victims had been killed by a US-made Hellfire missile,[80] thus contradicting the Pakistani government's official explanation that Rabia was killed by a blast caused by explosives stored in the house.[81] Khan was kidnapped the day after his story appeared. His body was found six months later, with five or six bullet wounds. It was unclear whether he had been killed by Pakistani security forces or the Taliban. A year later his widow was reported as killed by a bomb placed next to her bedroom.[82]

Given the risks and threats that investigative journalists can face in Pakistan, and especially in FATA, it seems reasonable to infer that it takes great courage for Behram to speak out about drone strikes.

No doubt we could pass other aspects of Behram's experience through the analytical grid Foucault offers us when discussing *parrhēsia*. That is, we could also consider it under the headings of criticism and duty or responsibility to oneself and to others. But rather than emphasise the specific ways in which this particular act of fearless speech might be isomorphic with the *parrhēsia* of Ancient Greece, I want to use my remaining space to examine some important shifts in *parrhēsia*.

In the case of Behram's intrepid photojournalism I want to suggest that we are faced not with the eternal recurrence of *parrhēsia* across the ages but with a novel constellation of elements. Let's call it *parrhesiastic exposure*. Here I want to play upon the full, if not fullest, range of meanings that can be attached to the word "exposure." As we all know, one set of meanings of exposure is "the action of bringing to light (something discreditable); the 'showing up' of an error ... or evil" (Oxford English Dictionary online). This overlaps with an understanding that exposure can also mean "presentation or disclosure to view; public exhibition."

Now in nearly all the instances and contexts in which Foucault discusses political *parrhēsia*, it entails a direct confrontation with a ruler. Or if it's a public, it's the bounded, finite public of the agora where the parrhesiast confronts the citizens with an uncomfortable truth. But, as I argued above, in liberal democracies *and* autocracies today the truth teller is rarely in a situation where they can address

79. Chris Woods and Christina Lamb, "Obama Terror Drones: CIA Tactics in Pakistan Include Targeting Rescuers and Funerals", The Bureau of Investigative Journalism, 4 February 2012, available: <http://www.thebureauinvestigates.com/2012/02/04/obama-terror-drones-cia-tactics-in-pakistan-include-targeting-rescuers-and-funerals/> (accessed 11 July 2013).

80. Amnesty International, "Hayatullah Khan—Justice Denied One Year On", ASA 33/011/2007, 16 June 2007, available: <http://www.amnesty.org/en/library/asset/ASA33/011/2007/en/c38d9612-d385-11dd-a329-2f46302a8cc6/asa330112007en.html> (accessed 11 July 2013).

81. Bob Dietz, "The Last Story: Hayatullah Khan", Committee to Protect Journalists: Special Report, 20 September 2006, available: <http://cpj.org/reports/2006/09/khan.php> (accessed 11 July 2013).

82. "Slain Tribal Area Journalist's Widow Murdered", Reporters without Borders, 17 November 2007, available: <http://en.rsf.org/pakistan-slain-tribal-area-journalist-s-17-11-2007,24417.html> (accessed 11 July 2013).

the ruler in such a direct fashion. This is especially so when it is not their own sovereign or people they seek to confront but that of a foreign power. Behram states that his agenda is "to show taxpayers in the Western world what their tax money is doing to people in another part of the world: killing civilians, innocent victims, children."[83] Noor Behram doesn't really need to address Barack Obama or the US Congress directly. For he offers his criticisms under conditions where, at least since the time of the Enlightenment,[84] the addressee of truth telling is a different kind of audience: the "virtual social object" and "indefinite audience" convened by modern modes of publicity.[85]

But if the public to which this truth is addressed is typically diffuse, then so are the source and the form of danger that the truth teller confronts. In Foucault's examples the parrhesiast runs the risk that the tyrant or the people will turn on the speaker. There is a definite, identifiable source of danger. The danger in Behram's case is of a different kind. It is at this point we need to note another meaning of exposure: an "unsheltered or undefended condition." Behram's attempts to reveal a truth about the killing of civilians by US drones exposes him to the threat of being injured or killed by a number of different factors and circumstances – by a follow-up strike, by angry residents, by secretive intelligence agents or by Taliban militants. The risks and dangers are multiple and complex.

That said (and recalling Foucault's frequent references to *parrhēsia* as *game*), there is also the possibility that these two senses of exposure can play off one another. The visibility a parrhesiast acquires before a public can sometimes offer a degree of security, and lessen their exposure to danger.[86] Indeed, Behram makes this point himself. "Now, he says—since he's known by the locals, since he's become a public figure—nothing can happen to him."[87]

But the term exposure also carries a third set of meanings, this time more technical. Exposure is, of course, an absolutely key technique and variable in photography where it indexes the amount of light that is allowed to fall upon a photographic film or image sensor. Exposure can be automated, as any amateur photographer will tell you, but for the expert photographer it is a matter of skill, judgement and experience. For example, a long exposure time will capture movement and dynamism in the way that a short exposure cannot. But it comes at the cost of blurring and loss of sharpness. In short, exposure constitutes a way in which the photographer, through a combination of skill and technology, can consciously manipulate an image in pursuit of particular effects.

By invoking parrhesiastic exposure in this third sense I want to highlight the fact that Behram's principle medium for truth telling is not just the verbal activity that Foucault makes so central to his understanding of *parrhēsia* but instead verbal

83. Ackerman, *op. cit.*

84. Jürgen Habermas, *The Structural Transformation of the Public Sphere: An Inquiry into a Category of Bourgeois Society* (Cambridge, MA: MIT Press, 1989).

85. Warner, *op. cit.*, pp. 55–56.

86. I owe this point to Anelynda Mielke.

87. Kazim, *op. cit.* A corroborating point was made to me by a journalist with extensive knowledge of the region and its conflicts (interview, London, 25 June 2012). The more that drone attacks in Waziristan have become public knowledge in western media, the less that the means of controlling information relies on killing and silencing rather than influencing and shaping the way events are reported. In a complex situation where there are multiple interested "players," including the CIA, Pakistan's Inter-Services Intelligence (ISI) and the Taliban, perhaps the danger attendant upon speaking out becomes attenuated.

activity combined with the visual image.[88] More pointedly, I am suggesting that *parrhēsia* can be visual as well as verbal. This is a matter that the eminent scholar of politics and vision, Martin Jay, has addressed at some length.

> There are ways ... in which resistance to power may take visual form, but these are understood by Foucault in largely negative terms, as disturbances in the hegemonic visuality of an era, like Manet's challenge to traditional perspectivalist painting. They rarely, if ever, translate into positive expressions of another visual order that comes closer to a truth grounded in a form of life, a critical practice whose effects Foucault came to value, both theoretically and in his own life as a deeply engaged intellectual.[89]

Certainly we can agree with Jay that "there is no visual *parrhēsia* for Michel Foucault"[90] if by visual *parrhēsia* one means a practice that "could somehow do an end run around discursivity and provide a basis for a truth that was not merely an effect of a specific discursive regime."[91] But if by *parrhēsia* we mean a truth that confronts authorities with uncomfortable realities, a truth that is not simply some facts but "me saying this,"[92] then it seems we should be willing to accept that *parrhēsia* today will only occasionally take the form of pure verbal expression. Much more likely, as with Behram's photography, we will encounter it as some combination of words, sounds and images. Indeed, we could go so far as to speculate that in a social world for which communication has become so bound up with the visual, in a modern environment ever more "thickened" by photographs and other communicative objects,[93] that "speaking out" with words alone is the exception rather than the norm.

In speaking of exposure in this way, in drawing analogies with the art and even the chemistry of photographic exposure, I am suggesting that the exercise of fearless speech has an entire technical dimension that we should not ignore. *Parrhēsia* is not a skill or a technique, as Foucault noted. One does not become an expert in this form of truth telling. But it does nevertheless have its "technical aspects,"[94] a point Foucault makes but fails to elaborate on. This is especially so in contemporary societies: to tell the truth in public requires all manner of props, mediators, technological prosthetics and social connections.[95] Foucault's account of *parrhēsia* veers towards a somewhat heroic conception of the speaker. This is quite understandable given the way in which great courage is a defining characteristic in the definition of the figure of the parrhesiast. Without wishing to downplay the necessary and irreducible element of courage, I do wish to emphasise that in

88. An extensive body of work has explored the power of visual images to construct and contest security worlds and identities. See, *inter alia*, Elspeth Van Veeren, "Captured by the Camera's Eye: Guantánamo and the Shifting Frame of the Global War on Terror", *Review of International Studies*, Vol. 37, No. 4 (2011), pp. 1721–1749; James Der Derian, *Virtuous War: Mapping the Military-Industrial-Media-Entertainment-Network* (Boulder, CO: Westview Press, 2001); and Williams, *op. cit.*

89. Jay, "Visual Parrhēsia?", *op. cit.*, p. 89.

90. *Ibid.*

91. *Ibid.*, pp. 81–82.

92. Vandekerckhove and Langenberg, *op. cit.*, p. 40.

93. Susan Sonntag, *On Photography* (New York: Picador, 2001), p. 3.

94. Foucault, *The Courage of Truth*, *op. cit.*, p. 14.

95. Barry, *op. cit.*

addition to courage, fearless speech calls upon a set of sociotechnical associations—the associative and rather banal side that serves as the counterpart to the individual and heroic.

In Behram's case his photography, his truth did not come to the attention of the press in the UK or US through the sheer force of its content. Instead, it required allies of various kinds who arranged events, publicity and so on. Behram has received support from a number of actors and groups who are actively campaigning to bring transparency and justice for the people who are on the receiving end of the US drone campaign in Waziristan. Prominent among these are the lawyer Shahzad Akbar, based in Islamabad where he heads the Foundation for Fundamental Human Rights, and the UK-based legal campaign group Reprieve, directed by Clive Stafford Smith. It was the latter, for instance, who was instrumental in staging the art exhibition in London. Meanwhile, *Wired* recounts some of the contributions of Akbar. For instance, Behram has not only taken photographs but also collected materials from the drone strikes. Survivors of drone strikes have given him pieces of the AGM-114 Hellfire missiles with which the drones obliterate their targets. It was Akbar who assisted in transporting these parts to a city in Punjab and then on to Islamabad. *Wired* reports Akbar saying it was "a 'hassle' to get the missile parts out of North Waziristan, as it would have been difficult to explain to a soldier or a policeman what they were doing with missile fragments in their car." "Hassle" is perhaps an understatement! In light of this one remark, and more generally as a way of complicating the image of fearless speech as the singular activity of one individual or even group, perhaps it might be useful, following Vandekerckhove and Langenberg, to speak of a "parrhesiastic chain." Sometimes it takes an interactive play of courageous acts and connections in order for the truth to be spoken and, crucially, heard.[96]

There is one final sense in which I want to work the notion of exposure. What happens to materials when they are exposed to the environment: to the actions of wind, sunlight, ice and rain? They can become weathered. If they are shiny they may lose their lustre. If brightly painted, they may become faded and worn. At the risk of overworking this metaphor, we might also observe that once exposed, a particular truth may also undergo a certain weathering process. It may also, with time, and subject to the social and political forces that greet it, undergo a change in appearance. It may lose some of the critical charge that it first carried into the public domain. Fearless speech may provoke disquiet; it may open a certain space of freedom where something can be posed in a different light. But we should not overlook the fact that the truth revealed may also undergo certain operations which may have the effect of blunting or transforming it. Let us return to Behram's photographs and missile parts one last time. At the start of its feature, *Wired* offers the following statement:

> Before posting Behram's photos we took a number of measures to confirm as best we could what was being shown. We verified Behram's *bona fides*

96. Analysing whistleblowing within the corporate world, Vandekerckhove and Langenberg (*op. cit.*, p. 39) argue: "[B]ecause most organizations are layered hierarchically, critique might have to travel upwards. This implies that the disorganising impact of [*parrhēsia*] can require a number of steps in a speaker-hearer/speaker chain, where a middle management hearer will need to become a speaker to top management."

> with other news organizations. We sifted through the images, tossing out any pictures that couldn't correlate with previously reported drone attacks. Then we grilled Behram in a series of lengthy Skype interviews from Pakistan, translated by Akbar, about the circumstances surrounding each of the images.[97]

With this remark it seems we are returned to the theme of Foucault's "grafts," of combinations between the different truth-telling modalities that I mentioned earlier. For media organisations to find the resolve to relay Behram's uncomfortable truths, to place them before a wider audience, these truths and their bearer have to be fact-checked. Behram's words and images carry a certain force due to the fact that, like all parrhesiasts, he risks so much in order to be heard. But at the same time, they only get into circulation if they can satisfy certain scientific and journalistic criteria of veracity. The embodied, motivated truth of *parrhēsia* becomes entangled within the disembodied, abstract methods of *tekhnē* and its regime of truth production.

Do the referent objects of Behram's exposure become weathered as a result of this entanglement? Do the injustices he catalogues lose some of their aura, and with it their capacity to shame and shock a public? Do they now derive their power to unsettle less from the fact that these are personal, embodied experiences, and more on the basis that they have been independently verified? Perhaps any given truth, once it is exposed and reproduced may ultimately fade or, if it endures, do so only through its translation into the modern regime of knowledge. No doubt a whole essay could be written on the theme of *parrhēsia* in the age of mechanical reproduction, to adapt Benjamin's famous thesis.[98] This article has pursued the more modest task of explaining *parrhēsia* and analysing some of its connections to the present. It is to something like a history of whistleblowing that we might look in order to answer the questions I have just raised about the weathering of truth. That history remains, for now, unwritten.

Concluding Remarks

At the outset I suggested that there are at least three areas in which engaging with the question of *parrhēsia* can advance our understanding of the contentious politics of security: the impact of the individual within contentious politics; the place of courage within the politics of resistance; and the contemporary politics of secrecy. By way of a conclusion I now revisit these areas in light of the preceding discussion.

First, *parrhēsia* provides a frame to analyse more clearly the place of individual action within the field of contentious politics. More specifically, it offers tools to study the act of speaking out. Research on social movements and non-governmental organisations (NGOs) has documented at length the tactics such social actors use to bear witness to injustice and to identify wrongs before a public.[99] These

97. Ackerman, *op. cit.*

98. See Walter Benjamin, "The Work of Art in the Age of Mechanical Reproduction", in Hannah Arendt (ed.), *Illuminations: Essays and Reflections* (New York: Schocken Books, 1968).

99. For example, see Fuyuki Kurasawa, *The Work of Global Justice: Human Rights as Practices* (New York: Cambridge University Press, 2007), esp. ch. 1.

collective agents are in key respects the descendants of the truth-telling modality that Foucault called *tekhnē*. Many invoke the authority of law, medicine, psychology and other expert knowledges when they campaign. But things are somewhat different when a person speaks out not as a representative for an organisation or an expert but unexpectedly and at great risk to themselves, as a principled conscientious subject. It means a name, a face, a conscience, a fate can become attached to an injustice in the public eye. *Parrhēsia* allows us to bring greater analytical precision to certain situations when protest takes the form of an individual who bears witness, or engages in some act of refusal or dissent.

The contentious politics of security and surveillance is today visibly contoured by some very public controversies involving individuals—Assange, Manning, Snowden and others—who have spoken out about the excesses of security practices, in some cases disclosing highly secretive information and facing the wrath of powerful sovereigns as a consequence. There is clearly a need for theoretical tools that can sharpen our accounts of political situations where political controversy crystallises around individual action. I argue that *parrhēsia* can be helpful here.

That said, we should not overgeneralise about *parrhēsia*. Like any concept it becomes rather blunt if stretched to cover all manner of acts of resistance and counter-conduct. Better to use it to make distinctions. For example, we might speculate that the truth telling of Daniel Ellsberg, Noor Behram, Edward Snowden or Malala Yousafzai is closer to the history of *parrhēsia* than the radical transparency of Julian Assange. To better understand Assange's place within the field of contentious politics one would surely look, at least initially, to other practices of dissent and their lineage. For example, one might fruitfully contextualise Assange and his political practice by relating them to the history of secret societies,[100] but equally to the history of those bourgeois groups who mobilised their polemics against the principles of *arcana imperii* upheld by the absolutist state.[101]

The bigger point here is not to suggest that political practices be placed in tidy little boxes, or that there is a hierarchy of political virtue with *parrhēsia* at the top. Rather, it is to suggest that a better account of *individualised* truth telling (for the subject is not just a bearer but an effect of these practices) and its relationship to the politics of security will benefit from a fuller grasp of *parrhēsia*. But equally it will require a clearer understanding of other, cognate practices of truth telling and counter-conduct. With his sketch of other modalities of truth telling pertinent to the Ancient world—the practice of the sage, the prophet and the technician—we saw how Foucault offers some coordinates for just this kind of wider understanding. But Foucault's should not, of course, be the last word. We do not live in Ancient Greece; we also need to fashion new concepts to register emergent forms and practices. How to make sense, for instance, of the anti-individualised truth-telling practices that are today associated with the moniker Anonymous?

100. For example, note Assange's background in anonymous hacking or his likening of Wikileaks to "an intelligence agency of the people"; see Mark Jenkins, "'We Steal Secrets': A Sidelong Look at Wikileaks", National Public Radio, 23 May 2013, available: <http://www.npr.org/2013/05/23/185533081/we-steal-secrets-a-sidelong-look-at-wikileaks> (accessed 11 July 2013).

101. Habermas, *op. cit.*, pp. 52–54. On secret societies as incubators for "modern political man," see Horn, *op. cit.*, pp. 111–112.

Unlike the parrhesiast who assumes "ownership for [her] words,"[102] it would seem that with Anonymous the ambiguous figure of the masked man/woman (Conspirator? Bandit? Superhero?) is reinstated within the public sphere.

Turning now to my second theme: what does a focus on *parrhēsia* bring to our understanding of the relationship between emotions and politics? This special issue has analysed the connection between affective economies and governmentality, a nexus of some interest to scholars of security. Recent studies have explored the governmentality of love in the area of migration,[103] the intertwining of compassion and repression that characterises many projects of humanitarian government,[104] and most of all the politics of fear and alienation animating many programmes of securitisation.[105] These undertakings all attest to a growing scholarly interest in emotions and governmentality, affect and power.

Certainly we could throw courage into this affective mix. One could perhaps speak of a *governmentality of courage.* This might draw attention to the various ways in which experts and authorities have sought to foster courage and manage fear, whether on the scale of a platoon of soldiers or a public at war. Courage might be read in this sense alongside studies in the engineering of resilience and morale.[106]

I argue that the kind of courage at stake with *parrhēsia* is not reducible to governmentality but neither does it entirely escape the realm of programmatic calculation and technologies of administration. Security studies tends to privilege the analysis of situations where emotions become entangled within calculative practices and function within administrative programmes—the *management* of morale, *technologies* of fear, etc. This is a legitimate and necessary focus. Yet I want to insist on the possibility of affective energies which exceed, if only temporarily, frameworks of capture and instrumentality.

To understand how *parrhēsia* overlaps with programmes of governmentality one only has to consider the powerful symbolic appeal that courage has in contemporary societies. Whether the focus is on survivors of terrorism, breast cancer or a tsunami, it is clear that tales of courage sell newspapers and raise charitable funds.[107] As a virtue, courage has great symbolic value in western public culture, much more than, say, humility. Events often get scripted in terms of a narrative of courageous action.

It is public respect for heroism that furnishes parrhesiastic action with what Hacking would call its "ecological niche."[108] No doubt many complex social, political and psychological forces and contingent elements affected Noor Behram in his decision to photograph and document drone strikes in Waziristan. To single

102. Foucault, *The Government of Self and Others, op. cit.*, p. 65.

103. Anne-Marie D'Aoust, "Circulations of Desire: The Security Governance of the International 'Mail-Order Brides' Industry", in M. de Larrinaga and M.G. Doucet (eds.), *Security and Global Governmentality: Globalization, Governance and the State* (Abingdon/New York: Routledge, 2010).

104. Didier Fassin, *Humanitarian Reason: A Moral History of the Present* (Berkeley, CA: University of California Press, 2012).

105. Jennifer Hyndman, "The Securitization of Fear in Post-Tsunami Sri Lanka", *Annals of the Association of American Geographers*, Vol. 97, No. 2 (2007), pp. 361–372.

106. Ben Anderson, "Morale and the Affective Geographies of the 'War on Terror'", *Cultural Geographies*, Vol. 17, No. 2 (2010), pp. 219–236.

107. I owe this point about the commodification of courage to one of my anonymous reviewers.

108. Ian Hacking, *Mad Travelers: Reflections on the Reality of Transient Mental Illnesses* (Charlottesville, VA: University of Virginia Press, 1998).

out his courage risks a kind of simplistic reduction: we fit him into a familiar hero narrative.[109] But in the dominant representation of his activity in western media—and within my own account here in terms of parrhesiastic exposure—this is precisely how his activity is coded. This becomes its dominant mode of signification. The larger point is that when *parrhēsia* takes place under contemporary conditions of mass-mediated publicity, it is subject to and even complicit in the same processes of selection, reduction and reification that shape most other forms of public communication. *Parrhēsia* does not enjoy a status that entirely escapes or transgresses the norms of governmentality and the grammar of the public sphere.

And yet to leave our assessment at that would risk a rather gloomy and somewhat fatalist account of *parrhēsia*. It might imply that *parrhēsia* today is subject to the same kind of instrumentalisation that Habermas and others associate with the decline of the modern public sphere.[110] This is not my intent. While *parrhēsia* mutates it does not vanish. I want to hold open the possibility that despite, or even in conjunction with forces of instrumentalisation and recuperation, there is an excess to *parrhēsia*, a surplus energy that can sometimes overflow governmentality and unsettle, however briefly, a given state of affairs. It is perhaps a matter of marking those occasions when an individual or a group risks their life or livelihood to exercise a freedom, a freedom that exceeds whatever right of freedom or promise of life a given regime holds on offer to its subjects. The Obama administration is reported as prosecuting whistleblowers in the security and intelligence domain at "double the number of all [US] presidents combined."[111] This fact alone suggests that *parrhēsia* today is still, in whatever modified form, a significant and viable source of political energy.

Finally, there is the question of *parrhēsia* and regime types, specifically its relationship to liberal democracies. As we noted earlier, Foucault observes that for the Greeks democracy was "the place in which *parrhēsia* is most difficult to practice."[112] This had much to do with the institutionalisation of freedom of speech among citizens. When a certain right to speak freely is guaranteed, the potential for speech to shock and unsettle is perhaps lessened. Does the guarantee of freedom of speech that liberal democracies promise us make *parrhēsia* more difficult and more rare today? Perhaps. But that is a question I cannot satisfactorily address in the space that remains. What can be said is that freedom of speech is not only institutionalised but exercised very unevenly in our societies. It is of course not a supreme value that trumps all others so much as a principle that exists in tension with other imperatives, none more so than national security. As Galison has documented so effectively, while the history of political secrecy is very long indeed, the regime of modern governmental secrecy only takes shape during World War II.[113] It is then, in conjunction with the rise of nuclear weapons research, that a vast "modern secrecy system" comes into being. One of its

109. The public acclamation of heroism is of course not exclusive to modernity. On the importance of narratives of heroism in Ancient Greece and the role of dramatic arts in conveying the "full meaning" of the hero to the public, see Hannah Arendt, *The Human Condition* (Chicago, IL: University of Chicago Press, 1998), pp. 186–187.

110. Habermas, *op. cit.*

111. Glenn Greenwald, "On Whistleblowers and Government Threats of Investigation", *The Guardian*, 7 June 2013.

112. Foucault, *The Courage of Truth, op. cit.*, p. 57.

113. Galison, *op. cit.*, p. 590.

consequences is that when it comes to published knowledge, "the classified universe ... is certainly not smaller, and very probably much larger than the unclassified one."[114] When we consider the extent of this classified universe, and the other associated ways in which speech is suppressed, (self-)censored and distorted in the name of security, when we take stock of the redacted state of our public sphere, it seems reasonable to conclude that there is ample scope and subject matter for *parrhēsia* today.

About the Author

William Walters is cross-appointed in the Department of Political Science and the Department of Sociology / Anthropology at Carleton University, Canada. His most recent book is *Governmentality: Critical Encounters* (Routledge, 2012). He is currently researching the material politics of secrecy.

114. *Ibid.*

The Capitalisation of 'Excess Life' through Life Insurance

LUIS LOBO-GUERRERO

The role of life insurance, as portrayed by the industry, is to get individuals and heirs back in financial circulation after accidents and catastrophic events. This role, however, is not innocent. It involves a complex problematisation of what it means to render life as valuable, commodifiable and securable. Life insurance effects a translation of the current and potential economic value of a life into investment capital. In return, it offers a form of security that promises compensation against insurable events. While insuring, the industry creates economies of security that have a historical dimension as they are anchored to the development of liberal economies. These economies are possible by what is here termed the "excess of life," which in turn becomes potential for resisting the biopolitical order of insurance. This article critically engages with the film Code 46 as an empirical site from which to make evident the political possibility of "excess life." After an analytical depiction of the film, the article offers an analysis of the valuation of life as practices of inclusion, which involve a vital ontology and which produce moral economies. The article concludes with a reflection on the immanent resistance to life's valuation.

> If we had enough information we could predict the consequences of our actions. If we know what would happen in the end, would we be able to take the first step, to make the first move?[1]

Life insurance, a 2.52 trillion USD industry by 2010,[2] is usually presented as a set of financial instruments through which the security of livelihoods and lifestyles can be protected. The Association of British Insurers (ABI) defines life insurance and pensions as "products that protect your income/lifestyle, and in some cases your family, in the event of premature death or even just once you reach retirement age and are no longer working."[3]

---

*This article was originally presented at the panel "Cultural Circuits of Capitalism and the Rise of the Symbolic Economy: Territoriality, Capital Flows and Emotions," International Studies Annual Convention, Montreal, March 2011. I am grateful to the editors of this special issue and participants of the panel for useful comments. Funding for research leading to this article was provided by The Leverhulme Trust grant F/00 130/Q, "Capitalising Security through Life Insurance in the UK."

1. M. Winterbottom, *Code 46* (Verve Pictures: Revolutions Films Ltd. / BBC / UK Film Council, 2003), preface. Subsequent citations to the film refer to time points in the film.

2. D. Staib and L. Bevere, "World Insurance in 2010: Premiums Back to Growth, Capital Increases", *Swiss Re, Sigma*, Vol. 2 (2011), pp. 1–42.

3. ABI, "Life Insurance", available: <http://www.abi.org.uk/Information/Consumers/Life/Life_Insurance.aspx> (accessed 24 February 2011).

> Life insurance offers valuable financial protection in the event of your early death if you have family dependent on your earnings. But it can also be a means of saving. This combination of protection and saving makes life insurance unlike any other financial product. Some policies protect, some help you to save and some do both.[4]

Operating a financial form of security that promises reparation in case "things go wrong," life insurance is an industry that profits from the possibility of mobilising fear with regards to the death or illness of a breadwinner. Parents are constantly reminded of their duty of care towards their family's future. The message is portrayed through advertisements with questions such as: What would happen to your family or your home should you die unexpectedly? How would you and your family cope if you suffered serious illness such as a heart attack? If you were ill and off work for a long period of time, how would this affect your lifestyle?[5] In other cases family protection is equated with the need to protect assets.

> Protect your family not just your belongings. Many of us take out insurance for our mobiles, cars, homes or holidays. But what about your family's future? Protecting the people we love is more important than anything else.[6]

This kind of protection against fear of the uncertain is not a one-off event; it is a lifelong journey which the life insurance business transforms into a market for protection. An important insurance company in the United Kingdom uses the motto "For the journey" as a way to remind its clients that life insurance is part of a way of life, a lifelong requirement/companion that generates "peace of mind." For a couple beginning their life together and buying their first home, mortgage life insurance and income protection are presented as indispensable. As they enter their 30 s, the couple who begin to have babies are reminded to revise their insurance cover to include a level term assurance plan and critical illness cover to provide for the needs of the growing family and to anticipate life contingencies. When the couple enter their 40 s, a new form of life insurance with a savings element should be introduced, and in their 50 s preparing for retirement might involve some form of annuity to cover the contingencies of old age.

There is, however, nothing natural or innocent about life insurance and its promises. They are entrenched within political imaginaries of protection, imaginaries that entail institutionalised ways of understanding what it means to promote and safeguard a way of life. They are embedded within a very particular capitalist appreciation of economics in which insurance operates a technology of financial reparation by means of creating markets of security. Economy is here understood, following Daston, as "an organised system that displays certain regularities, regularities that are explicable but not always predictable in their details."[7]

4. ABI, "Life (Non-investment) Insurance", available: <http://www.abi.org.uk/Information/Consumers/Life/Life_Noninvestment_Insurance.aspx> (accessed 24 February 2011).

5. Natwest, "Why Is Protection Important?", available: <http://www.natwest.com/personal/insurance/g1/life-insurance/why-life-insurance.ashx> (accessed 26 July 2012).

6. Aviva, "A Guide to Protecting Your Family's Future", p. 6, available: <http://www.aviva.co.uk/adviser/life-insurance-documents/view-document.cgi?f=pt15366c.pdf&lid=prod-lit-New Parent Free Life Cover&lpos=pt15366c.pdf2010> (accessed 26 July 2012).

7. L. Daston, "The Moral Economy of Science", *Osiris*, 2nd Series, Vol. 10 (1995), pp. 2–24, at p. 4.

The logic of these economies of security is not exclusive to insurance. It resembles other better-known and well-studied technologies of protection such as defence and national security, a resemblance that is locked into what others have analysed as a western metaphysics of thinking security.[8] Whereas defence and national security operate on the fear of threats to the stability and survival of states and political regimes,[9] insurance instantiates economies of security based on a different problematisation of fear: the fear of individuals and their families being exposed to the uncertainties of life and of the life-course.[10]

The economies of security that result from insurance practices and imaginaries are developed and presented to the public as security portfolios to protect against the financial uncertainties derived from the unforeseen "events" of life. The outstanding feature of these economies is not only that they are premised on an understanding of life as "evental," a feature that calls for the interrogation of the conditions of possibility of its regularities. It is also that life insurance effects a translation of life into capital that can be invested and profited from. While operating economies of security, insurers extract value from the life-course (aging process) and life-potential (career and economic development) of their clients and transform them into investment capital. The instrument through which this process is possible is the insurance policy, a device that renders the life of the client fungible as a security that can be traded and exchanged.[11] The policy, in turn, generates a premium, a cash payment which generates a flow of income that insurance companies invest into a portfolio of assets and securities to generate the funds with which to honour claims, but also to generate profit for the company stockholders.[12]

Francois Ewald, writing in the early 1990s, had already recognised this feature and noted that "[b]y objectivizing certain events as risks, insurance can invert their meanings; it can make what was previously an obstacle into a possibility. Insurance assigns a new mode of existence to previously dreaded events; it creates value."[13] This is not a new phenomenon in the liberal world. A quote

8. For example, M. Dillon, *Politics of Security: Towards a Political Philosophy of Continental Thought* (London: Routledge, 1996); D. Campbell, *Writing Security: United States Foreign Policy and the Politics of Identity* (Manchester: Manchester University Press, 1998); M. Neocleous, *Critique of Security* (Edinburgh: Edinburgh University Press, 2008); J. Reid, *The Biopolitics of the War on Terror: Life Struggles, Liberal Modernity and the Defence of Logistical Societies* (Manchester: Manchester University Press, 2009); M. Dillon and J. Reid, *The Liberal Way of War: Killing to Make Life Live* (London: Routledge, 2009); M. Foucault, *Security, Territory, Population: Lectures at the Collège de France* (Houndmills, Basingstoke: Palgrave Macmillan, 2009); S. Weber, *Targets of Opportunity: On the Militarization of Thinking* (New York: Fordham University Press, 2005).

9. For example, J. Baylis, J.W. Wirtz and C.S. Gray, *Strategy in the Contemporary World: An Introduction to Strategic Studies* (Oxford: Oxford University Press, 2009); C. v. Clausewitz, *On War* (Princeton, NJ: Princeton University Press, 1989); B. Buzan, *People, States, and Fear: The National Security Problem In International Relations* (Chapel Hill, NC: University of North Carolina Press, 1983).

10. For example, P. O'Malley, *Risk, Uncertainty and Government* (London: Glasshouse Press, 2004); R. Ericson, A. Doyle and D. Barry, *Insurance as Governance* (Toronto: University of Toronto Press, 2003); F. Ewald, "Insurance and Risk", in G. Burchell (ed.), *The Foucault Effect: Studies in Governmental Rationality* (Hemel Hempstead: Harvester Wheatsheaf, 1991), pp. 197–210; S. French and J. Kneale, "Excessive Financialisation: Insuring Lifestyles, Enlivening Subjects, and Everyday Spaces of Biosocial Excess", *Environment and Planning D: Society and Space*, Vol. 27, No. 6 (2009), pp. 1030–1053.

11. See L. Lobo-Guerrero, *Insuring Security: Biopolitics, Security and Risk* (London: Routledge, 2011).

12. M. Kirova and L. Steinmann, "Understanding Profitability in Life Insurance", *Sigma - Swiss Re*, Vol. 1 (2012), pp. 1–35.

13. Ewald, "Insurance and Risk", *op. cit.*, p. 200.

copied by him from an insurance text written in 1884 is evidence that such an understanding of the role of insurance was already clear to commentators on the field in the late nineteenth century.

> Insurance is eminently creative where, completing the interrupted work snatched by death from the hands of the family man, it instantly realizes the capital which was to have been the fruit of savings; it is eminently creative when it gives the aged man with inadequate resources the pension needed to sustain his declining years.[14]

The quote acts as a reminder that life insurance is and has been a central element in the history of liberalism, a phenomenon that invites a question on the relationship between life insurance and the creation of value under liberal regimes. It is important to note in passing that the analysis offered in this piece relates to private forms of insurance, those premised on a principle of mutuality as compared to public insurance schemes which rely on principles of solidarity.

Denoting regularity in the appreciation of life as capital, life insurance can be interrogated with regards to the role that the idea of "value" performs in constituting economies of security. In creating this form of value, which could accurately be referred to as biovalue if the term had not already been colonised by authors such as Rose and Waldby when referring to the capitalisation of genes and human tissue,[15] insurers perform a security effect in the form of moral economies. Moral economies are understood in this article as an efficient way of governing conduct collectively and from a distance. They are a form of economic government whereby the "common sense" of individuals is acted upon, silently, to ensure an order with clearly defined rules and expectations.

Making explicit what those rules and expectations are is not simply a matter of interrogating the terms and conditions of insurance contracts but demands an engagement with what gets sacrificed by insurers in the process of ascribing "value" to life. The *excess* that results from valuing life as capital is not understood here as exceeding in amount or degree, but instead as that which escapes the imaginaries and practices of valuation through which lived life and life-potential are rendered as capital; a remainder, which is not waste. Life's excess is a source of resistance to the ensembles of power/knowledge that problematise and govern life.[16] How to visualise that excess constitutes a challenge which is approached in this article by engaging with what Rancière referred to as "the aesthetic regime of the arts."[17]

---

14. A. Chaufton, *Les Assurances leur passe, leur present, leur avenir* (Paris, 1884), p. 209.

15. See C. Waldby and R. Mitchell, *Tissue Economies: Blood, Organs, and Cell Lines in Late Capitalism* (Durham, NC: Duke University Press, 2006); N. Rose, *The Politics of Life Itself: Biomedicine, Power, and Subjectivity in The Twenty-First Century* (Princeton, NJ: Princeton University Press, 2007).

16. M. Vatter, "Biopolitics: From Surplus Value to Surplus Life", *Theory and Event*, Vol. 12, No. 2 (2009), doi: 10.1353/tae.0.0062; S. Prozorov, "The Unrequited Love of Power: Biopolitical Investment and the Refusal of Care", *Foucault Studies*, Vol. 1, No. 4 (2007), pp. 53–77; M. Dillon and L. Lobo-Guerrero, "Biopolitics of Security in the 21st Century", *Review of International Studies*, Vol. 34, No. 2 (2008), pp. 265–292.

17. J. Rancière, *The Politics of Aesthetics* (New York: Continuum, 2004), p. 13. The aesthetic regime of the arts has been explored within International Relations with regards to film, most notably by Shapiro. See M. Shapiro, *Cinematic Political Thought* (Edinburgh: Edinburgh University Press, 1999); M. Shapiro, *Cinematic Geopolitics* (London: Routledge, 2009); M. Shapiro, *Studies in Trans-Disciplinary Method: After the Aesthetic Turn* (London: Routledge, 2013).

For Rancière, the aesthetic regime of the arts was a result of his interrogation of critical artistic practices. As analysed by Michael Shapiro, the role of these "practices [is to] 'disturb' accepted relationships between 'the sayable and the visible' and [...] effectively repartition the 'distribution of the sensible'."[18] From this perspective, critical artistic practices constitute sites for critical thinking, as put by Shapiro, "[t]o think rather than to reproduce accepted knowledge frames [...] to create the conditions of possibility for imagining alternative worlds (and thus be able to recognize the political commitments sequestered in every political imaginary."[19]

Taking the film *Code 46*, directed by Michael Winterbottom in 2003 and written by Frank Cotrell Boyce, as a critical artistic practice, this article explores the excess of biopolitics present in, and constitutive of, life insurance. Although a work of science fiction, albeit not a traditional one,[20] *Code 46* reveals several aspects of the role that insurance in general, but life insurance in particular, plays in the valuation of life as capital. The film operates as a work of art that performs an immanent critique of insurance as a provider of security for contemporary liberal life, a critique that invites a reflection on its technological role in modulating agency, desire, behaviour and responsibility.

The article proceeds in three parts. It begins by offering a detailed analytical narrative of the argument of the film focused on what is here termed a "rape" of biopolitics.[21] The richness of detail in this section is required as the empirical base for the next part devoted to analysing three dimensions of valuation immanent to the ways in which life insurance transforms livelihoods and lifestyles into investment capital: valuation as a practice of inclusion; valuation as vital ontology; and valuation as the basis for moral economies. The article concludes with a reflection on the relationship between the "vital excess" and the resistance to life's valuation immanent in life insurance practices.

Code 46 and the Rape of Biopolitical Security

In the imaginary futuristic world of *Code 46* liberal governance in the developed world was overtaken by insurance. There, insurance provided the technology for authorising or denying all forms of human interaction and circulation, from sexual intercourse and birth, to exit and entrance into areas of the civilised world. The inside world was one in which risks were kept under strict control and infringements to the established order were punished with exile. Insurance "cover" was a prerequisite for human circulation and modulated individuals' behaviour by linking biometric identifiers such as fingerprints with credit ratings in the form of a card that replaced passports and visas. The kind of "cover" protecting an individual would be displayed by a card which turned red as cover expired. It could be extended to allow its holder to circulate outside of the protected liberal area, referred to in the film as *afuera*, but cover outside would be limited in time and granted only if the risks involved were deemed "manageable".

18. Shapiro, *Studies in Trans-Disciplinary Method, op. cit.*, p. xiii.

19. *Ibid.*, p. xiv.

20. B.M. Goss, "Taking Cover From Progress: Michael Winterbottom's Code 46", *Journal of Communication Inquiry*, Vol. 31, No. 1 (2007), pp. 62–78.

21. For a more descriptive approach to the film, see Goss, *op. cit.*

Afuera—the Spanish word for outside—was the world where people did not, or could not, measure and manage uncertainty in terms of risks. Risks in the imaginary of *Code 46* were tightly linked to a set of human scientific disasters, for example high exposure to the risk of incest as the result of decades of *in vitro* fertilisation based on a batch of only 24 cloned foetuses. To manage the risk of accidental incest among couples, the authorities of that imaginary world issued Code 46, a law that established strict rules on human reproduction and which in its first article stated:

> any human being who shares the same nuclear gene set as another human being is deemed to be genetically identical; the relations of one are the relations of all... Due to IVF, DI [donor insemination] embryo splitting and cloning techniques it is necessary to prevent any accidental or deliberately incestuous reproduction.[22]

Code 46 was an overwhelming instrument of birth authorisation and moral order. It asked all prospective parents to undergo genetic screening before even trying to conceive, and matches of 100, 50 or 25% led to a prohibition to reproduce. Unplanned pregnancies incurring a violation of the code would be terminated. If prospective parents were ignorant of their mutual genetic relationship at the moment of conception, medical intervention was authorised to prevent further breaches to the code. Conscientious breaches were treated as criminal offences and led, potentially, to the exile of parents into the world of *afuera*.

Experimentation with artificial fertilisation, embryo splitting and cloning in the imaginary of *Code 46* played the role of original sin for Christianity. Disastrous consequences in the artificial creation of life provided the foundation for a moral narrative that authorised the governance of reproduction and of human interaction, two related dimensions of life deemed to be dangerous. The risk of incest became a principle of operability for a moral order that fostered genetic diversity as a condition for insurability. Genetic similarity was seen as a threat to the security of a wide pool of genetically diverse individuals, the "covered" citizens. The danger consisted not only of a threat to the health tissue of society—a consequence of which was the condemnation of genetic criminals and illegally conceived babies to living *afuera*—but it also challenged the governmental possibility of harvesting a healthy gene pool in the liberal world, the very possibility of a form of governance that relied almost entirely on the agency of insurers. While endangering the technology that enabled genetic and moral order in society, breaches to the code were treated as a security matter which warranted, as illustrated towards the end of the film, the immediate attention of the authorities. Jurisdiction in relation to the code included both the worlds of inside and *afuera*.

The moral economy instantiated by insurance in the world of *Code 46*, however, transcended the authorisation of births and the freedom of movement. It operated at the level of the deep dreams and wishes of individuals in an urge to protect them from events that would compromise the security of their genetic disposition. In this respect, the authority of *Code 46* was directed at colonising the imaginaries of individuals. Imaginaries are understood here as planes which are liberated from the rational strictures of moral governance and are motivated instead on

22. Winterbottom, *op. cit.*, 1–20.

the realm of emotion. They relate to Deleuze's idea of planes of immanence, where the wildest dreams driven by feelings and affects have the capacity to materialise into possible disruptions of order. The authority of *Code 46* intervenes in that realm pre-empting disruption, an intervention which is not wholly successful, as will be analysed later when referring to the rape of Maria.

Damian Alekan, a black man living in Shanghai—a city included in the inside (liberal) world but surrounded by the world of *afuera*—and whose passion in life was bats, had struggled over a period of eight years to get cover to fulfil his lifelong dream, to visit a particular colony of bats in Delhi. The Sphinx, a Shanghai-based insurance corporation specialising in the issue of short-term cover certificates for specific activities such as dangerous travel, had systematically denied Damian the *papel* (insurance certificates) required to travel *afuera*. Maria (played by Samantha Morton), a printer of *papels* at the Sphinx and who had lived *afuera* for 10 years as a result of her father's loss of cover due to financial irregularities, produced for him a faked *papel* which he used to go to Delhi, only to die of an ineluctable disposition to Wards disease. The Sphinx, whose motto was "Always knows best," was aware of his disposition to the disease, a disease to which most people in Delhi were immune, "which is why he could not get cover."[23]

William (played by Tim Robbins) was a fraud investigator based in Seattle working for a security consultancy hired by the Sphinx to look at an event of fraud at the company. A faked *papel* had been issued by one of the printers and as a consequence its bearer died performing a dangerous activity in the world of *afuera*. William had been tasked with identifying the guilty printer. To do his job, which consisted of intruding into people's thoughts to find out "factual truths," he was provided by his employer with an "empathy virus." Under the influence of the virus, all William had to do was ask his interlocutors to tell him something about their personal lives and he would then be able to intrude into their thoughts and know if they were guilty of having printed the fake *papel*. At the Sphinx he interviewed all staff of the printing department and had identified Maria as the culprit. The problem was, however, that he felt more than empathy for her and decided instead to identify one of her colleagues as the guilty printer.

Seduced by his liking of Maria, William reported the results of his investigation to the Sphinx's manager.

> "Are you sure it's him?" asked the manager. "I thought it might be her," pointing at Maria's picture. "I don't think so," replied William. "Do you have evidence?" insisted the manager. "I don't need to give you evidence, it's intuition you're paying me for," replied William.[24]

In the world of *Code 46*, viruses were not only vectors of disease but had also been genetically manipulated into instruments that could influence body reactions or enhance individuals' senses. Although the Sphinx claimed to know it all, it hired a consultant with enhanced intuition to identify who had manufactured the fake *papel*. The empathy virus enhanced "intuitive guessing." This virus-enhanced intuitive knowledge rivalled the "objective evidence-base" used by

23. *Ibid.*, 37:38–38:03.
24. *Ibid.*, 12:50–13:06.

the Sphinx to claim "it knew best." Intuition, as a "direct perception of truth, fact [. . .], independent of any reasoning process,"[25] revealed, however, a form of *faith* which was necessary for its success. This became evident in a dialogue between Maria and William when he coincidentally met her on the train on the way back to the hotel. During the interview at the Sphinx, Maria had told William it was her birthday and during their encounter on the train Maria asked him to take her to dinner. She also suggested going to a club afterwards; her intention was not to sleep throughout the day since she was afraid of a dream she had been having every birthday. At the club William revealed to Maria the secret of his job.

> "I'm on a virus right now, an empathy virus. I take an empathy virus to help with my work," said William. "I don't like that, that's weird. You could pick up stuff about me," replied Maria. "I could," said William. "That's like wearing x-ray specs, to look at girls' underwear," replied Maria. "I got x-ray specs, they don't work," added William. "But you bought them. You wanted them to work," argued Maria. "I was six years old. I was interested in skeletons, not underwear," replied William.[26]

After revealing his secret, they both met Damian who had come to the club. Conscious of his complicity in what was about to happen—witnessing Maria giving the fake *papel* to Damian—William wanted to know of Damian's reason for needing fake cover. En route from the airport to Shanghai, at an entry point, William had made conversation with a street vendor who had asked him, jokingly, if he would agree to change places with him so that the vendor could come into Shanghai. Having heard the conversation, William's driver told him, "if people don't have cover, there's a reason." That's exactly what William mentioned to Damian.[27]

> "Yes," Damian replied, "the Sphinx knows best. Best. The Sphinx knows a lot. It doesn't know what I know. Anyone who has ever wanted something knows you have to be prepared to risk. I think I'll be okay. Some things in life can be worth the risk to get it."[28]

The risk Damian spoke of, however, differed from the Sphinx's understanding of this concept. As far as they were concerned, what he wanted to do, the event for which he needed cover, was nothing but certain uncertainty, that is, an activity which would in all likelihood lead to his death and therefore to a claim and a loss of profit for the Sphinx. For this reason they had consistently refused Damian's *papel* under a simple principle of risk management through which they aimed at protecting the lives of those insured and the interests of the company's shareholders. He was, however, never informed of this reason. The Sphinx knows best, he was told, and "if people are refused cover, it's for a reason."

---

25. As defined by dictionary.com (accessed 17 February 2011); See also <http://dictionary.reference.com/browse/intuition>.

26. Winterbottom, *op. cit.*, 18:09–18:35.

27. *Ibid.*, 19:54–19:56.

28. *Ibid.*, 19:58–20:11.

Damian's knowledge of what was best for him was premised on a different base than that of the Sphinx. For him, life was more than managed and controlled risk. It involved the thrill of doing what he had always wanted to even if the apparent price to pay was high. It was the thrill of playing outside the system, of embracing the possibility of being responsible for his own actions and being free to bear the uncertainty involved in what was presented as "risky." It was an attitude of liberation, a way of being beyond itself, of breaking away from the self that the world of *Code 46* had instilled in him and a self of which he wanted to take control, even if it meant a one-way ticket to *afuera* and then to death. This knowledge was not comprehensible to the rationality of protection underlying the business model and corporate responsibility of the Sphinx where life could only be "if insured." Paradoxically, once again, it was the existence of an *afuera* that operated as the contrast against which the Sphinx could provide order and security. Knowing that a life *afuera* entailed no protection, exposure to the dangers of natural light (people in the world of inside lived at night and slept during the day to protect themselves from dangerous sunlight) and no support in case things went wrong, allowed the Sphinx and other insurance providers to design cover for a lifestyle free from those dangers. In other words, the Sphinx and the wider insurance complex created an *inside* as a space of security. After all, a world of risk, as managed and controlled uncertainty, was only possible in the film—as in real life—in contrast to an imagined state of certainty, of death, for example.

When William's boss in Seattle asked him to return to Shanghai to investigate the death of Damian, which had been identified as related to a fake *papel* produced by the same printer he had been sent to investigate in the past, William discovered that Maria was no longer working for the Sphinx. He found out she had been removed to a clinic *afuera* where she was allegedly being treated for a lost finger and provided with a prosthesis. He realised, however, that she had been "intervened" in relation to a violation of Code 46 and the replaced finger acted as placebo, an "intervention" enabled through and covered by her "insurance cover." They had removed the foetus as well as her memories of the man with whom she had slept and unknowingly violated the code. Claiming to be dealing with a fraud investigation—although at this stage he was dealing with his private business—William demanded that Maria be released from the clinic and he then drove her to her flat in Shanghai.

While she slept, William had his and her DNA tested, only to find out that Maria and his mother were genetically identical, hence the unwanted violation of Code 46 that led to Maria's "intervention." He explained this to Maria when she woke up but she could not remember anything apart from a strange dream of which she could not make sense.

Meanwhile, William had spent most of his period of cover in Shanghai and by the time he decided to return home his credit card had turned red, indicating that his cover had expired and he was not allowed to "circulate" back home. Ironically, he was still covered in Seattle, but not for the journey to get there. He returned to Maria seeking help with a fake *papel* to get him home, which she managed to provide on an exit-only basis. When Maria delivered the *papel* to William at the airport, she told him she now remembered having seen him in her dream. William, under the seduction that had led him to protect Maria in the past, decided to change his plans and travel not to Seattle but to *afuera*, to the free port of Jebel Ali, together with Maria.

Once at Jebel Ali, Maria asked him to have sexual intercourse with her. Her body, however, resisted any contact with William. When going to kiss him, she felt flu-like symptoms induced by a virus instilled in her at the clinic to prevent future liaisons with the forbidden man.

> "The Sphinx gave you a virus," explained William. "Like what? An anti-William virus?" replied Maria. "It's involuntary, it's like adrenalin. When you're scared of something, your body gets ready to run away," added William. "I'm not scared of you," Maria replied. "I know, but your body is," said William. "I want you to make love to me. Make me make love to you. I love you," whispered Maria.[29]

William helped Maria to act against her virus-induced will by tying her to the bed. He then took her body and mind in what amounted to an act of rape against the world of *Code 46*. The morning after, Maria, following the instinct induced by the virus, got up and phoned the authorities in Shanghai to report a violation of Code 46. She did so as if requesting a service from a friendly authority. With a feeling of satisfaction at having done her duty, she then returned to William who knew that they should start to run. While driving an old rented car through a desert road, they crashed in their attempt to dodge a caravan of camels and both of them lost consciousness.

The crash site was soon visited by authorities responding to the Code 46 violation and both Maria and William were taken into care. After the incident, William was exonerated by a tribunal who decided that his actions had been induced by the empathy virus. As a consequence of the ruling, his memory of the events was removed and all he could remember was that he had crashed a car in Shanghai. He was then returned to his wife and children in Seattle.

Maria, in contrast, was exiled to the world of *afuera* and left to her own resources.

> "I was exiled because I tried to cheat the Sphinx. They left me my memories. They don't care what you think if you're outside. Why bother? To them, it's as if we don't exist."[30]

Valuing Life as Capital

In the analytical narrative offered above it is possible to identify three dimensions that are immanent to contemporary life insurance practices: valuation as a practice of inclusion; valuation as vital ontology; and valuation as the basis for moral economies.

The first of these refers to its role in creating spaces of inclusion and exclusion, traditionally analysed in post-structuralist International Relations theory as the inside/outside.[31] These spaces are, however, not geographically determined,

29. *Ibid.*, 1:13–1:14.

30. *Ibid.*, 1:23:41–1:24:02.

31. See R.B.J. Walker, *One World, Many Worlds: Struggles for a Just World Peace* (London: L. Rienner Publishers, 1988); R.B.J. Walker, *Inside/Outside: International Rrelations as Political Theory* (Cambridge

although they are territorially related. They operate practices of governance in relation to the needs of circulation and interaction of the individual being insured. In so doing, they operate a clear distinction between which forms of circulation are covered and which are not, for example exclusions in life policies from travelling to particular countries and regions of the world. As clearly depicted in the film, inside spaces are those where risks are deemed manageable and controllable through technologies of insurance. The outside, or the world of *afuera*, is the realm of uncontrollable risks and feral uncertainty. The role of insurance in providing cover for some, and not all, forms of circulation, including and excluding some lifestyles (e.g. smokers, heavy drinkers), contributes to creating spaces of governance where activities and behaviours are relatively "secure". In so doing, however, a space of insecure governance is simultaneously constituted either as its radical opposite or as a gradient of opposition to the order of the insured world where insurers would try to penetrate while seeking market opportunities.

Value in this respect acquires a dimension of inclusion, of including lives within a political community. Whereas the operation of insurance in constituting the boundary of inside/outside is usually ignored or neglected in political analysis, insurance establishes boundaries without which it would not be possible to understand zones of protection.[32] Those insured are eligible for certain forms of circulation which are not accessible by default. Linking the idea of value to inclusion relates to the idea that only that which is considered valuable is worth protecting. An analysis of how value is constituted and how valuation processes proceed is therefore a way to explore a condition of possibility for political community, a link that is central to the possibility of liberalism and needs to be explored in great detail.

This element is intimately linked to a second one. Insurance, in its urge to render life fungible (i.e. amenable to trade and exchange), requires a vital ontology of value. Private insurance technologies, operating a principle of mutuality—or of actuarial "fairness"[33]—need an understanding of life that can be commodified. Livelihoods and lifestyles, as organic features of wider political economies, are under constant transformation and change. Insurers require a knowledge base that informs them on what to expect from life, from life processes, life-courses and lifestyles. Finding a base on which to anchor expectation is therefore an existential angst for insurers. Traditionally this has been done by calculating the probabilities of occurrence of future events based on statistical records. History has been approached by mainstream insurance companies as a depository of facts that if properly mined and interpreted can provide the knowledge with which to inform their expectations.[34] For example, in the case of life and health insurance products, issues such as family history have been used as an element with which

and New York: Cambridge University Press, 1993); R.B.J. Walker, *After the Globe, Before the World* (London and New York: Routledge, 2010); D. Bigo, S. Carrera, E. Guild and R.B.J. Walker (eds.), *Europe's 21st Century Challenge: Delivering Liberty* (Farnham, Surrey: Ashgate, 2010).

32. For example, L. Lobo-Guerrero, *Insuring War: Sovereignty, Security and Risk* (London: Routledge, 2012).

33. D.A. Stone, "The Struggle for the Soul of Health Insurance", *Journal of Health Politics Policy and Law*, Vol. 18, No. 2 (1993), pp. 287–317.

34. A distinction must be made here with specialist forms of insurance which demand specialist underwriting. These are used to insure against new events such as machines based on or exposed to new technologies (e.g. nanotechnological devices) and are underwritten at specialist markets such as

to prognosticate health and life events.[35] Family histories of breast cancer, stroke and heart disease, to name a few, are used as indicators of a heightened risk which translate, potentially, into higher premium levels.

Immanent to that understanding of history is a desire for a solid and irrefutable ontology to source actuarial practice as an evidence-based science. The hype of genetic determinism that followed the sequencing of the human genome at the turn of the twenty-first century, revealed, however, that such ontology would not be found by putting trust in a genetic imaginary.[36] If individuals were indeed genetically determined and scientific research could detail all the possible gene combinations and their implications in terms of future disease, insurers would only be approached by individuals with clear illness prospects. Not being able to balance good and bad risks, the business model on which private insurance operates would fail to work.

In the world of *Code 46*, genetic determinism plays a double role as an ontological condition. On the one hand it becomes an instrument through which incest, as the unacceptable way of conceiving life, can be prevented and in the process decisions on who can procreate with whom can be micro-managed. An imaginary of genetic determinism gives rise to the authority to procreate. On the other hand, genetic determinism enables *expectation*. The Sphinx was certain that Damian Alekan had a predisposition towards Wards disease and therefore insurance cover to travel to Delhi, where exposure to bats would certainly kill him, should certainly be denied. Correlating the genetic make-up of individuals with the logical risks associated with specific genes allowed the Sphinx to claim the protection of its pool of insurable subjects from the dangers of risky environments and lifestyles. Belief in genetic determinism provided the "security of expectation" that supports the very possibility of economies of security. Security of expectation serves as the pivot on which to anchor the valuation of life. With such a pivot in place it is possible then to design and develop insurance products to protect against normal and specialist risks.

In the film, however, such a notion of value rendered on rational expectation is radically disrupted. When William decides to leave his family to travel with Maria to Jebel Ali, and when Maria begs William to make her make love to him while knowing that her virus induces her body to physically reject him, the value of

---

Lloyd's of London. T. Maynard and D. Baxter, *Nanotechnology: Recent Developments, Risks and Opportunities* (London: Lloyd's of London, 2007).

35. M.A. Rothstein, *Genetics and Life Insurance: Medical Underwriting and Social Policy* (Cambridge, MA: Massachusetts Institute for Technology, 2004).

36. See H.W. Baillie and T.K. Casey, *Is Human Nature Obsolete? Genetics, Bioengineering, and the Future of the Human Condition* (Cambridge, MA: MIT Press, 2004); P.L. Brockett and S.E. Tankersley, "The Genetics Revolution: Economics, Ethics and Insurance", *Journal of Business Ethics*, Vol. 16, No. 15 (1997), pp. 1661–1676; M. Cooper, *Life as Surplus: Biotechnology and Capitalism in the Neoliberal Era* (London: University of Washington Press, 2008); J. Liukko, "Genetic Discrimination, Insurance, and Solidarity: An Analysis of the Argumentation for Fair Risk Classification", *New Genetics and Society*, Vol. 29, No. 4 (2010), pp. 457–475; T. McGleenan, V. Wiesing and F. Ewald (eds.), *Genetics and Insurance* (Oxford: BIOS, 1999); J. Mittra, "Genetic Exceptionalism and Precautionary Politics: Regulating for Uncertainty in Britain's Genetics and Insurance Policy Process", *Science and Public Policy*, Vol. 33 (2006), pp. 585–600; J. Mittra, "Predictive Genetic Information and Access to Life Assurance: The Poverty of 'Genetic Exceptionalism'", *BioSocieties*, Vol. 2, No. 3 (2007), pp. 349–373; Lobo-Guerrero, *Insuring Security, op. cit.*; K. Armstrong, B. Weber, G. FitzGerald, J.C. Hershey, M.V. Pauly, J. Lemaire, *et al.*, "Life Insurance and Breast Cancer Risk Assessment: Adverse Selection, Genetic Testing Decisions, and Discrimination", *American Journal of Medical Genetics*, Vol. 120A, No. 3 (2003), pp. 359–364.

life is driven not by the utility of production but by passion and affect. The temporality of economic production also gets disrupted in the process and the time of passion and affect take over, making the realisation of instances of love the structure of existence. Such a dimension of the value of life escapes reasonable calculability and predictability; it cancels out the possibility of expectation upon which liberal governance relies. In doing so it transforms the otherwise reliable expectation of the individual's maximisation of utility into a morality where responsibility is devoid of political community. In other words, life becomes accountable to its emotional sense, a sense that is not necessarily individualised and that operates in the realm of the imaginary.

The third dimension through which life is rendered as valuable evident in the film is its role in aiding the constitution of moral economies. These differ from those enlightened secular ideas of morality derived from Kant's categorical imperative and concentrate instead on the effects of organised systems of regular behaviour based on particular rationalities for the management of uncertainty. In this case, life insurance provides a technology that influences the behaviour of individuals and collectives down to the detail, which, as illustrated in the case of Damian Alekan in the world of *Code 46*, relates to modulating the dreams and vital prospects of action carved deep into the subjectivity of insured lives. Such moral economies relate directly to Foucault's idea of governmentality as the conduct of conduct and displace the focus of analysis from the government to the epistemology of governance where sets of ideas and beliefs underpin a logic supporting political action. The outcome of the moral economies of life insurance is the rendering of life as insurable or uninsurable and protecting the likelihood of loss, damage, injury or death in insured lives. This rendering of course has profound implications for the lifestyles and livelihoods life insurance aims to protect and promote.

A particular effect of this role is evidenced in the expectation of life insurance of repairing "damaged lives" and getting them back in circulation. For example, and in a radical way, the world of *Code 46* illustrates what happens to a life that has unknowingly breached the limits of acceptable behaviour if that life is protected by a life insurance policy. In the case of Maria, who slept with William in complete ignorance of their genetic incompatibility, life insurance provided the means to sanitise her behaviour and remove any traces of wrongdoing from her mind, a memory which might operate as an incentive or justification for future unacceptable behaviour. When the foetus and the memories of illicit procreation were removed from her mind, and a memory of an industrial accident for which she required an artificial finger was introduced in their stead, the Sphinx operated a technology of reparation which not only got Maria's life back into acceptable circulation but also repaired the temporality upon which behaviour relied, the continuous present.

This relates to the moral aspect of life insurance as a certification of acceptable life. Insurable life is considered to be "good life." However, insurable life is predictable and expectable life, not a life exposed to the nuances of desire, emotion and affect. A life prone to emotional and passionate drives is life exposed to the unknown, to accidents and dangers. Emotional and passion-driven behaviour disables the life-turned-capital premise upon which life insurance products transform expectable life into an enabler of credit. Life insurance operates a role of constraining desire, or at the very least, of modulating it into normalised behaviour.

Contemporary life insurance does not of course go to those extremes. It focuses instead on preventing, as much as possible, what is known in the industry as moral hazard and adverse selection. The former relates to risks derived from the unacceptable behaviour of a policyholder who seeks cover knowing there will be a certain claim. A radical example of moral hazard is a person who buys life insurance while wanting to commit suicide. To prevent that risk, companies tend to exclude suicide for the first two years of a policy on the understanding that someone who is thinking of taking his or her own life will not wait that long. Adverse selection refers to insuring lives that are known to be too risky and likely to cause costly claims. Those lives, however, are still insurable, that is, susceptible to be repaired in their capacity to circulate within a particular risk regime, for example an obese person who is also a heavy smoker and consumes alcohol beyond the agreed safe standards established by the government. If insurable, and likely to be so at a high premium, that individual is probably asked to reduce their risk factors by, for example, attending a gym regularly, seeking help to quit smoking, or undergoing therapy to control their drinking.[37] It might be the case that incentives are offered to that person in the form of a reduced premium if risk factors are reduced.[38] The likelihood of a higher premium or the possibility of being rejected completely from insurance cover if risk factors do not improve become incentives for "acceptable" behaviour. If the financial standing of that person depends on the insurability of his/her own life, for example as security for (re)mortgaging their home or for providing financial protection for their family in case of death or old age, adapting to the moral order dictated by the insurer becomes an imperative.

A more complex aspect of getting lives back in circulation refers to the insurability of lives in relation to activities considered to be of high risk and nonetheless in demand by certain populations.[39] A case in point is that of high mountain climbing, which attracts entrepreneurs addicted to the ecstasy of pushing the capacity of their bodies beyond their normal boundaries.[40] Activities of this kind are usually excluded from standard life insurance policies but are, regardless of the added risk, insurable under specialist policies. The very existence of these specialist products points to the fact that insurance does offer a great degree of flexibility to adapt to the changing demands of circulation of individuals seeking cover. For example, at the advent of space tourism in the early 2010s, a plethora of specialist products are being offered by the industry, sometimes in partnership with international organisations, to cover the uncertainties of space travel.[41] Although some of these activities have historically been located in the realm of *afuera* (or of uninsurable risks), what the history of insurance institutions, technologies and products shows is an incredible capacity to offer forms of protection for the changing conditions of life. However, by rendering these limit lifestyles insurable,

37. Swiss Re, *Too Big to Ignore: The Impact of Obesity on Mortality Trends* (Zurich: Swiss Re, 2004).

38. Munich Re, *Obesity – A Challenge for Global Healthcare Systems* (Munich: Munich Re, 2008).

39. See D. Laster and C. Schmidt, "Innovating to Insure the Uninsurable", *Sigma*, Vol. 4 (2005), pp. 1–36.

40. See J. Simon, "Taking Risks: Extreme Sports and the Embrace of Risk in Advanced Liberal Societies", in T. Baker and J. Simon (eds.), *Embracing Risk: The Changing Culture of Insurance and Responsibility* (Chicago: University of Chicago Press, 2002), pp. 177–208.

41. A case in point is that of 'Allianz Global Assistance', a provider of travel insurance and assistance solutions, which has entered into partnership with the International Space Transport Association (ISTA) anticipating the growth of space tourism. See <https://www.allianz.com/en/press/news/business/insurance/news_2011-11-15.html?search.query=international%20OR%20space%20OR%20transport%20OR%20association&search.filter=-_contentType:editorial> (accessed 24 March 2014).

insurers expand the horizon of insurability, influencing the behaviour of risk-thirsty individuals. This continuous widening of the moral economies instantiated through insurance effects a governmentalisation of life which must begin to figure prominently in studies of how liberal life is secured.

The "Vital Excess" and the Immanent Resistance to Life's Valuation

"Making reality intelligible" by "showing [how] it was possible"[42] opens up the possibility to engage with the resistance of "life" to the processes of valuation employed by life insurers.

In *Code 46* Damian's wish to challenge the secure order of the inside world by insisting on going to see his bats, and Maria's wish to disrupt the insurantial order of the Sphinx by creating windows to the *afuera*, constitute efforts to escape the biopolitical logic that supported the system. In the case of Damian it was made evident that insured subjects remain ignorant of the logics and reasons underlying certain underwriting decisions. When a quote on an insurance premium is offered, the client is not given the reasons why s/he was included in a particular risk pool and why the price quoted corresponds to that level of risk. This is not always a problem of fault or an intention to hide information from the customer, although cases of mis-selling of insurance products do happen.[43] It is partly related to what can be called, following the mathematical instruments through which insurance premiums are calculated, "algorithmic logic."[44]

Algorithms are designed as instruments that allow for the calculation of multiple variables taking into account what is known about particular events and particular kinds of risks. Providing an articulated answer to why a particular quote was given would require analysing the not-so-technical processes that took place in the computing of data through the algorithm. This involves, for example, questioning the assumptions immanent to its design such as the three dimensions of valuation analysed in this article (i.e. valuation as a practice of inclusion, valuation as vital ontology, and valuation as the basis for moral economies). In the case of the film, both Damian and Maria remained ignorant as to why the Sphinx insisted on denying cover for a particular activity and in their own ethic had no problem disrupting the system once they had found a way of doing so. While disrupting the system, the value ascribed to their lives changed, and Maria, whose life was deemed no longer worthy of protection, was left to exist in the realm of *afuera* deprived of the protection of insurance. Although the consequence of challenging the biopolitical order of insurance was exclusion from a political community ordered through the management of risk, resistance to that order highlights the excess to the biopolitical valuation of life. Love, thrill, adventure ... feral dreams.

The case of Maria and William's "rape" of Code 46 highlights the role of the vital excess as the core of the artistic performance of this film. William, in a professional capacity, was in effect playing the role of guardian of the insurantial order

42. M. Foucault, *The Birth of Biopolitics* (London: Palgrave Macmillan, 2008), p. 34.

43. L. Lobo-Guerrero, "*Uberrima Fides*, Foucault and the Security of Uncertainty", *International Journal for the Semiotics of Law*, Vol. 26, No. 1 (2012), pp. 23–37.

44. See L. Amoore, "Vigilant Visualities: The Watchful Politics of the War on Terror", *Security Dialogue*, Vol. 38, No. 2 (2007), pp. 215–232; L. Introna and D. Wood, "Picturing Algorithmic Surveillance: The Politics of Facial Recognition Systems", *Surveillance & Society*, Vol. 2, No. 2/3 (2004), pp. 177–198.

produced by companies such as the Sphinx. His duty was to identify fraudsters and denounce them so that the system could correct itself. When investigating the fraud case for which Maria was presumed guilty, he fell in love and by liaising emotionally with the culprit ended up contributing to what amounted in the film to a capital violation of order. Maria, on the other hand, knew through her father's and her own experience what living *afuera* meant and nonetheless decided to help others either get inside or outside as their wishes—and passions—commanded them. For her the problem of access/non-access was not a moral one but one related to holding the right certificate, the *papel*, something she could produce for them if she wanted. When William and Maria decided to travel together to Jebel Ali—the symbol of the free *afuera* in the world of *Code 46*—they did so knowing they were violating the biopolitical order. William's decision entailed leaving his family; without cover he would not be able to return to Seattle. Maria, who had been made to forget she had a history of disrupting order, was now wilfully running away from her job driven by the adventure of loving William and getting away from the boredom of life. When Maria asked William to make love to her, to make her make love to him, she did so driven by the thrill of enjoyment, adventure and the pleasure of being in control of her body and mind, a control that eluded her regular and secure, insured life. They both chose to engage in the crazy adventure of "raping" the system to be able to enjoy the satisfaction of their liberation from the norm that the insurantial order in which they lived imposed on them. The everyday routine of waking up and going to work and then getting back home to a perfectly regulated apartment was to be disrupted by the enjoyment of uncertainty of life in the world of *afuera*, the unregulated chaos in which life exceeded the biopolitical constraints of the world of *Code 46*.

The raping of the system, the very act of asking to be raped, denotes a well-known feature of resistance where the raper is the system and not the rapist, where the rape becomes an act of liberation, of exstatic existence. The evocations of domination, power, control, fear, but also fantasy that traditional ideas of rape bring along, assume an inverted meaning in this case. The rape becomes an act of creation, of desire, of making things otherwise at the level of the imaginary. Hence the need in the world of *Code 46* to repair the rape, to delete its occurrence, to deny its existence as a way to prevent further resistance to order. In denying the rape, the system preserves its capacity to operate economies of security.

In the world of contemporary life insurance, the life that escapes the calculability employed by the algorithmic logic is anchored to an economy of security which simultaneously offers opportunities for profit while liberating the uncertain from the markers of "security" against which it is formulated. It provides a market space towards which insurers can expand in their endless appetite for creating value within a capitalist system. Uninsured lives constitute a horizon to be colonised and can be as infinite as insurance entrepreneurs want to see them. Uninsured life and lives—be it because the logic of insurability has not yet encompassed them, because these lives resist the moral orders of insurability or because they have not been identified as potential targets for insurers—constitute in other words opportunities for profit. On the other hand, uninsured life and lives represent a space of freedom, a space of wild uncertainty, of passionate existence where anything is possible, where anything could potentially be achieved, where the magical stands a chance. It is a space for a romantic understanding of being, where the possible, and not the risky, norms the opportunity for happiness.

In this way, the very insurability of life and lives constitutes a paradox of security. The paradox results from a dual process in which insurance seeks to promote and protect a particular way of life but it is precisely what gets excluded from that life in the process of securing it that enables the operation of the technology. Put differently, it is the excess of the life to be protected that makes insurance possible.

About the Author

Luis Lobo-Guerrero is Professor of History and Theory of International Relations at the University of Groningen, the Netherlands. He is the author of *Insuring Security: Biopolitics, Security and Risk* (Routledge, 2011) and *Insuring War: Sovereignty, Security and Risk* (Routledge, 2012).

Love as Project of (Im)Mobility: Love, Sovereignty and Governmentality in Marriage Migration Management Practices

ANNE-MARIE D'AOUST

Marriage migration has recently drawn some attention, notably to the ways in which third-country nationals face increased challenges compared to European citizens when it comes to reunite with their spouse or partner. Foregoing a detailed legal analysis, this article rather seeks to interrogate the following: what connections can be drawn between law, love, mobility and sovereignty? Relying on various instances of management practices in Europe, I examine what marriage migration regulations tell us about their entanglement. On the one hand, I claim that love can and should be accounted for in the governmentality of marriage migration. On the other hand, by being attuned to the ways in which love is connected to different marriage migration management practices, we can see that governmentality cannot fully capture the different forms of power deployed and enacted in specific settings. What we have instead are complex assemblages that highlight a productive tension, as love becomes both a target and object of governmental calculations in projects of immobility, and a movement that participates in projects of mobility. It thus intermeshes with, yet also challenges, attempts at fixity.

> The inability of the modern mind to see this connection between love and power is the measure of its inability to understand the true dimensions of either love or power.[1]
> —Hans J. Morgenthau

> Love or money, Marx tells us, that is our choice.[2]
> —Michael Hardt

---

*I would like to thank Michael Orsini for his close reading and insightful comments. An earlier version of this article was presented at the University of Ottawa's Observatoire des nouvelles pratiques symboliques in October 2013. I would like to thank all workshop participants for their support and suggestions. Finally, this article benefited greatly from a very close reading from two anonymous reviewers, along with productive exchanges with David Grondin and William Walters on different sections.

1. H.J. Morgenthau, "Love and Power", *Commentary*, Vol. 33 (March 1962), p. 247.

2. M. Hardt, in H. Davis and P. Sarlin, "No One is Sovereign in Love: A Conversation between Lauren Berlant and Michal Hardt", Nomorepotlucks, December 2011, available: <http://nomorepotlucks.org/site/no-one-is-sovereign-in-love-a-conversation-between-lauren-berlant-and-michael-hardt>.

In 2011, the Court of Justice of the European Union (EU) handed down its McCarthy judgement.[3] Its conclusion was clear: European nationals who had never moved outside their homeland could neither rely on their EU citizenship nor on their rights as a citizen of the Union to move and reside freely within the territory of the member states (Directive 2004/38) with their non-European spouses or partners. As a dual Irish/UK national, Ms. McCarthy never left the UK, and never worked under EU laws. Trying to circumvent stringent national requirements which prevented her from reuniting with her Jamaican husband, she applied for her Irish passport and sought a right of residence in the UK as an EU citizen, while her husband applied for a right of residence as the spouse of an EU national, rather than a UK national. Indeed, whereas British citizens wishing to reunite with a loved one must meet strict national requirements for family reunification,[4] European citizens can sidestep them and benefit from the right to family reunification, even with non-EU and non-EEA (European Economic Area) spouses, thanks to Directive 2003/86/EC of the Council of the European Union. As Helena Wray concludes, the McCarthy judgement "suggests that EU rights to family reunification hinge on the exercise of free movement rights and not on the fact of EU citizenship. At one level, that is coherent even if it relies on an economic vision of the European Union ... EU citizenship does not, on its own, bring with it the liberal rights to family reunification *associated with cross-border activity*."[5]

The McCarthy case is puzzling as it challenges the idea of the citizen as someone who, by virtue of citizenship privileges, "holds" or "possesses" specific rights. The case emphasises the idea of the citizen as right *bearer*, namely as a carrier, as rights get acquired through movement. It is precisely the lack of movement (within the European Union) that led to the non-activation of rights in the case of Ms. McCarthy, and a different kind of movement (an emotional one) that got denied: her love for her Jamaican husband. The political nature of bodily movement has long been acknowledged, but here I would like to investigate another kind of movement, namely that of love. Love as movement, as an emotional transport, albeit one that also moves people, and thus intermeshes and also confronts "projects of immobility," namely orderly and rationalised circulation.

At first neglected in studies of migration, marriage migration has recently drawn attention, notably to highlight the ways in which third-country nationals face increased challenges compared to European citizens when it comes to reunite with their spouse or partner.[6] The literature has emphasised the gaps in

3. Case C-434/09 McCarthy v Secretary of State for the Home Department.

4. For instance, in Great Britain, citizens and permanent residents wishing to sponsor a non-EU spouse or partner must prove since June 2012 a minimum income level of £18,600, which led to the conclusion in 2013 that "47% of the UK working population last year would have failed to meet the income level to sponsor a non-European Economic Area partner." (BBC News, "UK's New Visa Rules 'Causing Anguish' for Families", 10 June 2013, available <http://www.bbc.com/news/uk-22833136>). Europeans residing in the country though—a presence which testifies to their mobility inside the Union, and thus to the effective mobility of labour and capital—are exempted from any such *national* requirements.

5. H. Wray, "Family Life and EU Citizenship: A Commentary on McCarthy C-434/09 5 May 2011", *EUDO Citizenship*, 19 May 2011, available: <http://eudo-citizenship.eu/citizenship-news/479family-life-andeu-citizenship-a-commentary-on-mccarthy-c-43409-5-may-2011>. Author's emphasis.

6. See for instance Y. Pascouau, in collaboration with H. Labayle, *Conditions for Family Reunification under Strain: A Comparative Study in Nine EU Member States*, European Policy Centre/King Baudoin

rights between citizens and non-citizens. But paying attention to the McCarthy ruling detailed above complicates this picture between the "haves" and the "have nots" and raises questions about the ways in which marriage migration regulations highlight specific nodes between love, law, sovereignty and mobility.

Legal scholars of the European Union have long been familiar with the wide differential of rights existing within the European Union when it comes to spousal migration. But while such variations have been well documented in the European context and sometimes even contested in their legal complexities, "existing research largely is limited to a legal analysis of family related migration, while more theory informed approaches to the study of family migration policy are largely absent."[7] In an attempt to develop the latter, this article investigates the role of love in marriage migration management practices.[8] On the one hand, I suggest that love can and should be accounted for in the governmentality of marriage migration. Foucault understood governmentality to refer to the conduct of conduct, to "the ensemble formed by institutions, procedures, analyses and reflections, calculation, and tactics that allow the exercise of this very specific, albeit very complex, power that has the population as its target, political economy as its major form of knowledge and apparatuses of security as its essential technical instrument."[9]

Being attuned to what I call "technologies of love"[10] can help us see how emotions such as love can be included in the "matrix of practical reason" Foucault was concerned about when thinking about technologies inherent to governmentality. Thinking of technologies of love acknowledges the movement towards community implied by love, with its direction and diversions, while also taking into account how this movement is interwoven in other flows and assemblages (those of law and sovereignty, especially), whose material and spatial features should be addressed.

Foundation/Odysseus Network, Brussels, November 2011, available: <http://www.epc.eu/documents/uploads/pub_1369_conditionsforfamily.pdf>; A. Staver, "Free Movement and the Fragmentation of Family Reunification Rights", *European Journal of Migration and Law,* Vol. 15, No. 1 (2013), pp. 69–89; L. Block and S. Bonjour, "Fortress Europe or Europe of Rights? The Europeanisation of Family Migration Policies in France, Germany and the Netherlands", *European Journal of Migration and Law,* Vol. 15, No. 2 (2013), pp. 203–224; P.V. Elsuwege and D. Kochenov, "On the Limits of Judicial Intervention: EU Citizenship and Family Reunification Rights", *European Journal of Migration and Law,* Vol. 13, No. 5 (2011), pp. 443–466.

7. A. Kraler, "Civic Stratification, Gender and Family Migration Policies in Europe. Final Report", revised and updated public version (Vienna: BMWF/ICMPD, NODE, 2010), p. 10. What Kraler seems to imply here is not so much that legal analyses cannot be or are never theory informed, but rather that theorising has been limited to analyses of the consequences of actual policies and of the current legal apparatus. Rather than trying to challenge and reconfigure ways of conceiving family migration altogether, most analyses work inside these pre-established parameters.

8. For more on the how migration management is underpinned by a neoliberal rationale of government, see M. Geiger and A. Pécoud (eds.), *The Politics of International Migration Management* (Basingstoke and New York: Palgrave Macmillan, 2010).

9. M. Foucault, *Security, Territory, Population: Lectures at the Collège de France, 1977–1978,* trans. Graham Burchell (Basingstoke: Palgrave Macmillan, 2007), p. 108.

10. For a thorough discussion of the concept, see A.-M. D'Aoust, "In the Name of Love: Marriage Migration, Governmentality and Technologies of Love", *International Political Sociology,* Vol. 7, No. 3 (2013), pp. 258–274 and A.-M. D'Aoust, "'Take a Chance on Me': Premediation, Technologies of Love, and Marriage Migration Management", in M. Geiger and A. Pécoud (eds.), *Disciplining the Transnational Movement of People* (London and New York: Palgrave Macmillan, 2013), pp. 103–125.

On the other hand, being mindful of the ways in which love is connected to different migration management practices reminds us that governmentality cannot fully capture the different forms of power deployed and enacted in specific settings. Saying that love relates to governmentality should not make us oblivious to other non-liberal forms of governance that remain present and central. Such assemblages, as will be shown throughout the article, highlight a productive tension, as love becomes both a *target* and *object* of governmental calculations in projects of immobility and stability,[11] and *a movement* that participates in projects of mobility. It thus exceeds and constantly challenges such attempts at fixity. In other words, sovereign and governmental powers do not appear as clearly differentiated when it comes to mobilising love in marriage migration management practices. What we see instead are assemblages that "bring together and even combine different forms of sovereign and disciplinary power in contextual formations."[12]

In light of these claims, two cautionary notes are worth mentioning. First, though examining some specific management practices, this article does not purport to engage in a genealogy of all the forms, deployments and effects of the rationalisation of love in a specific site, an empirical endeavour some might see as being the main task of any analysis that aims to put governmentality to work. Rather, by raising the issue of love in relation to law and sovereignty, this article explores what an engagement with love *does* to governmentality, pointing to its usefulness and limits as a concept when we turn to the issue of marriage migration management practices. This engagement could thus be best described as a productive critical encounter with governmentality, as William Walters would suggest. This means veering away from "applicationism" to openness to "unexpected meetings" that can lead to "new ways of understanding social and political problems" in such a way that the toolbox offered by governmentality, far from being settled, can be imagined as "a dynamic and transactional place."[13]

Second, though not engaged in a genealogical analysis proper, this article favours a relational approach that problematises the relationships between love, law and sovereignty.[14] Such an approach allows for the study of different dynamics and spaces created by relations between objects or sites. I thus look at love, law and sovereignty as an evolving constellation in relation to issues of (im)mobility: it is the changing shape of their meaning and recognition that emerges through their interrelationship in marriage migration management practices that interests me here.

To better situate my two claims that love can and should be accounted for in the analysis of the governmentality of marriage migration, and that sovereign and

11. The idea of "project of immobility" emphasises *attempts* at stability (in the case of a desired order or circulation) or actual immobility (in ensuring that some people, some movements are stopped or kept still).

12. S. Mezzadra and B. Neilson, *Border as Method or, The Multiplication of Labour* (Durham, NC and London: Duke University Press, 2013), p. 195.

13. W. Walters, *Governmentality: Critical Encounters* (New York: Routledge, 2012), p. 5.

14. As Foucault explained: "Problematization doesn't mean the representation of a pre-existing object, nor the creation through discourse of an object that doesn't exist. It's the set of discursive or non-discursive practices that makes something enter into the play of true and false, and constitutes it as an object for thought (whether under the form of moral reflection, scientific knowledge, political analysis, etc.)." M. Foucault, "The Concern for Truth", in S. Lotringer (ed.), *Foucault Live: Collected Interviews 1961–1984* (New York: Semiotexte/Smart Art, 1996), pp. 456–457.

governmental powers both co-exist and mobilise love when it comes to management practices, this article is divided into five parts. The first two parts offer a theoretical engagement with the idea of love as a political concept, one that could be related to governmentality. I first briefly appraise the notion of love as a political concept. In this section, I take seriously Michael Hardt's recent call for "a properly political concept of love,"[15] while distancing myself from his own reading of love in relation to capital. This discussion allows for a better understanding of the ways in which love should be seen as being political, while not necessarily opposed to or distinct from capital as a mode of relationality.

From there, I take up Hardt's discussion of this relationship by making the case for exploring love in relation to governmentality. Here, I propose to use the notion of technologies of love to help us think about the constellation formed by love, law and sovereignty, and the need for orderly circulation, be it of goods, bodies or feelings. Technologies of love, I suggest, enable us to highlight a productive tension between these three sites, as love becomes both a target and object of governmental calculations in projects of immobility, but also a movement that exceeds and constantly challenges attempts at fixity, which are the hallmarks of law and sovereignty.

Building from this theoretical discussion, the third section examines marriage migration management through an emphasis on some of the dynamics that can be traced between the three sites that interest me here, namely love, law and sovereignty. This section highlights the ways in which law and sovereignty stand out as projects of immobility, of spatialisation in the face of movement—physical and emotional. It also points to several tensions, as legislation regarding mobility and family reunification at the EU level initially derives from concerns regarding the mobility of goods, not people, and the establishment of a "European" space. While this section establishes some connections between love, law and sovereignty, the fourth section zeroes in on the ways in which sovereign and governmental powers are both exercised in marriage migration management practices, especially in the UK. It draws our attention to "the co-presence of liberalism, illiberalism, violence, and force"[16] in the management of marriage migration, which precludes any understanding of the governmentality of marriage migration as being coherent and rational. Acknowledging this dual presence, the last section shows how sovereign and governmental powers are involved in adjudicating "true love" from marriage migrants and their spouses, a task that reveals the fragility of the institutionalised order of sovereignty and its bureaucratic practices.

Love as a Political Concept

Hannah Arendt famously argued that love, as a general human experience, was in fact *the* quintessential antipolitical force. Love, she said,

> is unconcerned to the point of total unworldliness with what the loved person may be, with his [sic] qualities and shortcomings no less than with his achievements, failings, and transgressions. . . . Love, by its very nature, is unworldly, and it is for this reason rather than its rarity that it

15. M. Hardt, "For Love or Money", *Cultural Anthropology*, Vol. 26, No. 4 (2011), p. 676.
16. Walters, *Governmentality, op. cit.*, p. 74.

> is not only apolitical but antipolitical, perhaps the most powerful of all antipolitical human forces.[17]

Such unworldliness has meant that love is often assumed to be the liberal hallmark of a universally and individually experienced freedom, a homogenising social force that bridges differences.[18] Love becomes an equaliser, one that subsumes the entire social field, solving the issue of difference. Explains Berlant: "Romance ideology participates in this project by depicting sentiment or *feeling* as the essential and universal truth of persons. *Feeling is what people have in common despite their apparent differences.*"[19]

A similar universalist impulse can be found in Michael Hardt's attempt to offer "a properly political concept of love"[20] that would address the nature of the political relationship between love and neoliberalism. Returning to the young Marx, Hardt suggests that love should be conceptualised as a viable substitute for money in organising social relations: "Love or money, Marx tells us, that is our choice. It is significant in my view that, by establishing this alternative, Marx poses love on the same level of money: love operates not only in terms of intimate relations but also in a primary role of social organization."[21] Money therefore appears here as a technology that unmakes social relations initially based on love, and replaces them with new (alienating) forms of social interaction. Hardt notes that Marx identifies love

> as one of the senses or organs by which humans relate to each other and the world that will have to be created anew in communism ... In this context Marx proposes that communism (and the abolition of private property) requires or implies a new sensorium, that is, a renewal or extension of the existing human senses ... The development of a new sensorium, increasing our power to love and the strength of the other social muscles, is inversely related to the rule of private property.[22]

Some Marxists have distanced themselves from this interpretation, mostly because it presents "love as a spiritual force that will heal social alienation without the transformation of material relations founded on private property and exploitation that produce alienation in the first place."[23] More troublesome, in my view, is that it simply reproduces a specifically romantic notion of love (while still purposively trying to veer away from it) as still being apart from money, as being *an essence* which, though experienced in many expanding forms (some not yet known), has the potential to be corrupted by money.

---

17. H. Arendt, *The Human Condition* (Chicago and London: University of Chicago Press, 1998 [1958]), p. 242.

18. E. Povinelli, *The Empire of Love: Toward a Theory of Intimacy, Genealogy, and Carnality* (Durham, NC: Duke University Press, 2006), p. 178.

19. L. Berlant, *Desire/Love* (Brooklyn, NY: Punctum Books, 2012), p. 110. My emphasis.

20. Hardt, *op. cit.*, p. 676.

21. *Ibid.*, p. 679.

22. *Ibid.*, p. 680.

23. J. Cotter, "Bio-Politics, Transspecies Love and/as Class Common-Sense", *The Red Critique*, Winter/Spring 2012, available: <http://redcritique.org/WinterSpring2012/biopoliticstransspeciesismandclasscommonssense.htm>.

Hardt indeed relies heavily on this idea of "love corrupted" or "love gone bad,"[24] a move that suggests some pure form of love, an idea that brings him closer to the romantic understanding of love he seeks to overcome. Anchoring his analysis in Spinoza, Hardt depicts love as a new form of relationality, one that is transformative, collective and external to oneself.[25] These features are in fact the hallmark of a distinctively Western romantic understanding of love, one that Niklas Luhmann documented and identified as developing in Europe in the 18th century and around the turn of the 19th century, when "the *sociality* of loving . . . came to be understood in terms of the *enhanced chance of a self-confident formation of the self*."[26] The narrative of romantic love precisely relies on universalism and a blindness to its political and material features. This is echoed in Hardt's idea that love is an ontological organ or sense that makes us human (more human than we actually are, in fact, through the development of a new sensorium), and brings love back in as a false universalism.

Hardt's political conception of love ends up substituting one ontological absolute (love) for another (money) while avoiding the deeper complex social relationship between love and neoliberalism. His politicisation of love, one anchored in a universalist sensibility to love, fails to acknowledge two important dimensions. First, it neglects how emotions and bodies connect in different ways that go beyond possibly alienating relations to capital, and thus affect one's ability to feel or be affected. Bodies are always situated, sexualised and racialised. Tolia-Kelly aptly notes that racial hierarchies notably entail that the "affective capacities of any body are signified unequally within social spaces of being and feeling. . . . A body that is signified as a source of fear through its markedness cannot be free to affect and be affected similarly to one that is not."[27]

Second, and as a corollary to the recognition that love is socially and spatially located, "love" necessarily entails various modes of being and feeling. An implicit universalist sensibility to love assumes an equal capacity for each and every one of us to be affective and affected, to love and be loved. This can be experienced now or, for someone like Hardt, perhaps later once specific barriers or impediments are removed. But "how love 'feels' depends on 'cultural dictionaries', which define what is 'pre-acknowledged, prenamed, pre-articulated, culturally available, to be felt'."[28] As Nietzsche explains, love, like music, is movement caught up, something that has to be learned *to be recognised as such*:

> This is what happens to us in music: First one has to *learn to hear* a figure and melody at all, to detect and distinguish it, to isolate it and delimit it as a separate life. Then it requires some exertion and good will to *tolerate* it in spite of its strangeness, to be patient with its appearance and expression,

24. See for instance L. Schartz, "A Conversation with Michael Hardt on the Politics of Love", *Inter-val(le)s*, No. 4–5 (2008/2009), pp. 810–821; and M. Hardt and A. Negri, *Commonwealth* (Cambridge, MA: The Belknap Press of Harvard University Press, 2009).

25. "On the Risk of a New Relationality: An Interview with Lauren Berlant and Michael Hardt", *Reviews in Cultural Theory*, Vol. 2, No. 3 (Special Issue: New Commons) (2011), p. 6 and p. 11.

26. *Ibid.*, p. 136. Emphasis in original.

27. D.P. Tolia-Kelly, "Affect—An Ethnocentric Encounter? Exploring the 'Universalist' Imperative of Emotional/Affectual Geographies", *Area*, Vol. 38, No. 2 (2006), p. 215.

28. S. Jackson, "Love, Social Change and Everyday Heterosexuality", in S. Strid and A. Jónasdóttir (eds.), *Proceedings from GEXcel Theme 10: Love in Our Time—A Question for Feminism*, 2010, p. 100, available: <http://www.genderexcel.org/?q=webfm_send/77>.

> and kindhearted about its oddity. Finally there comes a moment when we are *used* to, when we wait for it, when we sense that we should miss it if it were missing; and now it continues to compel and enchant us relentlessly until we have become its humble and enraptured lovers who desire nothing better from the world than it and only it. But that is what happens to us not only in music. That is how we have *learned to love* all things that we now love. . . . Even those who love themselves will have learned it in this way; for there is no other way. Love, too, has to be learned.[29]

Technologies of Love: Moving beyond Affective Governance

In this light, rather than being the "most powerful of all antipolitical human forces,"[30] love might instead be one of the main political sites and relays of power—a technology. And if love is not to be seen as a force running against power, but rather as being enmeshed in it, it needs to be explored in relation to governmentality.

What kind of technologies are technologies of love? Love, as "an acknowledgement and recognition of alterity and affiliation," which emerges through connection and "only within the moment and movement of exteriorization," is technical by definition.[31] Whereas several studies have examined the role of sexuality in relation to technologies of power and technologies of the self, engagements with emotions have usually been limited to the study of their rationalisation or governance. One explanation for this omission might be Foucault's own emphasis that governmentality entailed a "matrix of practical reason." For Foucault, technologies of power "determine the conduct of individuals and submit them to certain ends or domination, an objectivizing of the subject," whereas technologies of the self "permit individuals to effect by their own means or with the help of others a certain number of operations on their own bodies and soul, thought, conduct, and way of being, so as to transform themselves in order to attain a certain state of happiness, purity, wisdom, perfection, or immortality."[32] In both cases, technologies appear to be a matter of *the will*, one that precisely seems to run counter to the very idea of love; love cannot simply be effected by one's own individual means, determination, choice, despite the fact that they can still be part of it. Love thus sits uneasily with technologies of power and technologies of the self that characterise governmentality; certainly it can be involved in both, but it still exceeds them.

Does this mean that technologies of love are simply technologies of government?

They certainly can be, but again, they exceed it. As Nikolas Rose insists, "[t]echnologies of government are those technologies *imbued with aspirations* for

29. F. Nietzsche, *The Gay Science*, trans. W. Kaufmann (New York: Random House, 1974 [1887]), p. 262. Emphasis in original.

30. Arendt, *op. cit.*, p. 242.

31. D. Pettman, *Love and Other Technologies: Retrofitting Eros for the Information Age* (New York: Fordham University Press, 2006), p. 18.

32. M. Foucault, "Technologies of the Self", in L.H. Martin, H. Gutman and P.H. Hutton (eds.), *Technologies of the Self: A Seminar with Michel Foucault* (Amherst: University of Massachusetts Press, 1988), p. 18. My emphasis.

the shaping of conduct *in the hope of producing certain desired effects* and averting certain undesired events."[33] If love were solely a technology of government, it would then be reduced to an emotional economy of intimacy management or an affective governance, where the movement and impulse of affect get stirred in a specific direction to obtain certain results.[34] It would then lead us to inquire how political rationalities are also invested in "assessing appropriate sentiments and in fashioning techniques of affective control."[35] Such intimacy management, or what Ann Laura Stoler calls "desire education,"[36] has been widely documented by historians of race and colonial history. Key in such accounts is the open recognition that emotions do not run antithetical to the economic realm, but are in fact central to it:

> By shaping appropriate and reasoned affect, by directing affective judgment, by severing some affective bonds and establishing others, by adjudicating what constituted moral sentiments—that is, by educating the proper distribution of sentiments and desires, the emotional economy of colonialism was always central to strategies of labour control ... In this sense, the role of the states is not only in the business of educating consent ... but such concern is possible by the shaping of appropriate and reasoned affect, and placing "affective knowledge" at the core of political rationality.[37]

Love can certainly be shaped and stirred through various institutional practices and in specific directions to be recognised and acknowledged *as such*. After all, as Berlant aptly points out, "What does it mean about love that its expressions tend to be so *conventional*, so bound up in institutions like marriage and family, property relations, and stock phrases and plots?"[38] But technologies of love are no different from other technological artefacts: the movement they bring about and try to foster, the relations they establish, do not always work as anticipated. There can be gaps between what the technologies were designed to do or aimed to do, and what uses are made of them.[39] In short, the chain of movements created by technologies of love, the connections they establish between sites,

33. N. Rose, *Powers of Freedom: Reframing Political Thought* (New York: Cambridge University Press, 1999), p. 52.

34. For examples and discussions of this, see A.-M. Fortier, "Proximity by Design? Affective Citizenship and the Management of Unease", *Citizenship Studies*, Vol. 14, No. 1 (2010), pp. 17–30. For a different understanding of affective governance, see M.A. White, "Ambivalent Homonationalisms: Transnational Queer Intimacies and Territorialized Belongings", *Interventions: International Journal of Postcolonial Studies*, Vol. 15, No. 1 (2013), pp. 37–54.

35. A.L. Stoler, "Affective States", in D. Nugent and J. Vincent (eds.), *A Companion to the Anthropology of Politics* (Malden: Blackwell Publishers, 2004), p. 5.

36. A.L. Stoler, *Race and the Education of Desire: Foucault's History of Sexuality and the Colonial Order of Things* (Durham, NC: Duke University Press, 1995).

37. A. Ramos-Zayas, *Street Therapists: Race, Affect, and Neoliberal Personhood in Latino Newark* (Chicago, IL: Chicago University Press, 2012), p. 104.

38. Berlant, *op. cit.*, p. 7; emphasis original.

39. J. Huysmans, "What is in an Act? Dispersing Politics of Insecurity", p. 39, Paper prepared for The Politics of Securitization, Conference organised by the Centre for Advanced Security Theory (CAST), Copenhagen, 13–14 September 2010, available: <http://www.open.ac.uk/researchprojects/iccm/files/iccm/What%20is%20in%20an%20act%20v1.0.pdf>.

people and objects, do not always go in the direction of dominant emotional economies concomitant with political rationalities.

Technologies of Love and Governmentality: Ensuring Orderly Circulation

If it is necessary to think about love as movement taking place inside and cutting across different bodies and different spaces, this entails that the very landscape of marriage migration comprises economic relations that facilitate, foster or prevent economic flows, emotional transports and movement of people. Considering marriage migration regulations through the prism of technologies of love allows us to critically examine the role of love in relation to mobility and neoliberalism, two central features of governmentality. Of course, neoliberalism is not limited to governmentality, as it can be understood as a policy framework or as a political ideology.[40] But for Foucault, neoliberalism is first and foremost a specific form of liberalism. It is neither a theory nor an ideology. It is a practice, a rationalisation that obeys the internal rule of specificity in a maximised economy.

Governmentality emerged as a concern with orderly movement and circulation of goods and people when sovereign power gradually gave way to disciplinary power. For Foucault, the latter has become the feature of an age of individuality and objectification, characterised by a need for identification, classification and registration of things, persons and phenomena, all of this with the aim to order and optimise management and circulation through the identification of problematic objects/subjects. Thinking about technologies of love acknowledges the movement towards community implied by love in its different forms, with its directions and diversions, while also taking into account how this movement is interwoven in other flows and assemblages (those of law and sovereignty, especially), whose material, economic and spatial features should be accounted for. To say that love is not disconnected from these broader flows is not to deny "true love" between partners involved in a relationship, however they want to recognise its manifestation. It is rather to acknowledge, as Povinelli points out, the nexus between "micro-practices of love" and the "macro-practices of state governance ... capital production, circulation and consumption."[41]

In Europe, the "marriage migrant" is a bureaucratic figure that emerged in the post-war context, implicitly opposed to the "labour migrant."[42] This dichotomy is more the reflection of artificial divisions anchored in bureaucratic systems of regulation and classification than an accurate representation of the actual lives of migrants, who navigate these categories in fluid ways. But this legal complex rests on, constantly recreates and seeks to validate through procedures this dichotomy between love and labour. Economic flows and capital move labour migrants, love moves the others; the assumptions of the bureaucratic apparatus get displaced onto the migrants' claims for legitimacy. "Good marriage migrants" are expected to reunite with their partners for the sake of love, not for the sake of

40. See W. Larner, "Neo-Liberalism: Policy, Ideology, Governmentality", *Studies in Political Economy*, Vol. 63 (2000), pp. 5–25.

41. Povinelli, *op. cit.*, p. 191.

42. On this, see for example P. Raghuram, "The Difference that Skills Make: Gender, Family Migration Strategies and Regulated Labour Markets", *Journal of Ethnic and Migration Studies*, Vol. 30, No. 2 (2004), pp. 303–321; E. Kofman, "Family-Related Migration: A Critical Review of European Studies", *Journal of Ethnic and Migration Studies*, Vol. 30, No. 2 (2004), pp. 243–262.

other material benefits. It is the constant re-enactment of this loving movement that is being regulated, tested and assessed by the state.

Such assumptions about love and money as being distinct fields regulate and police mobility practices of specific marriage migrants, thus connecting love, law and sovereignty as three crucial nodes in marriage migration management. In the case of Russian–Norwegian marriages, for instance, we can see how assumptions about women being involved in what is presumed to be *capital* circuits (for instance, sex trade or the so-called "mail order brides industry") rather than being involved in *affective* ones, results in a differential in mobility controls. Such evaluation is not fixed in a firmly established security dispositif. Rather, it is negotiated in a sometimes ad hoc manner between different micro bordering sites. In the case of Norway, as Flemmen explains, couples involving a third-country national "must report to the police every year for the first three years of their marriage, and provide a written statement signed by witnesses who confirm that the couple lives together in a residence."[43] Yet she points out that this request for common residence is a demand that comes from national immigration law, not Norwegian marriage law, and that not all couples involving a non-Norwegian citizen need to report to the police: "This practice is limited to foreign spouses from countries considered to be 'migration inclined'. The local police authorities decide which countries represent such a risk. At present all marriages between Russian citizens and Norwegian citizens are suspected of not being 'real' in this sense."[44]

Love, Law and Sovereignty

Love is movement, an idea translated in the very idea of emotional transports. The very category of "marriage migrants" translates this emotional movement onto bodies as well. Indeed, when it comes to marriage migration and family reunification more generally, love becomes transport, a way of travelling: love moves people across borders. Yet law and sovereignty stand out as projects of immobility, of spatialisation in the face of movement, which is embodied by the marriage migrant, of course, but also by the idea of love itself.

As Christodoulidis suggests:

> Because love thrives on change, its existence over time is dynamic ... In contrast to any legal relationship, immobility is likely to be thematized as indifference, repetition as reluctance to unfold love further, to exceed the limit, which in turn signals the absence of love. ... Law is about ordering interaction and providing us with some security of expectations. And to order it must simplify. What was dynamic must now be *stilled*.[45]

We must remain suspicious of any defence of law as being fundamentally immune to technologies of love, and fight the tendency to see the latter as being law's

43. A.B. Flemmen, "Transnational Marriages—Empirical Complexities and Theoretical Challenges. An Exploration of Intersectionality", *NORA—Nordic Journal of Feminist and Gender Research*, Vol. 16, No. 2 (2008), p. 119

44. *Ibid.*

45. E.A. Christodoulidis, "Law, Love, and the Contestability of European Community", in H. Petersen (ed.), *Love and Law in Europe* (Dartmouth and Aldershot: Ashgate, 1998), p. 55. Emphasis in original.

"emotional outside." For instance, Raes notes that several sociologists of law took an interest in love as the very negation of law: "The good that is incorporated in the loving affection contradicts any conception of the right and the just that is embedded in reining legal institutions. The non legal topos is a topos of loving relationships, beyond contract or justice."[46] Such an understanding of the central role of love in relation to law reminds us that law is already central to governmentality. As Foucault explained,

> in the search for a liberal technology of government, it appeared that regulation through the juridical form constituted an efficient instrument, one different from wisdom or the moderation of those governing ... This regulation, it is in "law" that liberalism sought it. ... [T]he participation of the governed in the elaboration of law in a parliamentary system constitutes the most efficient system of governmental economy.[47]

Love is said to be extra-legal, yet legislation surrounding marriage migration shows that it is embedded in the legal complex that manages both mobility and the boundaries of sovereign identities, such as national or European ones. Consider for instance the so-called "rule of supposition" in Denmark adopted in 2003 to serve as a guideline for immigration officers to reject a spouse's application for reunification with a spouse. This guideline entails that the authorities "automatically treat a marriage between 'close relatives' (for example, first cousins) as forced, even though marriages between first cousins are legal under Danish law."[48] More than regulating mobility and conditions of entry and residence, such legislation anchors this governance of circulation in love, or namely its assumed impossibility in marriages between cousins who are not both Danish.

This example of an apparent break between a liberal idea of citizenship tied to an individual right to marry and the importance of love crystallises a tension at the heart of liberalism. In line with Foucault's reflection about the centrality of the legal complex to governmentality, Stolzenberg notes that the historical development of liberalism entailed that a rationalist conception of rights expanded alongside an increased recognition of a non-rationalistic "freedom of the heart"—a different, yet valid, form of "reasoning." Though developed during the Enlightenment, and anchored in the supreme value of "Reason," liberalism contains what she calls "a strong romantic impulse" where "matters of the heart" (such as religious or sexual freedom) uneasily cohabit with "matters of reason."[49] If anything, the Danish example indicates that technologies of love, far from opposing the rationality of liberalism or its affiliated legal complex, are "part of the techniques and mechanisms of regulation and control are or could in fact be used in the government of the populations of contemporary states."[50]

---

46. K. Raes, "On Love and Other Injustices: Love and Law as Improbable Communications", in Petersen, *Love and Law in Europe, op. cit.*, p. 39.

47. My translation. M. Foucault, *Dits et écrits, 1954–1988/Michel Foucault: Volume 2* (Paris: Gallimard, 2001), p. 822.

48. M. Rytter, "Semi-Legal Family Life: Pakistani Couples in the Borderlands of Denmark and Sweden", *Global Networks*, Vol. 12, No. 1 (2012), p. 100.

49. N.M. Stolzenberg, "Liberalism in Love", *Quinnipiac Law Review*, Vol. 28, No. 3 (2010), p. 614.

50. B. Hindess, "Liberalism: What's in a Name?", in W. Walters and W. Larner (eds.), *Global Governmentality: Governing International Spaces* (New York and London: Routledge, 2004), p. 26.

We might assume that the legal complex surrounding marriage migration in Europe emerged out of concern for individual rights: a right to love, for instance, concomitant with this "freedom of the heart" Stolzenberg linked with the development of the idea of human rights. In fact, the legal complex that has developed since the 1950s regarding marriage migration did not emerge as an answer to the perceived problem in the protection of a fundamental human right of migrants or citizens, such as the right to family or the right to marry. Legislation regarding family reunification at the EU level does not derive from the possessed rights of EU citizens. Rather, it derives from a translation of a concern for the mobility of goods to a concern for the mobility of persons, and should that mobility be hampered, economic productivity might suffer. As Petersen reminds us, "[l]ove and love relations that fall under the jurisdiction of EC law are not protected as a value in themselves, but as a requirement for productivity gains."[51] In the EU, the right to family is ancillary to the fundamental principal of market integration: "The underlying rationale is that if workers were not allowed to have their families accompanying them, many of them ... would most probably abandon all ambitions to be employed abroad. Such would hinder the further integration of the European market."[52]

Indeed, the right to family reunification, as the McCarthy case discussed in the introduction demonstrates, is not an inherently possessed right, even by European citizens. It derives from the circulation of capital, goods and labour. The right to family appeared for the first time in European legislation in 1961, with the first Regulation No. 15 on free movement outlining the rights of the spouse and children aged under 21 to join a worker.[53] If anything, it signals a movement from "object" rights to "human" rights (!). A genealogy of family reunification rights would show that even when it comes to the assumedly most intimate relations (family and spousal relations), we see a transfer from legislation concerning the freedom of movement of goods to the movement of workers and EU citizens. According to Schmidt, "provisions for the free movement of goods, services, workers and establishment were formulated and originally interpreted as prohibitions of discrimination," but then moved to a non-restrictive approach to trade.[54]

In the European Court of Justice, argues Schmidt, we see a favouring of an analogy between goods and people which strengthens legal certainty by relying on precedent and consolidating pre-existing legislations: "Since the logic of a prohibition of restrictions is transferred from goods to the other freedoms, there is much more pressure of pursuing a parallel approach to all freedoms in order to maintain the coherence of case law."[55] As a result, we see a double movement between the assumed dichotomy between "true love" and "capital," which gets reproduced and assessed through the bureaucratic categories of labour migrant

51. H. Petersen, "The Language of Emotions in the Language of Law", in Petersen, *Love and Law in Europe, op. cit.*, p. 21.

52. M.-C. Foblets, "Family Reunification: Who Pays for Love in Europe", in Petersen, *Love and Law in Europe, op. cit.*, p. 64.

53. K. Groenendijk, "Family Reunification as a Right under Community Law", *European Journal of Migration and Law*, Vol. 8, No. 2 (2006), p. 191.

54. S.K. Schmidt, "Who Cares about Nationality? The Path-Dependent Case Law of the ECJ from Goods to Citizens", *Journal of European Public Policy*, Vol. 19, No. 1 (2012), p. 10–11.

55. *Ibid.*, p. 15.

and family migrant, and the development of an intricate legal complex, where "the right to love" is directly enmeshed in and related to the orderly circulation of goods in a carefully delimitated "European" space.

Technologies of Love as Assemblages of Sovereign and Disciplinary Power

This last point is a reminder that technologies of love connect to law and (state) sovereignty in complex ways. Technologies of love participate in the ordering of different movements of feelings and people while also regulating and creating different cartographies. As the previous examples have shown, we can see through technologies of love the biopolitical regulation and creation of a national population by a sovereign nation state via marriage migration restrictions, but also the biopolitical regulation and creation of a European population and space by the European Union.[56] Such rationalities can intersect and connect, but they do not necessarily always converge.

If we accept that how, where and what we love is deeply political, what does this mean for a political understanding of technologies of love? Here, I want to take seriously Lauren Berlant's claim that "love always means non-sovereignty."[57] At the intersubjective level, Berlant's assertion recalls the idea of love as a force, as a movement that cannot be fully captured by the sheer force of individual will. It is about the composure you intended to keep, only to be betrayed by your uncontrollable smile or talking too fast. It is about this principle you may have secretly wished you could betray (be it reputation, fidelity, responsibility, etc.), but instead chose to retain. It is doing things because you *want* to or because you *have* to (wherever this imperative, this "ought," comes from and answers to: yourself, your family, God, destiny), as much about respecting boundaries as transgressing them. "Love," concludes Berlant, "is always about violating your own attachment to your intentionality, without being anti-intentional."[58] For her, love necessarily entails ambivalence, the idea that "something cannot be helped," escapes one's careful control and baffles the will of sovereign power, while also not being totally alien to it.

While focused on the intersubjective experience of love, Berlant's statements on love and sovereignty can be applied to the links between love and the sovereign state in relation to marriage migration management. What does it mean, then, to say that "love always means non-sovereignty?" Berlant's scheme maps well onto Foucault's idea of governmentality, as well as onto his point about our love/hate relationship with the state under neoliberal governance, which entails an emotional response, a drive which apparently cannot be helped either.[59] Her reflection that

56. I would like to thank one anonymous reviewer for spelling out this distinction so clearly. For more on the geographies of love resulting from these distinct but sometimes intersecting rationalities, see A.-M. D'Aoust, "Fractured Citizenships and Broken Hearts: Marriage Migration Regulations and Geographies of Love in Europe", *Environment and Planning D: Society and Space* (Special Issue: Geographies of Love), forthcoming).

57. L. Berlant, in Davis and Sarlin, op. cit.

58. *Ibid.*

59. "We know the fascination that the love or horror of the state exercises today: we know our attachment to the birth of the state, to its history, advance, power, and abuse. I think this overvaluation of the problem of the state is basically found in two forms. *An immediate, affective, and tragic form is the lyricism of the cold monster* confronting us." Foucault, *Security, Territory, Population, op. cit.*, p. 109. My emphasis.

love always entails non-sovereignty leads us to consider how technologies of love in relation to marriage migration are not reduced to one more mechanism inside neoliberalism, but are rather part of a complex assemblage, one that combines instances of sovereign and disciplinary power that combine with governmental ones. Assemblages, as Rabinow explains, are not *dispositifs*; they denote "a distinctive type of experimental matrix of heterogeneous elements, techniques and concepts . . . They are comparatively effervescent, disappear in years or decades rather than centuries."[60]

Technologies of love in marriage migration processes relate to sovereign practices and neoliberal rationalities in ways that are intentional yet simultaneously violated. The UK Border Agency (UKBA), for instance, issued guidelines for the clergy to help detect sham marriages and encourage denunciations. It notably offers training to clergy members to help them detect possibly fraudulent marriages. In doing so, it moves borderwork inside. As a spokeswoman explained, "[w]e advise our clergy . . . to insist on seeing valid identification such as passport or visa which shows a name and photograph and to interview both parties."[61] It illustrates the very process of the multiplication of inside borders that challenge the inside/outside fiction of stable state sovereignty. Moved from the checkpoint to the parish, such borders

> are no longer localizable in an unequivocal fashion. It also means that they no longer allow a superimposition of the set of functions of sovereignty, administration, cultural control, taxation and so on, and consequently a conferral on the territory, or better, on the duo of territory and population, of a simultaneously englobing, and univocal signification of "presuppositions" for all other social relations.[62]

Possible "official" indicators of fraud listed in the UKBA guidelines include "very few or no guests," "guests showing little participation in the ceremony," "wedding rings/dresses not being present or if present not being the correct size" or "the couple leaving separately following the ceremony."[63] Although the guidelines underline that "none of these reasons may in themselves necessarily indicate that the marriage is a sham and there may be other factors that may arouse suspicions," it still insists that "[m]aking such suspicions known to the Agency *would allow us to make a more informed decision* on whether the Third Country National is entitled to the leave that they are seeking."[64] Relying on the sovereign decision rather than the strict legal bureaucratic process creates new assemblages that reinforce sovereign power, while also consolidating the legal framework that frames and regulates what constitutes a "sham."

---

60. P. Rabinow, quoted in Walters, *Governmentality, op. cit.*, p. 77.

61. "Church in Wales Clergy Train to Spot Sham Marriages", BBC News Wales, 1 February 2011, available: <http://www.bbc.co.uk/news/uk-wales-12328026>.

62. É. Balibar, "The Borders of Europe", in P. Cheah and B. Robbins (eds.), *Cosmopolitics: Thinking and Feeling beyond the Nation* (Minneapolis: University of Minnesota Press, 1998), p. 219.

63. UK Border Agency, *Guidance for Clergy—Issued by UKBA—Foreign Nationals Seeking to Marry in the UK*, guidance issued 12 April 2011, available: <http://www.newcastle.anglican.org/userfiles/file/Newcastle%20Website/Mission%20and%20Ministry/Diocesan%20Handbook/Marriage%20ukba%20gdnce.pdf>.

64. *Ibid.* My emphasis.

This love/sovereignty/security nexus illustrated in the UKBA guidelines also finds a striking expression in the creation in France, in 1999, of the Association Nationale des Victimes de l'Insécurité (National Association of the Victims of Insecurity). No referent to insecurity is added here: it is insecurity altogether, in its ontological and existential dimensions. The association is devoted to the fight against so-called "grey marriages," a term coined in 2006[65] and a kind of marriage criminalised in 2011. Such marriages are depicted as being "sentimental frauds," namely marriages where one of the two parties involved "fake true love" to gain immigration benefits. The association thus "devotes the bulk of its efforts to supporting victims of grey marriages, primarily by providing the necessary help in getting repayment for *the primarily moral prejudice* suffered by people often left in a state of great distress."[66]

Adjudicating True Love

The regime of control pertaining to marriage migration also testifies to the fragility in the representational nature of the institutionalised order of sovereignty, as performances of sovereign power have become central to marriage migration management. Consider, for instance, the UKBA's decision to promote a politics of public naming and shaming by purposively circulating via social media several videos and pictures of "live" sham marriage crackdowns on Valentine's Day. These images include the interruption of a ceremony and "live" interrogations, along with handcuffed migrants being taking away in their wedding dresses, crying. Exposition of such public shaming contrasted the apparent helplessness and suffering of migrants with the state's strength, embodied through its law enforcement representatives. A state so "strong", in fact, that it can brag on Twitter: "Do you take this woman to be your sham bride? Flic.kr/p/8MVijo #happyvalentinesday" and "#rosesareredvioletsareblue if your marriage is sham we'll be on to you."[67]

The publicity and theatricality of punishment is central to sovereign power, as is the banning or deportation. On 28 May 2013, the UKBA announced that a "Pakistani man has been sentenced for attempting to cheat UK immigration rules by staging a sham marriage," and reported that "Judge McReynolds said: 'Your continued presence is detrimental to the country and flouting immigration law undermines confidence'. She also recommended that Zafran be deported when he has completed his sentence."[68]

More recently, in the UK, Australian activist Trenton Oldfield saw his application for a spousal visa denied after the Home Office evaluated that "his continued presence in Britain would not be conducive to the public good."[69] Oldfield

65. M.-A. Delauney, *L'immigration par escroquerie sentimentale* (Paris: Éditions Tatamis, 2006).

66. My translation, and my emphasis. Available: <http://mariagegris.fr/?page_id=16>.

67. National Coalition of Anti-Deportation Campaigns, "The Judges' Revolt and The Home Office's Assault on Love", 18 February 2013, available: <http://ncadc.org.uk/blog/2013/02/the-judges-revolt-and-thehome-offices-assault-on-love/>.

68. UK Border Agency, "Man Jailed for Sham Wedding Plot", 28 May 2013, available: <http://www.octf.gov.uk/News/Man-Jailed-For-Sham-Marriage-Plot-(1).aspx>.

69. Hugh Muir, "Boat Race Protester Trenton Oldfield Ordered to Leave UK", *The Guardian*, 23 June 2013, available: <http://www.theguardian.com/world/2013/jun/23/boat-race-protester-trenton-oldfield-ordered-leave-uk>.

had served a six-month jail sentence after he disrupted the annual Cambridge–Oxford boat race for 25 minutes in April 2012. His protest, as Oldfield explained then, "was designed to highlight elitism in British society."[70] Despite the fact that he had lived in the UK for 10 years, was married to a British woman, possessed a tier one working visa and expected to become a father in early July 2013, the Home Office remained inflexible: "Those who come to the UK must abide by our laws."[71] These exceptional prerogatives all express in different ways, as Carl Schmitt famously put it, at once the limit of sovereign power and its legitimation.

Such practices reaffirm sovereign power as protector and adjudicator of "true love"—true love between spouses, but also true love of one's country, as deportation and loss of citizenship can ensue. These examples illustrate the emergence of a governmentalisation of deportation, which not only serves to shape a national identity or protect the labour market, but also helps maintain the integrity of the governmental mechanism, the integrity of the immigration system.[72] Still, it does not necessarily signal a return to the past, before the rise of neoliberal governmentality, as it also ultimately relies on the processes of rationalisation proper to governmentality. It is noteworthy, for instance, that the term "mixed marriage" slowly moved from being used to refer to marriages between Catholics and non-Catholics, to interracial marriages, to now refer in Eurostat databases to a marriage "in which one partner is native-born and the other was born abroad,"[73] thus (re)producing through marriage the very fragile borders of the state to be protected. Similarly, in a detailed comparative study of marriages of convenience commissioned by the Norwegian Directorate of Immigration, the authors point to patterns of divorce rates and age difference as a key indicator of marriages of convenience. They identify that the average female applicant is seven years younger than her spouse/partner, whereas in marriages of convenience, she is on average 13 years younger. The average male applicant, by contrast, is about the same age as his spouse/partner, but about eight years younger in marriages of convenience.[74]

This appropriation and demand for love by the sovereign state is a performance of sovereignty, but also the recognition of a vulnerable one in the face of an excess that might escape its bureaucratised rationality. Marriage migration regulations invoke two apparently antithetical forces, traditionally seen as pitted against each other: the cold, repetitive, mechanical and dehumanising bureaucratic apparatus, versus the unique emotional dimensions assumed to be the proper and central feature of modern Western marriages. And while documents have become powerful technologies allowing for the control and management

70. *Ibid.*

71. *Ibid.* After months of fighting and gathering public support, Oldfield ultimately won his appeal against deportation in December 2013.

72. W. Walters, "Deportation, Expulsion, and the International Police of Aliens", in N. de Genova and N. Peutz (eds.), *The Deportation Regime: Sovereignty, Space, and the Freedom of Movement* (Durham, NC and London: Duke University Press, 2010), p. 87.

73. G. Lanzieri, "Merging Populations: A Look at Marriages With Foreign-Born Persons in European Countries", *Eurostat: Statistics in Focus*, Vol. 29 (2012), available: <http://epp.eurostat.ec.europa.eu/cache/ITY_OFFPUB/KS-SF-12-029/EN/KS-SF-12-029-EN.PDF>.

74. Pöyry Management Consulting, "Marriages of Convenience: A Comparative Study. Rules and Practices in Norway, Sweden, Germany, Denmark and the Netherlands", Commissioned by the Norwegian Directorate of Immigration, 8 November 2010, pp. 28–29, available: <http://www.udi.no/Global/upload/Publikasjoner/FOU/R-2010-053_SAA_Marriages_of_convenience.pdf>.

of legally authorised or criminalised migration flows, marriage migration management defies the assumed impassibility of the bureaucracy.

The very notion of a "sham marriage" creates an incongruence between "reality" and what has been called "papereality."[75] Whereas passports have become a trusted materialised substitute for their embodied carriers, the same truth correspondence is not sufficient when it comes to marriage migrants. In other words, producing the appropriate paperwork (for instance a marriage certificate) is not enough to judge whether a couple has entered into a bona fide marriage. What is deemed necessary to prove goes beyond the legibility of the paperwork, and requires an *emotional reading* of artefacts or practices. A "look of love" on photographs submitted with a visa application file, toothbrushes in bathrooms shared by the spouses under investigation, rings exchanged at wedding ceremonies, the presence of multiple guests during the wedding ceremony: these materialisations are said to validate the "true relationship" and suggest the legal expectations of couples' alignment with the dominant Western commodification of romantic intimacy.[76] More importantly, it testifies to the central role love plays, to paraphrase Rose and Valverde, as a conceptual code and criterion of judgement within which the problem of marriage migration is formed, and around which clashes and alliances between different explanatory logics and types of judgements take place.[77]

Conclusion

"Rather than organizing a stable map of the world," Mezzadra and Neilson argue, "the processes of proliferation and transformation of borders aim to manage the 'creative destruction' and constant recombination of spaces and times that lie at the heart of contemporary capitalist globalization."[78] This article has examined how love, far from being apolitical or a challenge to the realm of the political, is in fact central to migration management and bordering practices. As such, it can and should be accounted for in the governmentality of marriage migration. As a technology that emerges through movement, love can be shaped through various institutional practices. But technologies of love carry an excess that escapes intentionality, which means that they cannot be reduced to technologies of government. Rather, they are part of assemblages where they confront and exceed, but also at times collude with, projects of immobility integral to governmental calculations that aim at orderly circulation. The emotional mobility afforded, delineated and challenged by technologies of love is thus not disconnected from other regimes of mobility controls. Such movement is tied to bodily ones as well: "The freedom of movement . . . can only ever be a perpetual and troublesome affront to the self-anointed sovereignty of state power. It manifests a restless and inassimilable

75. J. Kim, "Establishing Identity: Documents, Performance, and Biometric Information in Immigration Proceedings", *Law & Social Inquiry*, Vol. 26, No. 3 (2011), p. 778.

76. See E. Illouz, *Consuming the Romantic Utopia: Love and the Cultural Contradictions of Capitalism* (Berkeley, Los Angeles and London: Berkeley University Press, 1997).

77. N. Rose and M. Valverde, "Governed by Law?", *Social and Legal Studies*, Vol. 7, No. 4 (1998), p. 546.

78. S. Mezzadra and B. Neilson, "Between Inclusion and Exclusion: On the Topology of Global Spaces and Orders", *Theory, Culture & Society*, Vol. 29, No. 4/5 (2012), p. 64.

alterity busily working both within and against state power's most cherished ideal: social order."[79]

A brief look at the "problem" of marriage migration management, especially in Europe, allowed us to examine how intermingled the domains of love, law and sovereignty actually are. Such concerns over marriage migrants show that love is a movement, a transport that is not only central to migration processes carried over by migrants, but also to management practices that aim to secure an imagined identity and space—that of Europe. Such space is not only political; it is assumed to have a peculiar emotional landscape tied to it, a specific geography of love. In that way, technologies of love are also integral to the constant recombination of spaces and times Mezzadra and Neilson are concerned about in relation to globalisation.

The McCarthy case mentioned at the beginning of this article points to the very heterogeneity of European citizenship, as citizens and non-citizens alike might end up not holding the rights we assume they possess or might be entitled to. Citizens living in their own country inside the EU might be unable to gain the right to family reunification, whereas their mobile European counterparts might be able to, simply due to their physical mobility, which rests on an assumption that the latter reflects a mobility of capital inside the European space as well. There is an ordering of feelings that is stirred to mimic the orderly circulation of capital. Such instances may indicate that we might indeed be witnessing a new disarticulation of citizenship and its space of definition, one that makes it even more pressing to ask "What makes the citizen?" More than clear belonging and fixity, in the European context, it is movement and love that distinguish the citizen from the non-citizen. Both might represent a challenge to sovereignty and law and their respective projects of immobility and stability. As movement and love have also become the hallmarks of "the manifestation (and precondition) of a *free* social *order*"[80] in Europe, we need to consider more carefully and critically what moves people, and in what directions, physically and emotionally.

About the Author

Anne-Marie D'Aoust is Assistant Professor in the Department of Political Science at the Université du Québec à Montréal. Her recent publications on marriage migration have appeared in *International Political Sociology* and in Martin Geiger and Antoine Pécoud's *Disciplining the Transnational Mobility of People* (Palgrave Macmillan, 2013). Her other projects include issues of language and the sociology of the discipline of IR, and an investigation of "Security and Its Publics," carried out in collaboration with William Walters.

79. N. de Genova, "The Deportation Regime: Sovereignty, Space, and the Freedom of Movement", in de Genova and Peutz, *The Deportation Regime, op. cit.*, p. 58.

80. H. Kotef, "Movement", *Political Concepts: A Critical Lexicon*, Vol. 2, No. 2 (2012), available: <http://www.politicalconcepts.org/movement-hagar-kotef/>; emphasis original.

No Good Deed Goes Unrewarded: The Values/Virtues of Transnational Volunteerism in Neoliberal Capital

WANDA VRASTI and JEAN MICHEL MONTSION

This article focuses on the value of volunteering in producing, sustaining and legitimising forms of subjectivity and social relations congruent with the ethos of neoliberal capital. Rather than treat it as a spontaneous act of virtue, we insist that volunteerism is a carefully designed technology of government the purpose of which is to align individual conduct with neoliberal capital's double injunction of market rationality and social responsibility. To this end we investigate two complementary case studies of transnational volunteerism, one dealing with Chinese international students volunteering in Vancouver seeking to obtain Canadian citizenship, the other looking at Western university students and graduates volunteering in Ghana to gather relevant professional skills and experience. In both cases we find that transnational volunteerism helps participating individuals assume cultural skills, affective competencies and citizenship prerogatives they could otherwise not have claimed through nationality or employment.

> Along with nihilists, we have to recognize that regardless of how brilliantly and trenchantly we critique it, we are destined to live in this world, not only subject to its powers of domination but also contaminated by its corruptions.[1]

In July 2010, at the very same time that the British government was announcing severe austerity cuts, Prime Minister David Cameron unveiled his "great passion": a programme that would trigger "the biggest, most dramatic redistribution of power from elites in Whitehall to the man and woman on the street."[2] Emphatically called Big Society, the initiative would roll back wasteful and demoralising public services, and empower communities to take charge of their own destinies by promoting volunteering, charitable giving and social entrepreneurship.

---

*This research was made possible through funding from the Social Sciences and Humanities Council of Canada (SSHRC). We would also like to thank the anonymous reviewers of the journal for their insightful comments.

1. Michael Hardt and Antonio Negri, *Commonwealth* (Cambridge, MA: Harvard University Press, 2009), p. ix.

2. David Cameron, "Big Society Speech", 19 July 2010, available: <http://www.number10.gov.uk/news/speeches-and-transcripts/2010/07/big-society-speech-53572> (accessed 11 January 2011).

> For a long time the way government has worked—top-down, top-heavy, controlling—has frequently had the effect of sapping responsibility, local innovation and civic action. It has turned many motivated public sector workers into disillusioned, weary puppets of government targets. It has turned able, capable individuals into passive recipients of state help with little hope for a better future. It has turned lively communities into dull, soulless clones of one another. So we need to turn government completely on its head.[3]

In using the lynchpin of individual responsibility to justify further spending cuts and privatisation measures, Cameron was echoing speeches heard 30 years earlier on both sides of the Atlantic: Ronald Reagan's promise to take "government off the backs of the American people" and Margret Thatcher's proclamation that "there is no such thing as society; only individuals and their families." Using the voluntarist and small-is-beautiful language of the counter-culture and pandering to their critiques of corporate capital and centralised government, neoconservative governments of the 1980s sold neoliberalism as an antidote to bureaucratic rigidities (read: government regulation and labour power) and a harbinger of personal freedom and prosperity.[4] Very soon though it turned out that behind the promise for flexible organisations, gratifying jobs and universal homeownership lay, in fact, a massive socio-economic overhaul designed to rid people of the kinds of social provisions and collective power that would enable them to resist precarious employment, overwork and private indebtedness.

Instead of embedding flexible accumulation in some sort of institutional fix, the solution offered at the turn of the millennium by Western social democratic governments was to dress up neoliberalism in a tolerable and therapeutic language[5] that could manage "the costs and contradictions of *earlier* waves of neoliberalization" without actually changing anything about its underlying logic.[6] Gradually, the general discourse of neoliberalism shifted "from dogmatic deregulation to market-friendly re-regulation, from structural adjustment to good governance, from budget cuts to regulation-by-audit, from welfare retrenchment to active social policy, from privatization to public-private partnerships, [and] from greed-is-good to markets-with-morals."[7] So-called "Third Way" neoliberalism

3. *Ibid.*

4. This is not to suggest that the neo-conservative Right has single-handedly invented and implemented the neoliberal doctrine. As David Harvey explains, the Reagan and Thatcher regimes, along with their Washington Consensus adepts, more or less "stumbled" towards neoliberalisation rather than following a predetermined policy path. See David Harvey, *A Brief History of Neoliberalism* (Oxford: Oxford University Press, 2005), p. 13. We do not want to perpetuate a history-less view of neoliberalism that locates the origins of this model of governance in the turmoil of the 1970s or attribute it solely to the policy decisions of a handful of political leaders and opinion makers. Rather, we acknowledge that neoliberalism is in fact the latest phase of a *longue durée* of capitalist accumulation that goes back to feudal land enclosures, the inquisition, 18th-century industrialisation and urbanisation, 19th-century institutions of liberal democracy, and 500 years of colonial and imperial subjugation. All of these things persist, in some form or another, under the banner of neoliberalism. Hence, we use the term neoliberalism less to suggest a rupture with the past than to point out capital's inexhaustible malleability and adaptability to changing historical conditions.

5. Eva Illouz, *Cold Intimacies: The Making of Emotional Capitalism* (Cambridge: Polity Press, 2007).

6. Jamie Peck, "Zombie Neoliberalism and the Ambidextruous State", *Theoretical Criminology*, Vol. 14, No. 1 (2010), p. 106.

7. *Ibid.*

sees no contradiction between market rationality and moral action. Free market principles, like profitability, performance, accounting, competition and entrepreneurship, in fact, require social responsibility and public legitimacy for their successful realisation.[8]

Volunteering, not coincidentally celebrated as one of the pillars of the Big Society approach, is an excellent illustration of this highly complex and duplicitous form of government. Situated at the intersection between the de-responsibilised post-Fordist state and the re-responsibilised entrepreneurial self (doubly responsible for its own wellbeing and that of its community), volunteerism is well poised to capture the great Foucauldian lesson on neoliberal government,[9] where the task of government is no longer to correct market imbalances through deficit spending, collective bargaining rights or full employment, like in the Fordist period, but to intervene in society to make sure it contains the necessary values, tastes and attitudes for flexible accumulation to run smoothly. In this view, volunteerism is being revalued as a key technique for disseminating appropriate forms of conduct. Of course, volunteering is not a new development. However, never before has this practice been riddled by so big a contradiction between the selfless aims it claims to pursue and the disciplinary task it in fact accomplishes.

Both a close reading of Marx[10] and a materialist feminist approach[11] will point out that capitalism has never been limited to producing commodities, but that this immediately economic task rests on the existence and reproduction of subjects and social relations congruent with the logic of private profit extraction. Thus, the task of (re)producing workers through language, communication, culture and other symbolic functions has always been at the core of capitalism. What changed perhaps is the *intensity* and *visibility* of this function. In advanced liberal economies, de-industrialisation and labour flexibilisation constitute an abrogation of the Fordist "norm." Capital no longer extracts value solely by producing and circulating commodities. It must also mobilise and valorise culture, social relations and affective dispositions. In this view, volunteering emerges as a useful subject-forming tool for producing the kinds of skills, emotions and normative orientations expected from neoliberal subjects.

Rather than "make a difference" or "give back" to the community, the main effect of institutionalised volunteering is to produce, sustain and legitimise subjects and social relations that are congruent with the ethos of neoliberal capital.

---

8. Stephan Lessernich, *Die Neuerfindung des Sozialen: Der Sozialstaat im flexiblen Kapitalusmus* (Bielefeld: Transcript Verlag, 2008).

9. Throughout this text we use the term government to refer not necessarily to the sum of state institutions and apparatuses, but rather to Foucault's concept of "governmentality" which describes a proliferation of governing bodies, strategies and techniques that go above and beyond the bureaucratic carcass of the state. This is not just a conceptual difference, but a historical shift from the centralised, bureaucratically organised Fordist government to the dispersed network of rules, norms and tactics of post-Fordism. See Andrew Barry, Thomas Osborne and Nikolas Rose (eds.), *Foucault and Political Reason: Liberalism, Neo-Liberalism and Rationalities of Government* (Chicago: University of Chicago Press, 1996) and Graham Burchell, Colin Gordon and Peter Miller (eds.), *The Foucault Effect: Studies in Governmentality* (Chicago: University of Chicago Press, 1991).

10. Jason Read, "A Fugitive Thread: The Production of Subjectivity in Marx", *Pli*, Vol. 13 (2002), pp. 125–146.

11. David Graeber, "The Sadness of Postworkerism", in David Graeber, *Revolutions in Reverse: Essays on Politics, Violence, Art, and Imagination* (Brooklyn, NY: Autonomedia, 2011), pp. 79–106.

This is not to say that volunteers are hypocrites looking to boost their résumés or that charity is nothing but an expression of "liberal guilt." In most cases volunteering is animated by veritable cosmopolitan impulses of care, compassion and even brotherly love. When deployed in a governmental context, however, these emotions, even if genuinely felt by participants, become mobilised for purposes not entirely under the control of those sharing them. In light of the works of Foucault and his followers,[12] we understand transnational volunteerism to be a strategy of government useful in performing the following tasks: governing communities without direct government intervention (and spending); equipping individuals with the social and emotional competencies necessary for producing value in communicative capitalism; and situating certain spaces, communities and identities as favourable junctions in the global flow of capital. Much of the versatility and efficacy of this strategy is owed to the fact that transnational volunteerism appears to be a spontaneous act of virtue independent from the disciplinary power of the state or the ideology of market forces.

In this article, we present two case studies of transnational volunteerism working at the intersection of neoliberal state practices, capital flows and global ethics. Whereas Montsion's research discusses Chinese international students volunteering in Canada to meet the social and moral requirements associated with the Canadian citizenship design, Vrasti's work focuses on Western students volunteering in Ghana to acquire professional experience and social capital. As authors, we present and participate in these case studies differently. Also, the emotional experiences of those participating in these volunteering projects vary. Still, our joint ambition is to highlight how, despite experiential differences, volunteerism operates as a form of subjectivation reaching beyond simple discipline and regulation to inaugurate a flexibilisation and stratification of neoliberal subjectivity, as discussed in the final section. But first we begin with an overview of the most recent uses of volunteerism in neoliberal government practices.

The Virtues/Values of Volunteerism

The virtue of volunteer work is not a new discovery. It has been celebrated in both liberal democracies and socialist countries for its reformative and restorative benefits. As early as Alexis de Tocqueville's *Democracy in America,*[13] volunteering or, more generally, participation in community associations and charity work has been recognised as vital for the functioning of republican liberal democracy. If during the Victorian age philanthropy and volunteering were mostly bourgeois paraphernalia meant to help the middle class distinguish itself from a morally corrupt aristocracy,[14] in the 20th century the merits of volunteering were recognised more generally. Political scientists and policy-makers alike have hailed service work as essential for disseminating the norms and habits of civil society

12. See Barry *et al., op. cit.;* Burchell *et al., op. cit.;* Thomas Lemke, "An Indigestible Meal? Foucault, Governmentality and State Theory", *Distinktion: Scandinavian Journal of Social Theory,* Vol. 15 (2007), pp. 43–64; Aihwa Ong, *Neoliberalism as Exception: Mutations in Citizenship and Sovereignty* (Durham, NC: Duke University Press, 2006).

13. Alexis de Tocqueville, *Democracy in America,* Vol. 1 (New York: Penguin Classics, 2003).

14. S. Amit Rai, *Rule of Sympathy: Sentiment, Race, and Power, 1750–1850* (New York: Palgrave, 2002).

and a key marker of a vibrant democratic culture.[15] In an age of neoliberal rule, volunteer work gains renewed importance for transmitting social and affective competencies that disseminate the kind of responsibility, both economic and moral, required for free markets to operate and expand. Under Third Way neoliberalism, charity work has been instrumental in filling the void left by the hollowing out of the state, especially in replacing the social bonds and safety provisions of the Fordist era with a more self-reliant, autonomous and flexible type of social organisation.[16]

The clearest indication of the revalorisation of volunteerism for capitalist purposes is the rise in recent years of so-called "philanthrocapitalism," that is, "the use of business thinking by large new donors to transform philanthropy, coupled with the deployment of market mechanisms on a much larger scale to promote development and social change."[17] We see this in non-governmental organisations (NGOs), private initiatives, international development assistance, and especially in the spectacular charity acts of celebrities and billionaires. Similar to the charity of 19th-century industrialists and capitalists, philanthrocapitalism celebrates individual acts of kindness that obscure how this work is "imbricated in and symptomatic of extreme inequality."[18] As Kapoor argues, this type of intervention has an ideological function. Spectacular acts of generosity are mobilised to attend to the most egregious instances of misery, as if these were mere exceptional instances, while the political relation between poverty and privilege remains untouched. Meanwhile, the consumption and accumulation practices of media and software giants participating in philantrocapitalism are allowed to carry on as usual.[19] What Third Way neoliberalism effectively tells us is "that we can have the global capitalist cake, i.e., thrive as profitable entrepreneurs, and eat it too, i.e., endorse the anti-capitalist causes of social responsibility and ecological concern."[20]

But this is not a practice exclusive to celebrities and wealthy entrepreneurs. Growing emphasis on charity, care and compassion as core components of civic conduct or citizenship is indicative of a broader transformation in political rationality, which can broadly be termed, following the work of Nikolas Rose, "ethopolitics." Ethopolitics encapsulates the logic of Third Way neoliberalism in that it blends traditional leftist aspirations for dignity and equal opportunity together with conservative values of individual responsibility and entrepreneurship to produce a subject, an ethical individual responsible for their own wellbeing and that of their relevant communities. Its purpose, as Rose argues, is to lend the

---

15. A. Gabriel Almond and Sydney Verba, *The Civic Culture. Political Attitudes and Democracy in Five Nations* (Princeton, NJ: Princeton University Press, 1963).

16. Suzan Ilcan and Tanya Basok, "Community Government: Voluntary Agencies, Social Justice, and the Responsibilization of Citizens", *Citizenship Studies*, Vol. 8, No. 2 (2004), pp. 129–144.

17. Michael Edwards, "Why Philantrocapitalism Is Not the Answer: Private Initiatives and International Development", in Monique Kremer, Peter van Lieshout and Robert Went (eds.), *Doing Good or Doing Better: Development Policies in a Globalized World* (Amsterdam: Amsterdam University Press, 2009), pp. 237–249, p. 237.

18. Jo Littler, "The New Victorians? Celebrity Charity and the Demise of the Welfare State", p. 1, Paper presented at the Capitalism, Democracy and Celebrity Advocacy Symposium, Manchester, 19–20 June 2012, available: <http://capitalismdemocracycelebrity.files.wordpress.com/2012/02/littler-the-new-victorians1.pdf> (accessed 18 January 2013).

19. Ilan Kapoor, *Celebrity Humanitarianism: The Ideology of Global Charity* (New York: Routledge, 2012).

20. Slavoj Zizek, *Violence* (New York: Picador, 2008), p. 16.

current regime of accumulation (and dispossession) a human face to make it more tolerable, download state power to the community level in the hopes of unburdening the former and disciplining the latter, and transform citizenship from a rights-based entitlement into a merit-based asset.[21]

With the post-Fordist state refusing or failing to assume responsibility for its citizens' lives through planning, calculation and steering, individuals are encouraged to bind themselves to their relevant communities and realise their destinies in congruence with these. Coined "government through community," this political rationality proposes that "[p]olitics is to be returned to society itself, but no longer in a social form: in the form of individual morality, organizational responsibility, and ethical community."[22] Government through community, that is, government away from the patronising and disabling structures of central government and back to the choices, energies and commitments of community members, sometimes even the global community, is supposed to cure all social ills which central government has been unable to address (e.g., poverty, crime, teen pregnancy, unemployment, drug abuse, urban decay) by activating personal self-reliance and responsibility.

Despite the welcome emphasis on sociality, autonomy and dignity, transformations in the rationality of government like ethopolitics and government through community render social life at once more inflexible and more uncertain. Suddenly, the relation of responsibility that ties individuals and their communities is no longer based on collective bonds and social obligations given through a national project so much as on capricious ethical and affective principles, like volunteerism. This has implications also for how we conduct and conceive ourselves. We are still dealing with the calculating and responsible subject we have come to expect under neoliberalism,[23] except that these dispositions are no longer limited to the economic terrain; they are "placing the affective subject at its centre."[24] While there is still a certain instrumentality to this mode of action, the ethopolitical subject is no longer exclusively informed by rational choice and cost-benefit calculations to the exclusion of all social and moral considerations. Demonstrating compassion, care and responsibility for our fellow human beings or the environment has become key to our understanding of a normative self. The same logic applies also for the transnational level, where images of a global community of care and responsibility are invoked with no attention to transnational relations of power pertaining to capitalism or imperialism, but phrased purely in moral terms dependent upon individual enlightenment and magnanimity.

This framing of the global volunteer necessarily speaks of the stratification of human life within global capital. Volunteerism contributes, alongside war and humanitarianism, to the "complex ontology of inequality [. . .] that differentiates in a hierarchical manner the values of human life."[25] Using the old Aristotelian

21. Nikolas Rose, "Community, Citizenship, and the Third Way", *American Behavioral Scientist*, Vol. 43, No. 9 (2000), pp. 1385–1411.

22. *Ibid.*, p. 1400.

23. Lemke, *op. cit.*

24. Anne-Marie Fortier, "Proximity by Design? Affective Citizenship and the Management of Unease", *Citizenship Studies*, Vol. 14, No. 1 (2010), p. 22.

25. Didier Fassin, "Humanitarianism as a Politics of Life", *Public Culture*, Vol. 19, No. 3 (2007), pp. 499–520, p. 519.

distinction between *zoe* and *bios*, between biological life and fully qualified political life, we can observe here a growing chasm between the passive populations waiting for help and rescue and the active individuals able to experience growth, accumulate skills and expand their field of possibility. This is not just the old distinction between haves and have-nots characteristic of global capitalism. It is also a normative difference between individuals able to live up to the demands of responsible self-government and those unable to do so. While the former come to enjoy ever more possibilities for action in terms of political rights and consumer freedoms, the latter are *de-subjectified,* included only by virtue of their exclusion from social protections and democratic participation.[26] Poor people, especially racialised ones, function as surplus populations, not entirely superfluous to capital but fully malleable to its needs. They can be made useful either as cheap labour, a trope against which to assert the superiority of the white man,[27] a "place for redemption for those with power,"[28] a learning ground for global citizens, or not at all. Either way, their chances to perform credible models of economic and moral conduct are drastically undermined by their position at the bottom of the hierarchy of human life.

We see here how this mode of government "actually seeks to inscribe the norms of self-control more deeply into the soul of each citizen."[29] It inaugurates new strategies of disciplinary rule at the same time that it downloads the classic obligations of the state onto the shoulders of private citizens. Still, this is not to suggest that volunteerism is nothing but an ideological cover for free labour, social cutbacks and privatisation. Despite it being unpaid labour, volunteerism rarely remains unrewarded. In its ability to fuse individual responsibility with social accountability and thus realise the injunctions of neoliberal government, volunteer work comes to function notably as symbolic capital, training ground and normative orientation.

Two Accounts of Transnational Volunteerism

In what follows we present two distinct instances of transnational volunteerism situated at the intersection between neoliberal capital, citizenship regimes and social responsibility. Although the cases have to be understood as eclectic in nature, we also focus on the unexpected crossovers between Chinese foreign students volunteering in Vancouver and Caucasian young adults volunteering in Ghana to better understand how social and moral responsibility is conceived, transmitted and lived in these encounters. As made clear in Montsion's research, for Chinese foreign students volunteering is an ideal opportunity to learn more about the cultural and social skills required to become a member of Canadian society. In an immigration system where citizenship rights are extended based on merit, voluntary agencies not only deliver much-needed social services to disadvantaged populations, they also teach volunteers the virtues of responsible

26. Andrew Neal, "Goodbye War on Terror? Foucault and Butler on Discourses of Law, War, and Exceptionalism", in M. Dillon and A.W. Neal (eds.), *Foucault on Politics, Security and War* (London: Palgrave, 2008), p. 51.

27. Achille Mbembe, *On the Postcolony* (Berkeley: University of California Press, 2001).

28. Kathryn Mathers, *Travel, Humanitarianism and Becoming American in Africa* (New York: Palgrave, 2010), p. 4.

29. Rose, *op. cit.*, p. 1409.

citizenship.[30] Relatedly, Vrasti's research demonstrates that for young adults looking for work in an increasingly flexible and precarious labour market, volunteering abroad counts as valuable professional experience. Living in a foreign country, with no language skills, modern amenities or support networks lends young professionals the types of immaterial and cognitive skills expected from the flexible workers: initiative, innovation, problem-solving, risk-taking, cultural awareness and global knowledge. In both cases, being a volunteer is not just about feeling responsible (read: "giving back") to the community so much as about becoming a subject responsible for its own skills and assets.

Although both of our research projects draw upon ethnographic evidence, our work is not ethnography per se, in the sense that we do not purport to capture and reconstruct the world of meaning of an entire people or community. Rather, our ethnographic sensibilities seek to communicate the itinerant nature of our object of inquiry as it moves between places, cultures and subject positions. It is not only volunteers who travel; research also moves back and forth between field sites and theory, experience and writing, as well as transversally between the two of us. As such, we have chosen ethnography and conversation as strategies for maintaining a degree of honesty and transparency concerning the journey knowledge production inevitably has to make before it can reach the public eye. Especially when the task at hand is connecting a quite specific issue, like transnational volunteering, to macro-level processes, like neoliberal government, transformations of capital and citizenship practices, we believe it important to keep some space open for movement, contingency and contestation.

Volunteering to Become Good Citizens

When I (Jean Michel Montsion) started doing field research in Vancouver for my doctoral dissertation on migratory flows at transient locations between China and Western societies in the spring of 2008, I decided to volunteer in local ethnic Chinese community associations not only to expand my contact base, but also to gain a different perspective on the research I was conducting. Most of these organisations are multi-service agencies that offer a variety of services from social assistance for vulnerable populations to support for the elderly, health services and more traditional immigration services, such as language and professional training. I soon became fascinated with the ways in which volunteering had been institutionalised by these community associations and instrumentalised by state authorities. More specifically, I noticed that community associations deploy volunteer work to strategically facilitate the integration of Chinese international students and newcomers to Canada into their ranks, where they can communicate values, norms and representations of what it means to be Chinese in Vancouver. Associations like the United Chinese Community Enrichment Services Society (SUCCESS), created in the 1970s to serve an exclusive but increasingly diversifying Hong Kongese population, are systematically using volunteer work to reinforce their position within local politics, notably by socialising newcomers in the specific affective competencies necessary to become a Canadian of Chinese origin in Vancouver.

30. Ilcan and Basok, *op. cit.*

As the closest North American metropolis to Asia, Vancouver is quickly becoming a key connection node in the restructuring of global networks of trade, mobility and communication. The city is particularly active in providing higher education, English as a Second Language (ESL) courses and other professional training programmes to Asia's growing elites, especially international students from mainland China. Volunteer work has expanded as a complementary branch to this growing demand for post-secondary education. Not coincidentally, Canadian state authorities have incorporated volunteering into the country's immigration policies. Since 1999, Citizenship and Immigration Canada has been advertising volunteer work experience,[31] even if still dissociated from legislations regulating labour, revenue and work, as a way to obtain Canadian permanent residency.[32] This is helpful for international students, as their visas might not allow them to work off campus. They may also not be able to legally find a job, depending on their age, or they may not have the time to take job.[33] For instance, four international Chinese students I met while volunteering at an event organised by a local ethnic Chinese community association shared with me that volunteer work not only allows them to meet people in a new city and gain a sense of self-worth, it was also a strategic component of their long-term plan to remain in Canada or perhaps return in the future.[34] As such, it reflected a close association between performing volunteer work, obtaining Canadian citizenship and having the individual freedom to choose opportunities leading to the good life.

If volunteering had a clear function with regards to Canadian society and authorities, within the Vancouver Chinese community volunteering became the terrain of contestation between older, more well-established (usually Hong Kongese) community associations and their newer counterparts from mainland China. In institutionalising volunteer work, especially by targeting international students coming from the mainland, well-established Hong Kongese agencies like SUCCESS remain relevant societal actors: they demand public funding and carve out a voice in local politics. Because the newly developed Volunteer Branch of SUCCESS has consolidated numerous partnership agreements and memoranda of understanding with post-secondary institutions in Vancouver, a large number of volunteers are being directed to SUCCESS by their counsellors.[35] This not only provides SUCCESS with a constantly renewable pool of volunteers, but the organisation can also appear to be opening its membership to mainlanders

31. To qualify for permanent residency status under the Canadian Experience Class, international students must accumulate the equivalent of one year full-time work experience in Canada, a requirement that can also be fulfilled through volunteer work. As with any other work experience, this has to be documented and certified by the employer or, in this case, voluntary association. See Citizenship and Immigration Canada, "Canadian Experience Class", January 2010, available: <http://www.cic.gc.ca/english/immigrate/cec/apply-who.asp> (accessed 27 January 2010).

32. British Council, "Visa and Immigration Requirements", 2009, available: <http://www.britishcouncil.org/usa-education-visas-entry-clearance.htm> (accessed 24 July 2009); Citizenship and Immigration Canada, "Q&A: Volunteer Experience", *CIC Newsletter*, March 1999, available: <http://www.cicnews.com/1999/03/volunteer-experience-03480.html> (accessed 24 July 2009).

33. Bruce [pseudonym]. Personal interview with a person involved in SUCCESS everyday operations, notebook of Montsion, Vancouver, 9 May 2008.

34. Collective interview with four international Chinese students, notebook of Montsion, Vancouver, 24 April 2008.

35. *Ibid.*

and adapt to new Chinese migration patterns.[36] Although a few concerned voices from mainlanders' associations have emerged over the last few years to dispute SUCCESS's claim of representing Vancouver's ethnic Chinese communities (notably as part of the "Big 5" Chinese community associations of Vancouver), the speed and ease with which SUCCESS incorporates newcomers privileges the organisation's social position and relevance against other community actors and their critics. This is especially important in a context where proliferating ethnic Chinese community associations have to compete for limited government funding.[37]

Through the systematic incorporation of volunteer work, community associations communicate specific representations of what a good Canadian citizen of Chinese origin is to their incoming members. Well-established ethnic Chinese community associations, for instance, cast volunteer work as an essential North American attitude which newcomers must practise if they want to integrate.[38] What is more, volunteer work is said to contain cultural and emotive lessons essential to pursuing the liberal ideals associated with Canadian citizenship, such as a strong career-oriented drive, a respect for personal boundaries, a desire to give back to the most vulnerable in the community, a social network to rely on and, most importantly, a will to learn and better oneself, notably by using every opportunity to practise one's English language skills. It also includes a strong ethos of framing the young international student as an active political agent who can help the most vulnerable populations of Canada, as a way to give back to the community he/she wants to join.

Volunteer work helps community associations to position themselves as (exclusive) bridges between the Canadian citizenship design and Chinese newcomers themselves. This is especially true for well-established Hong Kongese community associations opening up their membership to an increasing Canadian immigration from mainland China. Frank, for instance, a mid-level manager in a well-established Hong Kongese social services agency that uses a lot of volunteers in its daily activities, explained that volunteer work has very different cultural meanings in Canada and in mainland China: "In China, there is no volunteer work. They do not teach you how and why volunteer work is important [. . .] There is no fundraising because you are looked at by the government."[39] Working with increasing numbers of volunteers from mainland China for the last 12 years, he sets the motivations of mainlanders apart to suggest that their upbringing made a difference in how less committed they are to volunteer work, and how volunteer work can do them good in better understanding what it means to be a good Canadian citizen. He claims that culturally, *true* volunteer work is rather a Canadian than mainlander practice, hence reproducing the notion that there is an incommensurable divide between two social contexts that volunteer work in his association can help to bridge. As such, he recommends that mainlanders volunteer

36. Vince [pseudonym]. Personal interview with a Vancouver City social planner, notebook of Montsion, Vancouver, 12 June 2008.

37. Carl [pseudonym]. Personal interview with a local Chinese news director in the Greater Vancouver area, notebook of Montsion, Richmond, 3 November 2008.

38. Collective interview, *op. cit.*

39. Frank [pseudonym]. Personal interview with a person involved with SUCCESS everyday operations, notebook of Montsion, Vancouver, 22 May 2008.

when they arrive in Vancouver, as "volunteering is an eye-opener [for them], because of the work ethics."[40]

The interviews I conducted with mainlanders' community associations in Vancouver dispute these claims. Different from the narrative of Hong Kongese community associations, mainlanders claim volunteer work is an inherently Chinese practice and encourage mainland newcomers to join them to continue to participate in this Chinese reality. Even if volunteer work exists in North America, they consider their version of the term to be distinct and unique to their cultural practices, most notably a respect for the Motherland and its overseas representatives as well as an everyday use of Mandarin.[41] As such, participation in their associations as volunteers not only fulfils the requirements to work towards good Canadian citizenship, it also helps the participants to maintain and reproduce their cultural heritage, as Canadian multiculturalism encourages. In this context, subtle differences between competing notions of civic engagement are used by community associations to make strategic claims about identity politics, cultural translation and Canadian citizenship designs. While mainlanders' associations are fighting to carve out an autonomous and inherently Chinese political space in Vancouver, more established community associations use an equally essentialised notion of what it means to be Chinese to align their membership with certain Canadian notions of moral responsibility and civic duty.

These ethnic tensions aside, at the level of state practices and immigration policies, volunteerism remains useful in instrumentalising and pursuing Canada's vision of good citizenship. The legitimacy of volunteer work is reproduced through the workings of a well-oiled machine that stretches from post-secondary institutions encouraging international Chinese students to volunteer at agencies like SUCCESS, to Citizenship and Immigration Canada valorising volunteer work as valid work experience, and citizenship judges insisting on the importance for newcomers to "give back" to their community. In each of these cases, Canada being "a land of immigrants," civic participation is deemed vital for weaving newcomers into the social fabric. Prominent community associations like SUCCESS understand the pedagogical significance of volunteering and mobilise it to pursue their own ends. By presenting volunteer work as a Canadian practice rather than a shared or exclusively Chinese value, they can silence the most recent Chinese newcomers from the mainland and secure precious government funding in the name of minority representation. Furthermore, in using the rhetoric of multiculturalism to integrate newcomers from various cultural backgrounds, community organisations not only impress this foundational discourse upon their volunteers, they also use it to paper over the differences that separate their ethnically diverse membership. Still, none of this diminishes the emotional value of volunteerism. Community associations and international students alike are well aware that in a country where citizenship rights are "conditional on conduct," the spirit of personal responsibility, community involvement with the local vulnerable populations and civic initiative that volunteerism represents can go a long way in realising personal dreams of opportunity.[42]

40. *Ibid.*

41. Philip [pseudonym]. Personal interview with a Chinese international graduate student at the University of British Columbia, notebook of Montsion, Vancouver, 5 May 2008.

42. Rose, *op. cit.*, p. 1408.

In a context in which volunteer work has been imbricated with neoliberal citizenship designs, local community associations have become key in articulating and reproducing the coordinates of "good Canadian citizenship." Yet this example does not exhaust the possibilities of linking volunteer work and neoliberal capital, the next case study illustrating an entirely different juncture.

The Travails of Volunteer Tourism

Volunteer tourism refers to a rapidly growing phenomenon[43] which allows mostly white middle class students and graduates (18–25 years old) from Western countries, usually in exchange for a hefty price, to spend their summers building houses, teaching in schools, providing medical assistance or doing conservation work in the Global South. The phenomenon has blossomed over the past few years into a full-fledged branch of the tourism industry, including for-profit volunteer tourism agencies, all-inclusive packages and professional standards. On the one hand, the formula has its roots in the itineraries of religious pilgrims, healers and/or medical practitioners, and, most famously, colonial missionaries, educators and humanitarians. On the other hand, volunteer tourism borrows from consumer trends associated with the rise of post-Fordist "flexible accumulation" from the 1970s onwards. Like ecotourism, sustainable tourism, study abroad programmes and corporate social responsibility, volunteer tourism responds to a larger need for neoliberal capital to develop a "human face" capable of replacing or at least complementing its alienating, individualistic and competitive tendencies with more satisfying, meaningful and cooperative alternatives.[44]

The promotional but also scholarly literature on the topic (e.g. the volunteering brochures, websites, discussion forums, blogs and testimonies) describes volunteer tourism as a transformative practice with normative and therapeutic potential. By "putting travail back into travel,"[45] the formula presumably breaks with the vacuity of mass tourism to foster cultural exchange, social transformation and personal development.[46] But, as my research revealed, congruent with

43. Although not an unprecedented form of travel, never before has volunteer tourism been so popular and so vocal. In the United States over a quarter of the population is interested in signing up. Meanwhile, in the UK there are about 800 organisations offering volunteer services abroad. Tourism is the largest growth industry and volunteer tourism is its fastest growing sector. Over the past couple of years commercial travel agencies, such as Travelocity, Cheaptickets, GAP Adventures, Travel Cuts and First Choice Holidays, have jumped on board, crowding out or joining forces with not-for-profit organisations, such as Habitat for Humanity and United Way. See Aaron Dalton, "Voluntourism Trips for Do-Gooders: When Sipping Margaritas, Sunburning Yourself Poolside Loses its Luster", *MSNBC.com*, 4 February 2008, available: <http://www.msnbc.msn.com/id/19314446/> (accessed 18 May 2008) and Lucy Ward, "You're Better off Backpacking—VSO Warns about Perils of 'Voluntourism'", *The Guardian*, 14 August 2007, available: <http://www.guardian.co.uk/uk/2007/aug/14/students.charitablegiving> (accessed 13 March 2008).

44. Luc Boltanski and Eve Chiapello, *The New Spirit of Capitalism* (New York: Verso, 2005).

45. Debbie Lisle, "Joyless Cosmopolitans: The Moral Economy of Ethical Tourism", in J. Best and M. Paterson (eds.), *Cultural Political Economy* (New York: Routledge, 2009), pp. 139–158.

46. Daniel Guttentag, "The Possible Negative Impacts of Volunteer Tourism", *International Journal of Tourism Research*, Vol. 11, No. 6 (2009), p. 537; Nancy McGehee and C.A. Santos, "Social Change, Discourse and Volunteer Tourism", *Annals of Tourism Research*, Vol. 32 (2005), pp. 760–779; Stephen Wearing, *Volunteer Tourism: Experiences that Make a Difference* (Oxon, UK: CABI Publishing, 2001); Stephen Wearing, "Re-Centering the Self in Volunteer Tourism", in G.M. S. Dan (ed.), *The Tourist as a*

previous critiques of sustainable tourism, ecotourism and "recreational activism,"[47] volunteer tourism does more to consolidate the spirit of neoliberal capitalism and its attendant gendered and racialised fantasies than realise lasting social change or counter the exploitative dynamics underlying the global tourism industry.

In spring 2009, I (Wanda Vrasti) joined a teaching programme in Ghana for $1,400 per month organised by Projects Abroad, one of the world's largest volunteer tourism providers operating 166 projects in 20 countries.[48] Two reasons motivate volunteers to embark on this exorbitant experience: to "make a difference" in the lives of the local community and to add some professional experience to their education. Yet few of the participants were satisfied with the results. The place we lived in, the provincial town of Ho, many reproached, did not resemble the photogenic poverty shots many of us had seen on charity infomercials and fundraiser posters. There were no visible signs of starvation or malady. The locals did not seem to need or appreciate our assistance. Instead, there were constant frustrations relating to "culture shock" and the lack of modern amenities and Western cuisine. As a result, we often felt useless and somewhat deceived. As one volunteer aptly put it:

> They made it sound as if you weren't there, Ghana would fall apart, as if your presence was sought for. They painted a picture that's not in any way correct. [. . .] I don't think I've helped anyone while I was here. Only I benefited. I changed but I don't think I initiated any change. After I leave I'd have made a difference to myself but not to anyone else.[49]

It usually took volunteers no longer than two weeks to grow bored with their work responsibilities, which they were either unqualified for (as in the case of medical placements) or overwhelmed with (as with teaching programmes), and become full-time travellers instead.[50] Although the programme handbook we were given

Metaphor of the Social World (Oxon, UK: CABI Publishing, 2002), pp. 237–261; Stephen Wearing, Adrian Deville and Kevin Lyons, "The Volunteer's Journey Through Leisure into the Self", in K. Lyon and S. Wearing (eds.), *Journeys of Discovery in Volunteer Tourism* (Cambridge, MA: CABI Publishing, 2008), pp. 63–71.

47. Rosaleen Duffy, *Trip Too Far: Ecotourism, Politics, and Exploitation* (London: Earthscan, 2002); Rosaleen Duffy, "Neoliberalising Nature: Global Networks and Ecotourism Development in Madagascar", *Journal of Sustainable Tourism*, Vol. 16, No. 3 (2008), pp. 327–344; Rosaleen Duffy, *Nature Crime: How We're Getting Conservation Wrong* (New Haven, CT: Yale University Press, 2010); Rosaleen Duffy and Lorraine Moore, "Neoliberalising Nature? Elephant-Back Tourism in Thailand and Botswana", *Antipode*, Vol. 42, No. 3 (2010), pp. 742–766; Bruce Erickson, "Recreational Activism: Politics, Nature, and the Rise of Neoliberalism", *Leisure Studies*, Vol. 30, No. 4 (2011), pp. 477–494; Robert Fletcher, "Sustaining Tourism, Sustaining Capitalism? The Tourism Industry's Role in Global Capitalist Expansion", *Tourism Geographies*, Vol. 13, No. 3 (2011), pp. 443–461.

48. Projects Abroad, "Ghana Handbook", 2008, pp. 45–47, available: <http://www.projects-abroad.org/destinations/ghana/projects-abroad-in-ghana/> (accessed 13 March 2008).

49. Patricia [pseudonym]. Personal interview with a volunteer tourist in Ho, notebook of Vrasti, Ghana, 6 April 2009.

50. Certainly, Projects Abroad was partly to blame for these disappointments. From a strictly logistical point of view, Projects Abroad was not actively involved in managing work placements, communicating with the local staff or following up with volunteers. Often placements were poorly chosen, according to some cliché fantasies of humanitarian assistance, rather than organised around actual local needs and desires. On the other hand, however, the roots of volunteer apathy lie much deeper. For volunteers to feel "needed" the work must be continuous, it must be satisfying, challenging and

upon arrival discouraged extended travel during the work placement, it was clear from the organisation's website that exploring the cultural sites, major market towns and wildlife Ghana has to offer was very much a part of what made this the organisation's most popular destination (accounting for roughly 40% of its revenue). In fact, the website spent more time detailing the country's touristic attractions—its golden beaches, colonial fortresses, and bustling market towns—than explaining why Ghana required the urgent help of international volunteers.

Making sure volunteers enjoy their stay was in fact part of Project Abroad's official mission. For instance, the main responsibility of our local coordinator in Ghana was to help volunteers explore "the beaches and nightclubs in a different country without having any problems."[51] Ghana has no shortage of either. For white people, hungry for Western food, entertainment and service standards, Ghana offers an endless array of entertainment options to choose from, with the added bonus of a warm climate, servile people and lax law enforcement. But this should not suggest that tourism in Ghana is a purely relaxing and entertaining affair. Travelling through Ghana, a country with few modern amenities, a pervasive fascination for whiteness and plenty of opportunities for hilarious as well as painful moments of "culture shock," is part and parcel of the pedagogical function of volunteer tourism. Learning how to cope with recurrent frustrations and nervous conditions, in particular in the context of racialised encounters, is precisely how volunteer tourism retains its educational value despite its inability to "make a difference" or endow volunteers with practical skills and expertise.

Being white in Ghana means you are constantly on display. People shout "yevu" or "obruni" (white person in local dialects Ewe and Twi, respectively) after you in the streets, and they touch your skin and hair to check for a difference in texture. There are obvious advantages to being white: if you are white, Ghana is one huge resort where almost everyone works as an entertainer. You get the best seat on the bus, the biggest plate of food, the place at the front of the line. But the longer you stay in Ghana, the more bothersome this exchange becomes. With time, the proverbial Ghanaian friendliness becomes exhausting: your dress is scrutinised and your smoking habits reprimanded; your gestures and opinions awaken either curiosity or laughter; people ask for your name and contact information, they want their picture taken with you; they know you are wealthy and expect you to pay "white prices." Eventually, all that attention and attending becomes an unbearable form of what volunteers referred to as "reverse racism." As one volunteer explains:

> What is frustrating about travelling through Ghana is the constant haggle over taxi and tro-tro [minivan] prices where you are cheated because you're white. I understand the idea but I can't stand it anymore. I'm getting tired. At the end of our trip [my friend] Judith had to calm me down because I couldn't take it anymore. And it is more or less everywhere like this: in the market, in tros, it's always about the price. At first, everything was new. But step by step I hate the feeling of having

---

rewarding, it must address local deficiencies and it must show quick results. This is not an easy task to accomplish for any organisation, especially considering that volunteers stay for a relatively short time, they lack appropriate skills and training and also expect to have enough free time to travel and relax.

51. Charles [pseudonym]. Personal interview with a volunteer tourist in Ho, notebook of Vrasti, Ghana, 18 April 2009.

> to repeat myself. You lose a lot of time and energy. And it's the same with Ghanaian boys. The first time they ask you "can you take me home?" you joke that there is no room in your luggage. But after three months I overreact because I don't want to have this conversation again and again. They want to be your friend but that is not how you make friends. It's too easy to have friends here because I'm white, not because I'm interesting or I'm nice, only because I'm white. Being white can be funny, but I'm bored with it.[52]

The ability to know, speak about and gaze onto others has traditionally been the purview of white people, colonisers, scholars and later on tourists, who have limited their understanding of subaltern populations to essentialised images of innocence, passivity and exoticism. But this hegemony of the gaze can only be maintained in the world of knowledge production (writing, science, photography), where white people enjoy a tremendous advantage. When it comes to lived encounters, however, the gaze travels both ways, subjecting white bodies to the same act of ruthless objectification they believe is a normal instrument of the touristic repertoire.[53] Using the term "reverse racism" to describe this disturbance of tourist expectations strikes me as a misnomer. The fascination Ghanaians shared for the epidermal as well as the cultural properties of whiteness is not so much a form of "racism" than the racialisation of whiteness. Historically, whiteness has almost always been the unmarked centre of humanity, the *nomos* of normality and normativity, the standard of reference by which all other positions are assessed. When Ghanaians returned our gaze, even if only to idolise whiteness, we were asked to question their motives, aspirations and subject location and come to terms with the unnerving consequences of occupying the centre. For the first time in our lives, we existed for everyone to see, touch and assess. Being white in Ghana opened all sorts of doors for us, yet it also represented an obstacle. It aligned us with standards of beauty, civilisation and progress, but it also made us uncomfortable with inhabiting these undeserved privileges.[54]

Still, none of these frustrations and nervous conditions could have forced any of us to cut our trip short. Not only were volunteers reluctant to disappoint their friends and family members back home, who thought they were brave and selfless for being in "Africa," they were also determined to turn the painful experiences of culture shock and homesickness into pedagogical opportunities. For instance, the racialisation of whiteness in Ghana could have resulted in reconsideration, if not destabilisation, of white privilege. Ideally, experiencing first-hand the discomforts of being the object of the gaze would have encouraged volunteers to reflect upon the power relations involved in this act traditionally belonging to white colonisers and, later on, anthropologists, development experts and tourists. Instead, however, the anger and frustration of being gazed upon were channelled into a narrative of growth and self-development. Cultivating an attitude of enlightened indifference and emotional resilience in the face of "reverse racism" was what made up a large part of the learning experience volunteers always yearned for but were remiss to find in other aspects of the trip.

52. Marion [pseudonym]. Personal interview with a volunteer tourist in Ho, notebook of Vrasti, Ghana, 17 April 2009.

53. Edward M. Bruner, "Tourism in Ghana: The Representation of Slavery and the Return of the Black Diaspora", *American Anthropologist*, Vol. 98 (1996), pp. 290–304.

54. Sara Ahmed, *The Cultural Politics of Emotion* (Edinburgh: Edinburgh University Press, 2004), p. 132.

Phrases like "expand your horizons," "fulfil your potential" or "come back a changed individual" may sound like empty platitudes, but in fact they express the sincere pedagogical ambition of volunteer tourism. Whether it is by allowing volunteers to experiment with various professional identities or gather the necessary linguistic and cultural competencies to confidently navigate a foreign setting, volunteering in the Global South is ripe with affective and aesthetic lessons that can be easily translated into valuable entrepreneurial competencies. Living and travelling independently, making multinational friends, having work responsibilities, confronting cultural differences, narrativising daily adventures in a diary or blog, learning how to survive without modern amenities—all of these human (expertise, experience, capacities), social (emotionality, trust, charity) and cultural forms of capital (mobility, experience, civility) pave the path towards professional advancement and cosmopolitan citizenship.[55]

So it is less that volunteers are self-interested careerist individuals, as they are often portrayed in the media,[56] but that the merits of volunteering abroad, especially in the Global South, are perfectly congruent with the exigencies of cognitive capitalism. Flexible labour markets, shrinking welfare provisions and an increasingly competitive economic climate demand that individuals, from an early age onwards, expand their human capital beyond professional expertise, academic credentials or classroom experience.[57] Higher education is not exempt from this transformation. As education is moving outside the classroom into study abroad programmes, language courses, internships and volunteering programmes, its emphasis falls on transferable skills and talents that can endow students with a "borderless neoliberal ethos."[58] While the formula may not be able to redress the material and ecological ails of the global poor or engender cross-cultural understanding, as it promises, it is also not its opposite, an exercise in liberal guilt or middle-class hypocrisy. Its transformative promises are realised otherwise. By allowing young adults to operate in multicultural settings and globalised sites, acquire various aesthetic and affective competencies and experiment with "alternative" modes of being, volunteer tourism enhances the employability and entrepreneurial versatility of those participating. It invests individuals with the same qualities expected from the self-directed workforce of the new economy, the self-reliant subject of financial capital and the conscious consumer.

Transnational Volunteerism and the Politics of Life

We would like to end our discussion with a brief consideration of how the two case studies we have presented, although quite different, play a mutually

55. Illouz, *op. cit.*; Engin Isin, "Governing Cities without Government", in E. Isin (ed.), *Democracy, Citizenship and the Global City* (New York: Routledge, 2000), pp. 148–168.

56. Ward, *op. cit.*; J.B. McKinnon, "The Dark Side of Voluntourism", *UTNE Reader 2009*, available: <http://www.utne.com/Politics/The-Dark-Side-of-Volunteer-Tourism-Voluntourism.aspx> (accessed 18 January 2013); Ian Birrell, "Before You Pay to Volunteer Abroad, Think of the Harm You Might Do", *The Guardian*, 14 November 2010, available: <http://www.guardian.co.uk/commentisfree/2010/nov/14/orphans-cambodia-aids-holidays-madonna> (accessed 18 January 2013).

57. Lois McNay, "Self as Enterprise: Dilemmas of Control and Resistance in Foucault's Birth of Biopolitics", *Theory, Culture & Society*, Vol. 26, No. 6 (2009), p. 63.

58. Ong, *Neoliberalism as Exception, op. cit.*, p. 148.

reinforcing, even complementary role in reproducing the kinds of social relations and subject positions required by neoliberal capital. At first sight, volunteerism seems like an act of selfless generosity that speaks to a basic desire for purposeful action and meaning. And we certainly do not seek to deny the crucial importance of social bonds of love, care and compassion for producing (and salvaging) what we have in common.[59] Transnational volunteerism, however, plays upon these fantasies of social usefulness, community and self-determination to push the otherwise political question for collective responsibility into a moral terrain of individual responsibility where it becomes a matter of aesthetic self-presentation.

In Vancouver, volunteer work functions as a site of struggle between competing ethnic Chinese community associations shaped by migration patterns that have shifted from Hong Kong to mainland China. Despite serving a similar function, namely to support the Canadian state in managing an increasingly diverse workforce—commonly known as multiculturalism—both types of community associations instrumentalise volunteer work for their own purposes. On the one hand, established Hong Kongese community associations appeals to feelings of moral responsibility to help their members internalise the values and conduct befitting good Canadian citizens. In doing so, they position their various volunteering experiences as a competitive advantage over other Chinese associations. On the other hand, mainlanders' associations use responsibility and its related affective competencies to signal closer ties to a rising China and loyalty to its current political and cultural systems. Whereas SUCCESS uses volunteer work to promote liberal norms of citizenship, mainlanders' community associations deploy it to preserve a distinct and exclusive understanding of being Chinese in Canada. Although in both cases volunteer work communicates specific forms of conduct related to education, discipline, and surveillance volunteerism, it has emerged among the Chinese community in Vancouver has emerged as an everyday international site of conflict over volunteers and how to mould them into good Canadian citizens of Chinese origin.

In Ghana, the pedagogical content of volunteering adopts a different form. By placing volunteers in a foreign cultural setting with few modern amenities, language skills and networks of institutional or familial support, young adults from Western countries are supposed to develop the social and emotional competencies needed in a regime of accumulation that relies mostly on general intellect and immaterial labour (e.g. socio-ecological awareness, multicultural literacy and a taste for risk-taking and experimentation). With the double flexibilisation of the labour market and higher education, university students and graduates are required to amass an increasing number of extra-curricular activities to set themselves apart from their peers. In this context, volunteering in the Global South becomes a "world-class" degree. Although it is difficult to quantify the benefits volunteers gain from this experience (in terms of access to graduate programmes and professional schools or better jobs), it is safe to say that the emotional and entrepreneurial competencies gathered on these trips allow volunteers to better navigate their social field, assert a credible professional identity, embody desirable cultural values and norms and live more fully in the global moment. Certainly, the same cannot be said about the objects of their intervention. Ghanaians remain objects of curiosity to be gazed at, backward life forms to be meddled with, or exotic backdrops to volunteers' journeys of self-discovery.

59. Hardt and Negri, *op. cit.*

There is no question about it: transnational volunteerism carries many concrete cultural, professional and personal advantages for its participants, but beyond these, the technique is instrumental to and exemplary of the increasing stratification of human life. One of the distortions of neoliberal globalisation has been an increasingly loose relation between political membership and territorial belonging, and wage labour has made room for various types of "flexible citizenship" that follow the mobile and transient paths of capital (e.g. global cities, cyberspace, refugee camps, regional labour markets, high-tech districts).[60] Following global flows of capital, citizenship has shifted from an entitlement deriving from territorial belonging and wage labour to a flexible prerogative earned on merit. While this is no time to mourn the advantages of national citizenship or Fordist modes of production, both of which were based on social exclusion and conformity, we can also not celebrate the new rights regime. What seems to be a more flexible form of participation and belonging is, in fact, the dawn of an economically and politically uncertain future where citizenship becomes "conditional on conduct,"[61] that is, conditional on how well one fulfils the injunctions of neoliberal statecraft and flexible accumulation in competition with others.

Those who possess the right civic attitudes, skill set and symbolic capital will be rewarded with a growing number of passports, residence permits and mobility incentives as well as increasing access to job markets, housing options and cultural goods around the world.[62] Those who fail to conform will become second-order citizens, confined to slums and ghettos, doomed to perform low-wage and tedious jobs, with little possibility of escape. While some individuals can organise their lives (quite enthusiastically) according to the double exigencies of economic proficiency and moral responsibility, others are de-subjectified, they are excluded only to become included as objects of suspicion, compassion and humanitarian intervention.

Transnational volunteerism is perfectly suited to fulfil the requirements of citizenship by merit. To begin with, it is free labour affordable only for the privileged. Whether it is university graduates from advanced liberal nations or foreign students living in the West, volunteering always presupposes and requires a deep racialised, gendered and class division between those who volunteer their help and those who receive it, whether organised through religious or secular institutions. After all, one has to enjoy a certain level of material comfort and leisure time to expend labour power for free. Automatically, the objects of care, the global poor, the unemployed, the elderly and the diseased, are exempt from civic virtue and must remain the passive recipients of benefaction or, worse, inspection and surveillance. Just like in the Victorian heyday of philanthropy, contemporary volunteerism remains a marker of white middle-class privilege.

---

60. Aihwa Ong, *Flexible Citizenship: The Cultural Logics of Transnationality* (Durham, NC: Duke University Press, 1999).

61. Hannah Arendt was quite explicit that forms of sociality based on emotion (whether it is pity or pride, collective suffering or communal empowerment) tend to encourage non-public, non-political forms of association that function only through the voluntary disposition of like-minded individuals. The importance of strong affective bonds aside, Arendt warns us that these attachments can never translate into universalistic ideals or broad-based political movements, but are bound to remain tied to exclusionary, even disciplinary, face-to-face interactions. See Hannah Arendt, *On Revolution* (New York: Penguin Classics, 1991).

62. Ong, *Flexible Citizenship, op. cit.*, p. 2.

This is not to say that only racially white people volunteer. Whiteness, in this context, refers to the social and human capital historically attached to the tastes, values and attitudes of white bodies and, more contemporarily, extended to all responsible, self-reliant and self-governing individuals conforming to the (neo)liberal injunctions of good citizenship. These are the flexible subjects who can assume responsibility for themselves and the welfare of their communities without burdening the state or blaming the economy for the free labour they have to perform, the social goods they must distribute and the ties of sociality and affectivity they need to build in the wake of shrinking social services. They are the active citizens of today's globalising world.

At a more general level, transnational volunteerism harbours the ambition to cultivate a way of acting and feeling in the world that can offset the injustices of neoliberal capital with more humane forms of government and social action. Volunteerism promises to enhance the sentimental education of individual subjects and weave a more authentic social fabric. Given how callous the forces of transnational production and speculation have become (resource extraction, debt peonage, political repression), it might seem like the only way forward is to inject economic logic with a moral consciousness and to replace bureaucratic control with face-to-face responsibilities. But we should remain sceptical of these populist appeals. For decades, corporate social responsibility, good governance, green consumption, urban regeneration and a host of other "markets-with-morals" strategies, like volunteerism, have proven to be nothing more than a repackaging of the old formula for accumulation and dispossession. The continuous attempt to download public responsibilities onto private shoulders and transfer central government onto the communal level only proves that, whenever questions of housing, education, health and security are not treated as collective goods but pre-political (authentic) matters, human dignity loses its universal imperative and is left to the discretion of other people's charity.

Again, we do not discount the transformative potential of charity and community work. Neither do we accuse volunteers of being hypocritical, purely self-interested individuals who participate in charitable work solely for the benefit of their résumés or residency status, nor do we deny the fact that volunteerism can be a genuine manifestation of love, care and generosity for one's fellow beings. What we do insist on, however, is the need to unpack the moralistic and sentimental pretensions of this practice precisely in order to make room for a politics of love that is not tainted by nationalist, identitarian or imperialist undertones.[63] Even when volunteer work is motivated by the most noble of sentiments, it falls short of realising its progressive ambition without a political consideration of who volunteers, for what purpose and under what circumstances.

About the Authors

Wanda Vrasti is Lecturer at the Humboldt University in Berlin. Her book *Volunteer Tourism in the Global South: Giving Back in Neoliberal Times* was published by Routledge in 2012. Other pieces have been published in *Millennium: Journal of International Relations*, *Review of International Studies* and *Theory & Event*.

63. Rose, *op. cit.*, p. 1408.

Jean Michel Montsion is Assistant Professor of International Studies at Glendon College, York University in Toronto. His research focuses on the implications of community-based politics in the development of neoliberal strategies for gateway cities. His work has notably been published in *Citizenship Studies, Environment and Planning D: Society and Space* and *Ethnic and Racial Studies.*

"Retail Therapy in the Dragon's Den": Neoliberalism and Affective Labour in the Popular Culture of Ireland's Financial Crisis

NICHOLAS J. KIERSEY

A range of scholars embrace the concept of economic subjectivity in their analysis of relations of economic power and knowledge. They tend to do so, however, in a way that focuses on the inculcation of norms of individual accountability and self-empowerment. Addressing cases drawn from Irish 'Reality TV' programming in the context of the current financial crisis, this article seeks to expand our understanding of the stakes of economic subjectification by looking at the importance Reality TV also ascribes to capacities of affective labour. The article borrows from Foucault, as well as several autonomist Marxist sources, to make an argument that these cases indicate not only the subsumption of a wide swathe of social life into the domain of neoliberal governmentality but also the self-conscious turn towards affective labour as a way of refloating the Irish economy. Such a move is significant insofar as it suggests the reinvestment of subjects in a regime of valorisation that has proven to be emotionally and financially oppressive, not to mention unstable, all at a time when the capacity of the institutions of the Irish state to equitably distribute social wealth has been called into question.

Introduction

In the 2010 series of the Irish business-oriented 'Reality Television' (Reality TV) show, *Retail Therapy*, host Feargal Quinn spends time with Kim Buckley, a florist working from a location in the heart of the Liberties district of Dublin, one of the oldest and most storied parts of the city. Quinn is a senator in the national parliament and the former owner of the Superquinn brand of grocery stores, a brand synonymous with quality and customer care in the Republic. Having founded Superquinn in the 1980s, at the height of an economic recession, Quinn is today a paragon figure in Irish retail, known as the "pope of customer service."[1] Buckley, on the other hand, is a fourth-generation flower seller trying to get by in the middle of what the International Monetary Fund (IMF) has recently termed the greatest economic dislocation "of any economy since the Great

*The author would like to thank Anne-Marie D'Aoust, Wanda Vrasti and Anna Selmeczi for their help and encouragement in writing this article.

1. Molly Labarre, "Leader—Feargal Quinn", *Fast Company*, October 2001, available: <http://www.fastcompany.com/43805/leader-feargal-quinn> (accessed 16 September 2012).

Depression."[2] As the show portrays it, Kim's self-esteem is as run down as her shop, and the deepening crisis is testing the limits of her will and her retail expertise alike. While poor, the people of the Liberties district are considered to be hardy and true. Indeed, we are told, Kim is of the area's "old stock," following in the footsteps of her great-grandmother, Biddy McGrail. In honour of this legacy, Kim tells us, she has never deviated from her core values, delivering quality over volume. It is hard times now, however, and the more volume-centric competitors that emerged in the fresh flower sector during the good times are now snapping at her heels. Valentine's Day transactions were down 40% this year, and she is falling heavily into debt.

Kim believes she has a quality product. Quinn believes so too. But Kim's spirit is broken. She says she is shy and doesn't have the confidence to go after the corporate contracts that she needs in order to survive long term. Quinn tells her the shop needs a "wow" factor, and her delivery van needs a professional livery. Above all, however, says Quinn, Kim needs to recognise the important place of her own self-esteem in the branding of her product. By way of explaining this to Kim, and to the audience at home, Quinn takes her to meet Terry Prone and her son, Anton Savage, two of the nation's leading experts in personal branding. Prone is co-owner of the "Communications Clinic," a Dublin-based public relations firm with an established reputation among Irish politicians. The duo specialise in political speechwriting and "spin" control, but they are also quite well known as media commentators among the Irish public in general, and they are no strangers to controversy.[3] Prone focuses on Kim's lack of confidence, suggesting that her nerves appear so shaken it is as if she "wants to have a catastrophe." Kim needs to realise that she is not just selling a thing, she is "selling a relationship." With Kim's very subjectivity thus now established as the root of the problem, Quinn takes Kim to a local bingo hall in her area and arranges for her to be the host for a portion of the evening. (Regular viewers will learn that Quinn has a tendency to reminisce fondly about the jobs he held as a young man, and how they helped to teach him the basics of customer service. Calling bingo numbers was in fact the first job he ever held, working for his dad at the camping caravan resort he ran in Skerries.)[4] Quinn returns to the shop again a month later to see how Kim is getting on. He discovers that the shop has been transformed (out of her own pocket) and that she is getting ready to give a major corporate presentation. The new Kim exudes confidence. After her pitch, we get to meet one of her potential new clients, a manager of the local Jury's hotel franchise. The manager is effusive: "Kim herself is the reason you want to shop here, because you care about her … She will succeed because she believes in herself. People like Kim can change Ireland."

---

2. Antoinette Kelly, "Ireland's Economic Collapse Worst Global Crash since the Great Depression", *IrishCentral*, 2 July 2012, available: <http://www.irishcentral.com/news/Irelands-economic-collapse-worst-global-crash-since-the-Great-Depression-161058395.html> (accessed 16 September 2012).

3. Daniel O'Carroll, "Irish TV Boss in Hot Water over Notorious RTÉ Documentary 'Mission to Prey'", *IrishCentral*, 2 July 2012, available: <http://www.irishcentral.com/story/news/danny_boy/irish-tv-boss-in-hot-water-over-notorious-rte-documentary-mission-to-prey-157188465.html> (accessed 17 September 2012).

4. See also his remarks in Labarre, *op. cit.*

If the above example is any indicator, the capacity to be confident and build relationships of care with customers is understood to be of central importance in Ireland's strategy for economic recovery. But what does it mean to premise an economic strategy on the ability to make people like *you* as much as, if not more than, the product you are trying to sell? Recent research into the role of affect and emotionality in contemporary political economy has brought attention to the symbiosis between governmental imperatives and affective dispositions across a gamut of social domains.[5] Perhaps more interestingly, it has also shown how neoliberal capitalism's expansion of "human capital" to encompass affective and linguistic capacities of production has radically shifted the locus of labour and, consequently, decentred the coordinating or "command" function of production.[6] For Hardt and Negri, contemporary production tends increasingly to involve the manipulation of symbolic resources, and thus requires of the worker a certain capacity for independent, non-linear thinking. This tendency in production is not necessarily new, they note, but it is today greatly intensified, implying a shift in the locus of value production "outside the factory" to a significant degree.[7] Thus, paradoxically, we find that customers are increasingly implicated in the process of valorisation, blurring the line between production and consumption. However, capitalism today actively seeks out the deep capacities of its subjects, especially those capacities relevant to subjectivation, such as the ability to solicit compassion and empathy, not only to generate surplus capital from them but also to sustain their emotional investment in a whole way of life. In a sense, then, to borrow from Read, we live in an era in which capitalism's *political* reproduction is predicated upon "the production of subjectivity by subjectivity."[8]

This article marks an attempt to grapple with the idea of what we might call affective subjectification and its place in relation both to capitalism's strategies of re-valorisation and its political longevity, in the context of the current financial crisis. A range of scholars embrace the concept of economic subjectivity in their analysis of the relations of economic power and knowledge. They tend to do so, however, in a way that focuses on the discourses of economic neoliberalism, and the way it promotes the development of impulses of self-government and accountability. Neoliberal theory, they note, is premised on an imagining of the free market as an exemplary technology of the self, and therefore necessary in the essential task of producing a population that is ever mindful of the "transactional reality" of its existence, and thus willing to accept the need for austerity in times of crisis. Approaching this matter from a Foucauldian perspective, for example, Hay suggests that Reality TV presents us with something of a laboratory

5. See, for example, Bob Jessop and Stijn Oosterlynck, "Cultural Political Economy: On Making the Cultural Turn without Falling into Soft Economic Sociology", *Geoforum*, No. 39 (2008), pp. 1155–1169; Maxime Oulette, "Cybernetic Capitalism and the Global Information Society; from the Global Panopticon to a 'Brand' New World", in Jacqueline Best and Matthew Paterson (eds.), *Cultural Political Economy* (New York: Routledge, 2010), pp. 177–196; Andrew A.G. Ross, "Coming in from the Cold: Constructivism and Emotions", *European Journal of International Relations*, Vol. 12, No. 2 (2006), pp. 197–222.

6. See, for example, Nick Dyer-Witheford and Greig de Peuter, *Games of Empire* (Minnesota: University of Minnesota Press, 2009); Wanda Vrasti, "How to Use Affective Competencies in Late Capitalism", Paper presented at the Annual Meeting of the International Studies Association, New Orleans, LA, 17 February 2010.

7. Michael Hardt and Antonio Negri, *Commonwealth* (Cambridge, MA: Belknap Harvard, 2009).

8. Jason Read, *The Micro-Politics of Capital* (Albany, NY: State University of New York Press, 2003), p. 18.

for appraising the "dispersed micrologics and microphysics of the knowledge-power nexus" of contemporary neoliberalism.[9] However, while Hay discusses "human capital" and other important concepts constituting the vocabulary of neoliberalism's "positive" strategies of neoliberal subjectification, he offers little to help us understand the significance of a case such as the one noted above, where the entrepreneur is also subject to the moral expectation, in the name of "doing her part" to sustain a nation's economic recovery, not only to be a self-disciplined and dynamic entrepreneur but also to be adept in the art of creating value through leveraging the emotions of others.

Pushing beyond Hay's analysis of the semiotic content of Reality TV's exemplary neoliberalism, then, this article marks an attempt to investigate how entrepreneurial Reality TV shows solicit the development of emotional valorisation from their participants. The article focuses on the Irish case specifically because it presents an interesting opportunity to examine these two aspects of contemporary economic subjectification operating in tandem. As I argue below, the Irish population has been acquiescent in accepting the terms of the austerity package that the government is implementing currently, as a condition for receipt of funds from the so-called 'Troika' (a partnership of the EU, IMF and European Central Bank) in the mission of recapitalising the nation's banks. Affirming Hay's argument, the first case study, *Dragon's Den*, presents an interesting example of a popular show that works to naturalise the ideal of transactional subject and model its behaviours so that the viewers at home might be able to replicate them. Beyond Hay, however, the second case examines *Retail Therapy*, the show mentioned in the case above, which draws our attention to the quotidian struggles and sacrifices of Irish retailers as they seek to create and sustain emotional relations with their consumers, bespeaking in the same moment the struggle of contemporary capitalism to sustain value, especially in times of crisis. Combined, the two cases are of no small significance in our understanding of the function of popular Irish economic culture in times of austerity. They indicate not only the explicit normalisation of neoliberal responsibility but also the self-conscious turn towards affective labour as a way of reinvesting the desire of the Irish population in an emotionally and financially oppressive mode of capitalist valorisation, all the while deflecting attention away from questions concerning the responsibility of the institutions of the Irish state to manage the country's wealth in a just and democratic manner.

Situating Reality TV in Crisis Ireland

The theme of responsibility has loomed large in mainstream accounts of the Irish crisis, both in terms of explaining its origins and, more recently, in justifying the strategies necessary for its resolution. At the EU level, figures like Angela Merkel have spoken openly of the duty of the "good European" to practise tough love, condemning a culture of profligacy on the periphery which she believes has now placed the euro itself "in danger."[10] Mainstream debate in

9. James Hay, "Too Good to Fail: Managing Financial Crisis through the Moral Economy of Reality TV", *Journal of Communication Inquiry*, Vol. 34, No. 4 (2010), p. 386.

10. "Merkel Says EU's Future at Stake in Greek Crisis", *The Local*, 5 May 2010, available: <http://www.thelocal.de/politics/20100505-26981.html> (accessed 30 June 2010); "Merkel: Crisis-Hit

Ireland has shown little if any deviation from this line, turning on a discourse of good citizenship, delineated in terms of economic responsibility and moral courage. Politicians and public figures regularly decry the hedonism which they believe was characteristic of the so-called "Celtic Tiger" years, with Minister of Finance Brian Lenihan going so far as to declare in a primetime news interview that the crisis was nobody's fault in particular because, as he put it, "we all partied."[11] Elsewhere, editorialists like Mary Kenny, someone who has long lamented the deleterious effects of consumerism on the nation's moral fabric, wrote hopefully of austerity as a mechanism that would auger the restoration of Ireland's traditional Catholic values.[12] Importantly, such discourse makes for a radical change in tone from that which circulated as common sense during the boom. Back then, the "Tiger" was seen not only as a vital remedy to Ireland's long-running economic impasse but as testament to the maturity and sophistication of a people determined to escape their traditional place on the margins of Western prosperity.[13]

In the context of their overwhelming support for the status quo explanation of the Irish financial crisis, it is apt to consider the ways in which the Irish public has been led to understand its relationship to economic necessity. After all, the roots of the Irish crisis can quite plausibly be traced back to poor planning decisions in the state's early economic history, not to mention the successive waves of neoliberal or "supply-side" deregulation in global finance, dating back at least as far as the 1970s.[14] Moreover, such reforms have hardly been unique to the Irish context. They constitute an important part of the backdrop for what is now a long string of financial crises around the world, from Argentina to Southeast Asia.[15] And, indeed, as the IMF has effectively conceded, the strategies pursued thus far in the hope of fixing the economy, all modelled on the neoliberal austerity approach, are not turning it around. To the contrary, even after four years of crippling austerity, the crisis is the "costliest ... in advanced economies since at least the Great Depression."[16] These terrible costs acknowledged, however, it cannot be gainsaid that Ireland's elites have been able to palm off their lopsided solutions to the crisis with relative ease. In February 2011, in the middle of what some have suggested to be the greatest crisis since the nation's founding, a general election in Ireland revealed massive support for centrist, pro-market political parties, all more or less committed to the austerity regime and one of the most spectacularly unjust, and undemocratically decided, transfers of wealth from the taxpayers of an advanced

---

Europe Needs 'New Stability Culture'", *EUbusiness*, 19 May 2010, available: <http://www.eubusiness.com/news-eu/finance-economy.4t5/?searchterm=None> (accessed 20 May 2010).

11. Brian Lenihan, "We All Partied", *Prime Time*, 24 November 2010, available: <http://www.youtube.com/watch?v=YK7w6fXoYxo> (accessed 18 March 2013).

12. Mary Kenny, "Ireland Faces a Choice between Lucre and Liberty", *The Guardian*, 25 May 2012, available: <http://www.guardian.co.uk/commentisfree/2012/may/25/ireland-faces-choice-lucre-liberty-eu/print> (accessed 19 June 2012).

13. See David McWilliams, *The Pope's Children: The Irish Economic Triumph and the Rise of Ireland's New Elite* (Hoboken, NJ: Wiley, 2005).

14. See Conor McCabe, *Sins of the Father: Tracing the Decisions that Shaped the Irish Economy* (Dublin: The History Press Ireland, 2011).

15. See Joseph E. Stiglitz, *Globalization and Its Discontents* (New York: W.W. Norton & Company, 2002).

16. Kelly, *op. cit.*

Western nation to foreign bondholders (in this case German, British and French banks) in history.[17]

In the below I focus on the Reality TV genre as just one vector through which the nation's pro-market predilections have been instilled. While hardly a phenomenon unique to Ireland, Reality TV shows are hugely popular with Irish audiences, and this is especially true for those that deal with the subject of entrepreneurialism. According to the website of Radio Telefís Éireann (RTÉ), the largest domestic TV network in the country, which is also government owned and operated (although, unlike the BBC, does still depend on commercial advertising for much of its revenue), last year's second series of *Dragon's Den* attracted an average of more than 409,000 viewers per week, across the eight episodes of the series. Similarly, Feargal Quinn's *Retail Therapy* ended its first season as a huge ratings winner: "An average of 453,000 viewers tuned in every week to watch the retail mastermind advise independent shop owners around the country how to improve their businesses, all of whom were battling to survive the economic downturn."[18]

Irish audiences will of course have been familiar with the Reality TV genre prior to the current recession. Indeed, at the height of Ireland's "Celtic Tiger" years, a homegrown Irish version of *The Apprentice: You're Fired* (featuring Bill Cullen, a well-known entrepreneur, in the place of Donald Trump) was already pulling in half a million viewers for the country's newest indigenous station, TV3.[19] Yet the marketing for the more recent shows has been quite explicit in situating them as germane "entertainment-pedagogy" products in relation to the crisis. As Steve Carson, RTÉ's Director of Television, has commented:

> It's entertainment with a purpose. In *Dragon's Den*, these are real businesses, which are receiving real money in what is, unfortunately, a very real recession. Feargal Quinn's wealth of experience in *Retail Therapy* delivered advice and insight to struggling businesses which had a direct impact on their bottom line. That both series are such a strong draw for audiences is the icing on the cake.[20]

The rhetoric here is, of course, transparently exceptionalistic. Nevertheless, in a country whose entire population is no more than 4.5 million, that *Dragon's Den* could draw 550,000 viewers for the first episode of the 2011 season suggests that the show resonates strongly with Irish viewers.

How might we appraise the significance of such resonance? As Weldes notes, cultural "texts," the artefacts yielded to us by popular culture, "are never read in isolation." Weldes is here focusing specifically on Science Fiction (SF) television programming, but the point is relevant for Reality TV too. As she puts it, "SF texts

17. See David McWilliams, "Bailout Will Sink Ireland before We Can Even Swim", *Irish Independent*, 1 December 2010; Fintan O'Toole, "The People Must Act or We Will Remain Irrelevant", *Irish Times*, 23 November 2010.

18. "Real Entrepreneurial Stories Dispel Recessionary Gloom for Huge TV Audiences", RTÉ Press Release, 19 April 2010, available: < http://www.rte.ie/about/en/press-office/press-releases/2010/0419/292815-dragonsden18042010/ > (accessed 17 September 2012).

19. Melanie Finn, "Celebrity Apprentice Fired before First Day", *Evening Herald*, 6 March 2010, available: <http://www.herald.ie/entertainment/tv-radio/celebrity-apprentice-fired-before-first-day-2091083.html> (accessed 31 August 2012).

20. "Real Entrepreneurial Stories", *op. cit.*

repeat and rework generic conventions, and readers bring knowledge of these conventions, their generic expectations, to their consumption and appreciation of any particular text."[21] These conventions, unconscious expectations or "myths" are the undisclosed assumptions about the world that allow theory to make sense of the world. They constitute the "unconscious ideologies," or the silent, sub-textual pillars that media texts must draw upon and reproduce if readers are to be able, on the one hand, to recognise the "truth" of what they are consuming and, on the other, to be instructed about the emergence of new problems and solutions over time.[22] In this sense, for Weldes, pop culture texts are actually "intertexts," or transmission belts, relaying social energies back and forth between the real and the imagined.[23] In similar spirit, we assume that entrepreneurial Reality TV programmes in Ireland also contain scripts, and that these can function to buttress prevailing social power relations through a kind of economic pedagogy, tacitly modelling and progressing the expectations of normal social behaviour upon which the population's economic imaginary is founded.

The production values of the shows examined in this article do clearly embrace aspects of the fictional. While they are not formally scripted, the interactions they portray are structured by a set of pre-imagined rules, staged as they are around the interactions of pre-selected "real" entrepreneurs as they pitch ideas to "hardened veterans" of the Irish business world. Within this "game show" structure, the majority of the dialogue is unscripted. Yet the participants must govern themselves according to this structure, even when the cameras are not rolling. Indeed, it is this intense focus of the shows on the behaviour of their participants which makes them so compelling, and tells us much about the nature of the intertext they constitute, between the imagined world of Irish commerce and the quotidian endeavours of participants in the real Irish economy. Notwithstanding the fact that the successes and failures of the shows are quite real (in the second season, 13 enterprises were supported by the dragons, with a sum of over €350,000 pledged across the series),[24] the scenarios they present are consciously intended by their producers to be homologous to the real life predicaments that Irish entrepreneurs might encounter, and to have instructive value insofar as they can explain or reveal aspects of reality that viewers might not otherwise be sensitive to. We see, therefore, a certain self-conscious sense of mission in these shows and, as such, we are alerted to their potentially constitutive role in the Irish culture and the diverse ways in which the "real" world of the Irish economy is itself a produced, textual affair.

Of course, Reality TV is not merely a constitutive force. It is itself a cultural product situated at the intersection of an array of historically specific discursive and technological forces. In a useful study, Ouellette and Hay describe two of these forces. First, the "reinvention of government," or the emergence of neoliberal ideology and the attendant shift it has overseen, since the 1970s, of a range of governmental responsibilities from the state to the individual. Second, the

---

21. Jutta Weldes, "Popular Culture, Science Fiction, and World Politics", in Jutta Weldes (ed.), *To Seek out New Worlds: Exploring Links between Science Fiction and World Politics* (New York: Palgrave Macmillan, 2003), p. 13.

22. Cynthia Weber, *International Relations Theory: A Critical Introduction* (London: Routtledge, 2009), p. 2.

23. Weldes, "Popular Culture", *op. cit.*, p. 15.

24. "Real Entrepreneurial Stories", *op. cit.*

"reinvention of television," its technological "convergence" with a range of newer and older media, "books, magazines, the web and mobile media," and the increasing potential these developments afford for viewers to participate in the shows they are watching.[25] With these changes has come a reimagining of the viewing subject at home and, by consequence, a reimagining of the educational potential of television. One specific development within this context has been the emergence of new "lifestyle streaming" networks, epitomised in the US market by channels like the Home and Garden Network, the Food Network, the Fine Living Channel, Fit TV and the Do-It-Yourself Network. These networks are remarkable for the finessed manner in which they create brand awareness and blend product marketing with entertainment. For Ouellette and Hay, the popularity of these networks has placed Reality TV in a preeminent position as "an integral relay" for a politics of "self-actualisation," wherein citizens are not merely produced but are recruited as partners in the much more reflexive task of producing and assessing themselves.[26] Ouellette and Hay are adamant that this is not merely a false consciousness or an ideological façade: "The citizen is now conceived as an individual whose most pressing obligation to society is to empower her or himself privately. TV assists by acting as a visible component of a dispersed network of supporting technologies geared to self-help and self-actualization."[27]

To what extent can such a politics of responsible, neoliberal citizenship also be said to play out on Irish television? It is important to recognise the locally specific conditions with which neoliberalism must contend in Ireland, as it struggles to gain traction. To wit, Irish neoliberalism is a historically specific phenomenon, one that must be understood as taking place within "a particular political culture and system inflected by the long history of Anglo-Irish relations and the country's emergence as an independent postcolonial state."[28] In this sense, neoliberalism in Ireland has followed a somewhat uncharacteristic path, needing to contend with, for example, the national tradition of government-coordinated wage deal "partnerships." For Kitchin *et al.*, the result has been a counter-intuitive process of "path amplification" wherein such local conditions, which might at first appear to serve as barriers, reveal themselves on closer inspection to encourage "responsible" self-government, serving therefore as "catalysts, lubricants, and wellsprings for neoliberal reforms."[29] As we will see below, this paradoxical tendency is clear in the case of RTÉ, the producer and broadcaster of the two shows under scrutiny here. Established by The Broadcasting Act of 1960, RTÉ is a state-supported independent broadcasting authority, funded by a combination of user-paid television licence fees and advertising revenues. For this reason, as Sheehan observes, RTÉ has traditionally enjoyed a measure of structural freedom to focus on public service broadcasting, though not without a certain anxiety about how it would pay its own way. Despite its status as a "state institution," then, its

25. Laurie Ouellette and James Hay, *Better Living through Reality TV: Television and Post-Welfare Citizenship* (New York: Blackwell, 2008), p. 2.

26. *Ibid.*, p. 31.

27. *Ibid.*, p. 3.

28. Rob Kitchin, Cian O'Callaghan, Justin Gleeson, Karen Keaveney, and Mark Boyle, "Placing Neoliberalism: The Rise and Fall of Ireland's Celtic Tiger", *Environment and Planning A*, Vol. 44, No. 6 (2012), p. 1305.

29. *Ibid.*, p. 1308.

production values have tended to be more conservative and, as such, while early programming displayed a degree of technical innovation, content managers have tended over time to favour historical and moral themes in their programming decisions, eschewing the sort of social realism and reportage that might have brought into relief something of the dynamic changes the country was experiencing.[30]

Of course, there are ambiguous moments in RTÉ's development as a relay of neoliberal ideology. In the 1970s, Gay Byrne's long-running (and hugely popular) *The Late Late Show* introduced many viewers to progressive themes, often stirring up great controversy in the process. So it is perhaps with some justification that Corcoran, himself a former RTÉ chairman (1995–2000), argues that we should avoid understating the preeminent historic position of RTÉ in shaping Irish culture:

> [RTÉ] has played a major role in dominating the symbolic environment in which Irish people construct their sense of identity and weave the "common sense" that underpins the everyday life of the community. RTÉ's social role has been to find ways of "narrating the social" that makes sense of their society for viewers and listeners, by drawing from the available stock of frameworks and narratives and marking the boundaries of what is permissible.[31]

However, even if this is perhaps an idealisation of RTÉ's preeminent role as an agent of citizenship production in the 1970s, it is unclear how the statement could be applied to the broadcaster as it evolved into the coming decades. By the 1980s, trouble in the global economy had catalysed a significant reimagining of the moral purpose of Irish broadcasting. One key discursive turning point for RTÉ was the publication in 1985 of a government-mandated report by consultancy firm Stokes Kennedy Crowley. Using language that made no provision for any specific pedagogical function for public broadcasting, speaking of viewers not as citizens but as consumers, the report had dire results for the funding of home-made content, setting off a trend that would continue into the next two decades at least.[32]

By the 1990s, RTÉ was facing significant increases in production costs and a changing competitive environment brought new players with much greater economies of scale into the market. The Broadcasting Act of 2001 created the Broadcasting Commission of Ireland, which licensed a slew of new, foreign television services via cable and satellite channels, allowing them to penetrate deeply into, and further divide, the advertising market. Since then, as Corcoran observes, RTÉ has had its hands largely tied in terms of its ability to respond to these newcomers, mandated as it is to direct any increase in licence funding to domestic production (whereas foreign channels are under no such obligation). Moreover, under the current regime of "light touch" regulation, newer local stations like TV3 have not been required to hold up fully to commitments to Irish production (TV3 gives

30. Helena Sheehan, "Irish Television Drama in the 1960s", *RTÉ*, 2001, available: <http://webpages.dcu.ie/~sheehanh/60s-itvd.htm> (accessed 1 August 2012).

31. Farrel Corcoran, *RTE and the Globalisation of Irish Television* (Bristol: Intellect Books, 2004), p. 1.

32. Helena Sheehan, "Irish Television Drama in the 1980s", *RTÉ*, 2001, available: <http://webpages.dcu.ie/~sheehanh/80s-itvd.htm> (accessed 17 September 2012).

merely 20% of its broadcast time to Irish produced material whereas RTÉ gives 50%, meaning it is a vital fiscal source for sustaining domestic media production).[33] With all these players seeking to minimise costs, not just in Ireland but elsewhere as well, "localisation" has become increasingly common. Referring to practices wherein global show franchises provide "do-it-yourself" kits and reusable sequences for companies in different countries showing versions of the same show, localisation signals the emergence of transnational "reality" texts inflected with local "accents."[34] RTÉ first adopted this approach in 1997 when it developed and aired *Treasure Island*, a *Survivor*-style show, itself originally modelled on a Swedish show, sharing the same production location with an Australian show of the same name. Since then a litany of Reality TV shows have appeared, from local iterations of more globally known franchises like *The Apprentice*, *MasterChef* and *The Secret Chef* to more homegrown ideas like *Fáilte Towers* and *Celebrity Bainisteoir*.

Certainly one can agree with Hay and Ouellette that the emergence of Reality TV has been a good "fit" with Irish neoliberalism. However, while much of the Reality TV programming in Ireland (as elsewhere) rotates more explicitly around themes to do with musical entertainment, sports and fitness or home improvement, and can certainly be said to share in this neoliberal fascination with self-transformation and management, the shows discussed here establish a much deeper connection, speaking directly to the fact that Ireland is in the midst of a terrible financial crisis, and situating the cause of this crisis in an insufficiency of the popular economic will. If, as per Kitchin *et al.*, Irish neoliberalism is best characterised as "ideologically concealed, piecemeal, serendipitous, pragmatic, and commonsensical,"[35] the discussion below will demonstrate the importance of Reality TV in providing cues through which key neoliberal norms are modelled while criticism of the state is marginalised.

Dragon's Den as Neoliberal Governmentality

Based on an originally Japanese hit show, *Dragon's Den* has since travelled to countless markets around the world. The basic structure of the show is straightforward enough. Budding entrepreneurs are admitted into a room and "pitch" their ideas for a product to a panel of hardened business veterans. The entrepreneurs are looking for a sum of money to help further their project. After the pitch, the dragons must decide whether or not to invest some of their own money into the project. There is time for the dragons to cross-examine the entrepreneur for details and clarifications, and then, should any of them be interested, they can make an offer in exchange for a degree of equity in the profits of the business. Often none of the dragons will be interested, and the "contestant" goes home with merely the memory of the dragons' caustic remarks as a reward for their time. In Ireland the show has gained a significant following, dramatically boosting the media profile of its "dragons," who have not hesitated to exploit their newfound status as entrepreneurial icons to support a range of personal endeavours, including their own private consultancy ventures, business-oriented talk radio programming, news appearances and campaigns for the presidency.

33. Corcoran, *op. cit.*, p. 214.
34. *Ibid.*, p. 200.
35. Kitchin *et al.*, *op. cit.*, p. 1306.

Importantly, as dragon Sean Gallagher has commented in a radio interview, the show is completely unscripted (Mooney Show, RTÉ Radio 1, 2 November 2011). Yet it appears that the dragons do adopt personas to some extent, as the show progresses. Indeed, part of the narrative structure of the show is the dragons' "hard core" attitude. For example, one dragon may be interested in a product concept but may press his or her advantage as the sole bidder by raising the equity stake, sometimes to rather high levels. Consider the case of "Izzy's Chocolates" from the first episode of Season 3, where the dragons more or less unanimously agree that while the product is of very high quality, it is a disaster in terms of its marketing strategy. The contestant, Izzy, is presented to the dragons as a recently retrained recession victim, having lost her job to the recession the previous year. Izzy is now a qualified *chocolatier,* supplying 40 stores in County Cork. She came onto the show looking for €20,000 to expand her product line and purchase display stands for the stores. In exchange for the money she is offering 20% of the business. She will also keep her own salary capped at the minimum wage level until such time as the business can be deemed a success. However, while the majority of the dragons are leery, one—Niall O'Farrell, himself a successful clothing retailer—does step in to make an offer: the full sum sought in exchange for 50% of the business. In the "narrative" structure of the show, the producers choose to present this as a dramatic moment. The music becomes tense, and the camera zooms in to show the anxiety on Izzy's face. As contestants may ask for a moment to reflect once a final offer has been made, Izzy chooses to take advantage of this. The camera tracks her as she walks into an alcove at the back of the room, purposely designed for this purpose, and backlit to silhouette the contestant as she paces back and forth. Returning to the centre stage, Izzy announces that she will accept the offer.

As per the show's convention when a contestant accepts a deal, she shakes the hand of the new investor and exits the stage. However, while not typical, during the contestant's exit there can be some banter between the dragons. In this instance, the other dragons seem rather shocked by the high equity stake that O'Farrell has eked from Izzy. But O'Farrell laughs this off, declaring that he was in fact acting providentially: "I like to give back." This judgement of Izzy is a figurative moment, suggesting something of the occasionally condescending and duplicitous nature of the show. In this instance, the show's producers had chosen to present Lizzy to the viewers as a victim of the recession who, despite bad fortune, was returning to the marketplace as someone embodying the virtue of hope and determination in the pursuit of self-transformation. In the end, however, her efforts fall short to some extent. She succeeds in obtaining her funding but fails to fight for the better deal which, from the reaction of the other dragons, was clearly a possibility.

This "Gordon Gecko-esque" mantle is something that dragons seem happy to wear on occasion, and the producers make it a point to play it up. Throughout the show each dragon is shown with tidy stacks of cash piled on small tables positioned beside their chairs. It is not clear whether these piles are literally the dragons' money or merely dramatic props. But the camera periodically draws our attention to them, especially at tense moments. Similarly, the promotional materials for the show all feature the dragons in business attire, glaring with wilful intensity into the camera or staring pensively into the distance. The show's opening credits feature various dramatic shots of the dragons on a dock in Dublin's Grand Canal Basin, itself something of a symbolic "ground zero" for the entire Celtic Tiger phenomenon, the area having undergone significant redevelopment since 2000 as part of the Dublin Docklands area renovation project. Clearly they are not called "dragons" for nothing. And, true to form, this "ideal type" emerges forcefully when multiple dragons express an interest in a project. In the widely watched first episode of Season 3, the presenter of the "Savvy Bear" project seemed to really pique the dragons' attention. The product was an online learning environment for young children, where each child would have a cartoon-style bear avatar they would have to guide through various tasks. After a flurry of competitive, but only partial, bidding between recruitment and training specialist Gavin Duffy and the token female dragon of the show, magazine publisher Norah Casey, Niall O'Farrell makes a full bid for 30%. Not to be outdone, however, Casey responds with a full bid for 24%, a move that prompts Duffy to draw the contestant's attention to the significance of the event as a kind of teaching moment: "Do you see what's happened here? Without so much as taking a breath, Norah has just sunk a knife in Niall O'Farrell!"

In this instance, the lesson is that it is sometimes important to be aggressive. And the show is replete with such moments. Yet one would not want to come away from these anecdotes with the impression that the ideal-type evangelised in *Dragon's Den* is incapable of subtlety. To the contrary, the dragons seem at pains to emphasise that they are human beings, after all. Invited to guest host the well-known daily current affairs programme, the Matt Cooper Show, on Ireland's Today FM radio station, *Dragon's Den* presenter Richard Curran was emphatic that the successful Irish entrepreneur is someone who knows how to balance an outward appearance of success with a certain modesty (22 March 2010). On the show's car talk slot, with regular guest motoring expert Anton Savage, the topic was raised as to what car a young entrepreneur should be seen driving. According to Savage, it would have to be a car that would say the dragon was "successful" and had "made it" without screaming that he or she was an arriviste, an image that would not go down well in the context of the financial crisis. Hummers and Ferraris were considered excessive, but an Alfa Romeo 8C, Ferrari-manufactured but not labelled as such, was acceptable. Interestingly, Savage himself is son of Tom Savage, chairman of Irish state broadcaster RTÉ, and Terry Prone (discussed above), a well-known public relations consultant in Ireland. He is also the presenter of the Irish version of *The Apprentice.*

In the context of an ongoing economic crisis, *Dragon's Den* models an idealised entrepreneurial subject capable of calculating the relative utility of different types of behaviour in the marketplace. To gain a better purchase on the significance of the show in this sense, we might turn briefly to Foucault's discussion of governmentality, a term he coined to speak not only to "the way in which one conducts the conduct of men" but also to the creation of "an analytical grid" for assessing the efficacy of this conduct.[36] As I use the term here, governmentality refers to the relationship between power and the conduct of subjects, both in terms of the body of knowledge that provides criteria for the behaviour of the *ideal subject* and the way that the actual subject is then led to self-assess and govern itself, relative to these criteria. As a form of critique, then, Foucault's theory of governmentality

36. Michel Foucault, *The Birth of Biopolitics; Lectures at the Collège De France, 1978–79* (New York: Palgrave Macmillan, 2008), p. 186.

allows for a kind of indirect analysis of social institutions, focusing less on the form of this or that institution and more on the abstract "technology of power" embedded in this practice of self-assessment, which gives it its functional coherence.[37] Such a technology can be quite widely distributed, manifesting itself in the operations of a host of institutions, including the state itself, all of which could thus be said to share a common genealogy vis-à-vis the efforts of a social formation to assess and manage certain problems. Of course, the history of specific modalities or iterations of such governmental regimes is vast and by no means exhausted by those discussed here. For the purposes of this article, however, we can focus specifically on Foucault's discussion of the emergence of political economy as a discourse capable of modifying practices of government, a development which he proposes was well and truly in place by the eighteenth century.[38] To be sure, this development changed the nature of government in the formal sense, but it also had ramifications for the way individuals perceived the range of ethical choices they had at their disposal in the task of their own self-management.

As Foucault tells it, the early modes of political economy had ambivalent understandings of their own need to intervene upon the subjectivity of their populations. The more contemporary "neoliberalism," however, has a fairly explicit understanding of the market as an essential technology of subjectification, allowing for "the strategic programming of the individuals' activity."[39] On this reading of neoliberalism, *every* facet of social life is encompassed as an ostensibly market-based interaction. This understanding is made possible through neoliberalism's theory of human capital, or the idea that all labour, not just waged labour, can be understood as a voluntary investment or entrepreneurial activity carried out in the individual pursuit of some sort of future return or surplus benefit.[40] As a result, economic analysis can be applied to almost any form of social activity: marriage, parenting, discrimination, education, fertility, population growth, crime and punishment, addiction, and even insanity. That is, any activity that involves "substitutable choices" or the application of a "limited means to one end among others."[41] In this sense, the human being is fundamentally enjoined with his capacities as a kind of assemblage with a dynamic productive potential. Foucault goes so far as to suggest that neoliberalism appraises man in the market as a "machine-stream ensemble" or even a "capital-ability."[42] Neoliberalism is thus a theory that normalises this idea that the subject ought to direct his or her life in a manner consistent with the strictures of the market.

If neoliberalism seeks to normalise the responsibility to develop one's life in accordance with the norms of the market, the role of *Dragon's Den* as a confessional aid becomes clear. While the ultimate test of the neoliberal subject is the market itself, what *Dragon's Den* offers is a series of actual entrepreneurial encounters wherein viewers can see, as in the case of Izzy, for example, just how damaging a poor investment choice might be. The fact that so many of the entrepreneurs

37. Michel Foucault, *Security, Territory, Population; Lectures at the Collège De France, 1977–1978* (New York: Palgrave Macmillan, 2007), p. 111.

38. *Ibid.*, p. 107.

39. Foucault, *The Birth of Biopolitics, op. cit.*, p. 223.

40. *Ibid.*, p. 224.

41. *Ibid.*, pp. 222, 268.

42. *Ibid.*, p. 225.

invited onto the show are victims of the recession in Ireland, and that they have worked to reskill themselves and forge new paths in their career, says much of their commitment to adaptation. This is consistent for, as Foucault reminds us, in neoliberalism the worker is in a very real sense "an active economic subject," not just while on the job but in terms of his disciplined attitude towards the entirety of his own life, treating every facet of his or her being as a potential source of capital.[43] This is significant, as Foucault notes, because other historical imaginings of the market have taken it merely as a space where a "process of exchange" takes place. The neoliberal entrepreneur, however, is actually an "entrepreneur of himself," constantly balancing costs and benefits, and constantly careful of the material impact of choices, even in seemingly non-economic spheres. The universality of this subject consists in the fact that he will, out of hope for some sort of return, pursue his own transformation into a useful form of capital, through enhancement of his basic physical capacities, mental skills and general attitude.[44]

The significance of *Dragon's Den* is that it presents us with a celebration of this managerial disposition towards oneself and makes this explicit within the context of the Irish financial crisis. As Foucault tells us, neoliberal governmentality works through the "market milieu" to create incentives and disincentives, shaping how entrepreneurs think and act towards others and themselves. By this account, to the extent that the neoliberal subject is expected to subscribe to any particular norms of behaviour, he is asked simply to be a participant in this milieu, guided by his own substitutable tastes. By showcasing real life entrepreneurial encounters in an actual marketplace context, *Dragon's Den* models for audiences just how the market functions as a technology of the self, and the sort of emotional resolve and discipline with one's very self that might be required in order to succeed in it. In this sense we might say shows like this function alongside the market, or as a pedagogical complement to it. Now, Foucault does not quite seem to develop the broader social implications of this universal yet contingent "subject-as-capital" but, as I will elaborate below, if we apply this category of human capital to currently existing capitalist techniques of value production, it is clear that neoliberalism makes a substantive difference within the history of governmentality precisely because it takes the subject not simply as something that must be produced but something that is also in fact itself productive, in a very broad sense.

Retail Therapy, Affective Command

If *Dragon's Den* shows us how better to govern ourselves as neoliberal subjects, as creatures who must know precisely when to be conniving and when to hold back in the market of life, it is *Feargal Quinn's Retail Therapy* which shows us how to survive, and thrive, in an affective economy. Analogous in some respects to the American TV show *Home Makeover: Extreme Edition*, this show eschews the *Dragon's Den*-style "game" format in favour of a more straightforward self--improvement or self-actualisation documentary approach. Named, somewhat ironically, after the psychological disorder of "oniomania," where one pursues the

43. *Ibid.*, p. 223.
44. *Ibid.*, pp. 226–229.

consumption of high fashion goods in order to forget or dissipate feelings of anxiety or depression, this show revolves around one of Ireland's best-known retailers, Senator Feargal Quinn, founder of the prestigious grocery store Superquinn, as he takes six small-time, recession-hit retail operations under his wing and tutors them in the subtle arts of remaining viable in a bearish market. Comparable to *Dragon's Den* in terms of viewership, *Retail Therapy* makes a concerted effort to avoid its more sensational affectations. Nevertheless, unlike the dragons, Quinn has a long-established, cult-like popularity among discerning grocery shoppers in Ireland. As an elected member of the Irish Senate, he also uses his status in the media to offer views on the nature of the financial crisis. His constant mantra in the show is that retailers can beat the crisis, but only if they become better at developing the emotional connection of the customer to the experience of buying. As with *Dragon's Den*, the producers are keen to point out the crisis-focused, pedagogical mission of the show, showing retailers how to "battle the downturn and remain relevant in a cut-throat and over-crowded market."[45]

Renowned for being one of the first to bring contemporary retail techniques to the Irish market, Quinn's soft-spoken style puts a far gentler accent on Irish capitalism than that of the dragons. He became a millionaire in the deep Irish recession of the 1980s by, in his own account, putting the customer first. Quinn is known for what he calls the five lessons in humility: "My customers know more than I do. My employees know more than I do. Neither my employees nor I can be creative all of the time. What I knew yesterday is not enough for today. I'm not responding fast enough for my customer."[46] In interviews, Quinn often repeats the story of his experience growing up on his father's "camping-caravanning" site. The customers were paying up front, he recalls, so one had to be constantly focused on ensuring that they had a good experience, thereby ensuring that they would come back the following year. This experience led Quinn to develop on his first lesson, which he calls the "boomerang principle."[47] That is to focus, in every deed, on persuading the customer to return to the store. Key to this idea is the principle that, even though it may not be quantifiable to the accountants, the customer's *emotional* experience is essential to making a profit. For example, in order to curry favour with mothers of young children, Quinn has prohibited the sale of sweets and candies at his stores' checkout counters. "They kick up blue murder until the mother buys them something from the display of goodies," he observes. And while his accountants might object, he believes that it is worth it in order to avoid the possibility that mothers might leave the store feeling harassed. Passing up on the opportunity to sell sweets to kids might seem like folly, he notes, but "it requires courage to take the unquantifiable option."[48]

The story of *Retail Therapy* is as much about the wisdom gleaned from Feargal Quinn's success in an affective economy as it is about the predicaments of the stores he visits. He constantly returns to the theme of the non-quantifiable nature of successful retail. To make this point he often cites the old Irish

45. "Feargal Quinn's Retail Therapy", *RTÉ*, 15 March 2010, available: <http://www.rte.ie/tv/theafternoonshow/2010/0315/fearghalquinnsretailtherapy884.html> (accessed 17 September 2012).

46. Labarre, *op. cit.*

47. "Crowning the Customer with Feargal Quinn", Business of Success Podcast, 19 February 2006, available: <http://businessofsuccess.typepad.com/business_of_success/2006/02/crownting_the_c.html> (accessed 17 September 2012).

48. Labarre, *op. cit.*

proverb, "Listen to the sound of the river if you want to catch a salmon." And it is this message that he takes to the operations he visits on the show, which appear to be chosen precisely because of their current ignorance of this valuable message. Above, we discussed the case of Quinn's 2010 visit with Kim Buckley, the fourth-generation inner-city Dublin flower seller, whose retail technique was pretty much identical to that used by her great-grandmother. Identical, that is, until Quinn introduced her to public relations professionals who revealed to her the importance of her ability to insert her own *self* into her sales technique. In other words, put "her heart" into it. But it must be emphasised that these moves to embrace affective sales techniques often come at tremendous material and emotional cost to the subject. In another episode, for example, Quinn meets Fionnuala Law and her husband, equal partners of X-IT Department Store in Dublin. The business is on its knees. A small, 18-year-old discount store operation, the firm has never put much effort into keeping up appearances. Quinn was suggesting that Law invest €10,000 in giving the store a complete makeover, but Fionnuala wanted to invest it in stock. The show includes emotional scenes in the couple's kitchen at home as they fight over the cost of Quinn's recommendations, and the fact that, if they follow through, there will be no going back to the comfortable existence they knew before. Indeed, interestingly, despite the warmth of Quinn's general approach, there are moments when the show's producers are unafraid to hint that the participants may need to be disciplined for their lack of commitment to the mission. Thus, when Quinn visits Burgess's in Athlone, which at 170 years old is Ireland's oldest continuously run department store, he finds a small, family-run business that is being put under huge pressure by larger, foreign-owned operations. He assigns an international retail store expert from Madison Avenue as an advisor. Dramatic scenes follow as the store's relaunch day approaches, however, as the owners are making only slow progress, and the expert threatens to quit in order to sanction them for their lack of discipline. After all, it is *her* reputation on the line too.

Understood in the context of the Foucauldian arguments presented above, the narrative structure of *Retail Therapy* insinuates the importance of skills of emotional labour in the turn towards human capital. But this premium attached to emotional labour should also give us pause to reflect on our understanding of what it is exactly that is in crisis in the first place. Consider, for example, Hardt and Negri's understanding of affective labour as a key pillar in their thesis that contemporary globalisation has achieved a certain political autonomy, over and above its various constituent elements. Referring to this mode of globalisation as "Empire," they note the preeminent role played in its development not just of neoliberal idealisations of the subject but of practices of communicative and "immaterial" labour. "Empire," they declare, "takes form when language and communication, or really immaterial labor and cooperation, become the dominant force."[49] The advent of this type of global communicative capitalism bespeaks, for Hardt and Negri, what they refer to as the passage to "real subsumption." Whereas in the era of classical imperialism nation-based European capitalism expanded to enshroud the entire world, thereby also expanding the political forms of European modernity, real subsumption suggests a shift away from the economic modernisation of the industrial era towards socialisation, or a change

49. Hardt and Negri, *Empire, op. cit.*, p. 385.

in quality of labour itself, as labour reconcentrates around the production of information goods and physically intangible "service" goods.

In a sense, Hardt and Negri are here elaborating on the implications of the hegemony of the neoliberal theory of human capital, as discussed by Foucault, above. For them, "real subsumption" in the contemporary capitalist conjecture is intimately connected to the creative potential of human capital. They agree with Foucault that neoliberal discourse idealises the subsumption of every form of social activity, from the household to the schoolyard to the family doctor's office to the university, making them accountable to metrics of behaviour determined by the rationality of the market. What they add, however, is a concern that the turn towards human capital has *in practice* also radically changed the stakes of capitalist life. That is, that the turn towards immaterial and affective production has created an indeterminacy in the location of capitalist command. As Negri observes, today, because capacities for producing and managing value are sourced in the non-linear creativity of the human being as opposed to the worker as traditionally conceived, "the factory spreads throughout the whole of society ... production is social and activities are productive."[50] Capacities of intuition and care that were once more or less irrelevant to the mundane tasks of industrial production are now referred to as indispensable forms of human capital, and are today directly implicated in the production process. Beyond this, however, Hardt and Negri are preoccupied with the basic political significance of these novel forms of labour insofar as they have a kind of ontological power, too. That is, by virtue of the way capitalism extracts surplus today, through the production of knowledge, desires and affects, the question of power is not simply a question of the production of this or that type of subjectivity but, rather, a question of the real and intense ways in which the "commanding heights" of the economy have become immanent through the hegemony of immaterial labour. In this sense, then, contemporary capitalism is staked upon a mode of control that is essentially immanent. That is, as Read puts it, the basic organisation of power in our era is staked upon "the production of subjectivity by subjectivity."[51]

If *Dragon's Den* highlights anything about the current Irish situation, it is the normative expectation of a "hard core" attitude towards oneself, and one's position in the market. *Retail Therapy,* on the other hand, points us towards the precise kinds of skills and competencies that Irish subjects are being led to recognise as necessary in producing value. Even in the absence of a crisis, such skills would of course be at a premium. In *Retail Therapy,* however, the advice for surviving the downturn is to "double down" on affective labour. For Hardt and Negri, this would suggest a certain desperation on the part of capitalism. Indeed, to them, as they discuss in recent work, what the crisis really indicates is the incommensurability of the traditional capitalist institutions for measuring and allocating wealth with the new realities of capitalist valorisation. Hardt and Negri offer the example of rent in an actual city to illustrate the point. Here, real estate agents pitch the value of high-value properties on the strength of their proximity to zones of affective intensity, the "cool" and "chic" parts of town. What they fail

50. Antonio Negri, "Interpretation of the Class Situation Today: Methodological Aspects", in Werner Bonefeld, Richard Gunn and Kosmas Psychopedis (eds.), *Open Marxism, Vol. 2: Theory and Practice* (London: Pluto, 1992), p. 85.

51. Read, *op. cit.*, p. 18.

to see, however, is that the additional value of the property over and above its bricks and mortar is linked to an external "common work" of the crowd.[52]

Rental properties situated close to such zones of "common work" are capable of generating tremendous wealth. The rub, however, is that once the zones become unpopular, the source of value disappears. And this is precisely the analysis that Hardt and Negri bring to the current financial crisis. Whereas goods might once have retained their value through the means of relative scarcity, thus allowing for the possibility of garnering surplus through the surreptitious withholding of *profit* from the worker, today capitalism's surplus is extracted through means of *rent*, from almost everyone.[53] No wonder, then, that with the neoliberal abandonment of the institutions of care previously guaranteed by the welfare services of the state, the subject of indebtedness has become the key figure of the current financial crisis. That this figure emerges in the context of the new regime of valorisation is no accident, as Marazzi argues, for capitalism is today desperate and necessarily must stoop to make "raw life a source of profit."[54] In this sense the world's financial system is both an affective phenomenon, an "enormous engine of abstraction" and the "paradigmatic economic instrument" of biopolitical capitalism's exploitation.[55] As much is clear in the narrative structure of *Retail Therapy* which, as we have seen, rests not only on the premise that affective labour is a necessary part of the process of running a successful retail operation in crisis Ireland. Rather, the necessity Feargal Quinn articulates is one of taking great risk and "digging deep" in one's human capital if the country is to be saved, costs to one's bank balance and psychological wellbeing notwithstanding.

Conclusion

Autonomist Marxists have taken an interest in the predatory rent economy of contemporary capitalism not only because it speaks to the fragility and cynicism of capitalist valorisation today but also because it explains to some extent the counter-intuitive return, and re-legitimisation, of the state. As Lazzarato argues, in the financial crisis, the state has emerged anew: "not a minimal state, but a state free from the control of workers, the unemployed, women, the poor." Here, both governmentality, "the 'management' of the population," and representative democracy "become definitively integrated in the economy in so far as they are reshaped as devices of neoliberal governance."[56] The Irish case would appear to be a particularly powerful example of this phenomenon, with the results of the last election attesting to the degree to which the population has internalised the status quo explanation of the reasons for the crisis. As noted above, Irish elites often try to narrate the Irish financial crisis as a uniquely homegrown problem ("we all partied"), having no necessary relationship either to elite behaviour or even the contemporaneous crises experienced in Greece, Spain or elsewhere. Sanctioning the austerity regime through the ballot box, the Irish have acquiesced in

52. *Ibid.*, p. 155.

53. *Ibid.*, p. 139.

54. C. Marazzi, *Capital and Language; from the New Economy to the War Economy* (Cambridge MA: The MIT Press, 2008), p. 33.

55. Hardt and Negri, *Commonwealth, op. cit.*, pp. 157, 258.

56. Maurizio Lazzarato, "Governmentality in the Current Crisis", *Generation Online*, March 2013, available: <http://www.generation-online.org/p/fp_lazzarato7.htm> (accessed 18 March 2013).

accepting this status quo account not only of the place of their own subjectivity in the destruction of their country's economy but of the role of their own state as nothing more than the manager-in-chief of the necessary dismantling of their country's welfare system.

Irish Reality TV programming partially explains the attractiveness of these choices. Its "heroes" are those who have been confronted by the harsh logic of the nation's economic woes but who nevertheless have eschewed protest and accepted instead that their economic fate is up to them. They are those who have been willing to take the risk of investing anew in their own "human capital" and returning to the marketplace. To viewers at home, *Dragon's Den* and *Retail Therapy* offer the promise that, by taking their message seriously, the subject can succeed, even in the midst of a terrible recession. Moreover, in narrating a linkage between these successful figures and the country's chances for economic recovery, they suggest that becoming entrepreneurial is a moral responsibility for the people of Ireland. In so doing, however, they also affirm the status quo account of what caused the Irish crisis in the first place, directing attention away from social explanations and encouraging Irish entrepreneurs to dig deep into their "human capital," often at great expense to themselves, as necessary penance for the excesses of the Celtic Tiger years.

About the Author

Nicholas J. Kiersey is Assistant Professor in Political Science at Ohio University's Chillicothe campus. His recent publications address the question of the status of power as a concept in "world state" theory, the "debate about Empire" in International Relations, and Foucault's understanding of the place of economic thought in the globalisation of liberal discourses of government. He recently co-edited the volume *Battlestar Galactica and International Relations* with Iver Neumann (Routledge, 2013). He is currently writing a book exploring the cultural political economy of the Irish financial crisis.

Affective Economies in the Governance of Trafficking and Sex Work in Vietnam

NADINE VOELKNER

Since Vietnam's advances in "capitalist globalisation" in the late 1980s, it is argued to have become a source and destination country of trafficking in men, women and children. Considered a global problem, human trafficking draws together an array of national and international actors, governing logics and practices in its global governance. This article examines how, in the prevention of trafficking in women and children in Vietnam, a global neoliberal governance logic converged with socialism. Specifically, it focuses on one site where this can be seen playing out, namely in the attempt to prevent trafficking in women and children in the Mekong Delta area in the mid-2000s. The article draws particular attention to the affective economies at play in the discursive regimes of Vietnamese femininity deployed to prevent the trafficking of women and girls. It thereby complements a Foucauldian reading of governance with Ahmed's work on the cultural politics of emotions.

In the context of Vietnam's increasing exchanges with other countries following its ground-breaking open-door policy *Đổi Mới* (renovation) in the late 1980s and its subsequent gradual integration into the global political economy, the country today also finds itself at the crossroads of global circuits of human trafficking.[1] According to the influential "Trafficking in Persons Report"[2] (TIP) of 2013, Vietnam is a source country for men, women and children "subjected to sex

*The field research carried out for this article was funded by the Economic and Social Research Council, UK. For their insightful comments, the author would like to thank Martin Coward, Stefan Elbe, Luis Lobo-Guerrero and the editors of this special issue.

1. Human trafficking, according to the UN Protocol to Prevent, Suppress and Punish Trafficking in Persons, Especially Women and Children (2000), supplementing the UN Convention against Transnational Organized Crime, is "the recruitment, transportation, transfer, harbouring or receipt of persons, by means of threat or use of force or other forms of coercion, of abduction, of fraud, or deception, of the abuse of power or of a position of vulnerability or of giving or receiving of payments or benefits to achieve the consent of a person having control over another person, for the purpose of exploitation. Exploitation shall include, at a minimum, the exploitation of the prostitution of others or other forms of sexual exploitation, forced labour or services, slavery or practices similar to slavery, servitude or the removal of organs." Available: <http://www.osce.org/odihr/19223?download=true> (accessed 25 March 2014).

2. The influential "Trafficking in Persons Report" (TIP) describes itself as representing "an updated, global look at the nature and scope of trafficking in persons and the broad range of government actions to confront and eliminate it. … Worldwide, the report is used by international organizations, foreign governments, and nongovernmental organizations alike as a tool to examine where resources are most needed." It is "the U.S. Government's principal diplomatic tool to engage foreign governments on human trafficking." Available: <http://www.state.gov/j/tip/rls/tiprpt/> (accessed 12 August 2013).

trafficking and forced labour" across Asia and beyond.[3] As the United Nations Inter-Agency Project on Human Trafficking (UNIAP)[4] operating across Southeast Asia has noted, research and experience in the region suggests that human trafficking is best understood mainly as "a fall-out from irregular migration."[5] Vietnamese migration is said to occur due to various factors, including uneven economic development.[6] Both Vietnamese men and women migrating for work can face various forms of trafficking. However, until recently the Vietnamese government only acted on the trafficking of women and children for sexual exploitation and prostitution. The emphasis on the prevention of the trafficking of women and children is reflected also in the initiatives by international organisations allowed to work in Vietnam. While human trafficking is today seen in Vietnam as a problem of illegal migration and prostitution more generally, the subject remains a "sensitive issue to be addressed with care."[7] As with the issues of prostitution, drug abuse and HIV/AIDS, the Vietnamese government has engaged human trafficking as a "social evil" that is rationalised as one of the negative consequences of Vietnam's dramatic transition to a market economy, urbanisation and increasing involvement with other countries.[8]

Governing the trafficking of women and children as a social evil, as this article goes on to elaborate, has involved cultivating an economy of shame in which young women and girls are discouraged from "shameful" immoral behaviour that is argued to put them in danger of trafficking. This has been set against an image of the traditional virtuous Vietnamese woman who is mindful of transgressing moral boundaries, an attitude that is taken to safeguard her from becoming trafficked. The social evil campaign has since converged in places with neoliberal programmes of preventing trafficking in women and children introduced into Vietnam by international organisations such as the International Labour Organization (ILO) and the International Organization for Migration (IOM) operating within the global anti-trafficking regime. The article discusses this encounter between the Vietnamese and neoliberal mode of preventing trafficking in its analysis of the implementation of an ILO International Programme on the Elimination of Child Labour (IPEC) programme in Hau Giang province in the Mekong Delta of Vietnam.[9] The neoliberal approach in question aimed at targeting women and

---

3. US Department of State, "Trafficking in Persons Report (TIP) 2013" (Washington, DC: USDS, 2013), p. 392.

4. UNIAP, "Siren Human Trafficking Data Sheet: Vietnam", SIREN: Strategic Information Response Network, UNIAP: Phase III, Hanoi, Vietnam, November 2008 (V.1.0) (Bangkok: UNIAP, 2008), available: <http://www.no-trafficking.org/content/SIREN/SIREN_pdf/vietnam%20datasheet%20final%20november%202008.pdf> (accessed 6 February 2014).

5. There is no agreed definition for irregular migration. The International Organization for Migration (IOM) defines it as the "movement that takes place outside the regulatory norms of the sending, transit and receiving countries." IOM, "Key Migration Terms", available: <http://www.iom.int/cms/en/sites/iom/home/about-migration/key-migration-terms-1.html> (accessed 5 February 2014). Quote from Phil Marshall, "Globalization, Migration and Trafficking: Some Thoughts from the South-East Asian Region", Paper presented at the Globalization Workshop, Kuala Lumpur, 8–10 May 2001, p. 10, available: <http://www.childtrafficking.com/Docs/marshall_uniap_mekong_2001_.pdf> (accessed 25 March 2014).

6. UNIAP, *op. cit.*

7. Annuska Derks, "Combating Trafficking in South-East Asia: A Review of Policy and Programme Responses", *IOM Migration Research Series* (Geneva: IOM, 2000), p. 46.

8. *Ibid.*, p. 46.

9. This article draws on field research carried out in Vietnam in 2008. The field research focused on tracing the implementation of the ILO IPEC project "Prevention of Trafficking in Children and

girls "at risk of trafficking" for self-responsibilisation exercises in which an entrepreneurial spirit was to be cultivated that was argued to reduce the need to migrate for work. Here, an economy of entrepreneurial spirit rather than shame comes into play. In both affective economies developed to prevent trafficking in women and children, the discourse of Vietnamese femininity served as a principle site for governmental intervention. It is here that it becomes possible to see the way the divergent economies of emotions in question converge.

In order to understand how the prevention of trafficking in women and children operates through emotions, the article complements Michel Foucault's thought on governmentality and the reasoned way of directing behaviour[10] with Sara Ahmed's work on the cultural politics of emotions.[11] According to Ahmed, emotions are economic and circulate between people in "relationships of difference and displacement."[12] In this way, rather than just being psychological dispositions, emotions do things "in concrete and particular ways, to mediate the relationship between the psychic and the social, and between the individual and the collective."[13] It is this which leads Ahmed to speak of "affective economies." In directing emotions, for example through "global economies of fear" in the War on Terror after 9/11,[14] or in the affective economies mentioned above to prevent the trafficking of women and children in Vietnam, "identities are produced and policies are legitimated *affectively*."[15] In fact, as Ahmed has also pointed out, it serves to create subjectivities of self and other, thus generating social relations, which delineate communities of belonging including national identities. Here, bringing Foucault's considerations together with Ahmed's helps to understand how Vietnamese femininity is reconstituted in attempting to minimise the risk of trafficking in women and children. It also helps towards understanding, as this article also notes, how the emotional investment of gender identities in the prevention of trafficking matters to the constitution of contemporary Vietnamese national identity in the major social transition since *Đổi Mới*.

Đổi Mới and the Social Evil of Trafficking

Many of the regular and irregular migrations (including human trafficking) within and outside of Vietnam today are the effect of *Đổi Mới*, the path-breaking governmental policy of market reform and the integration of the country into the global political economy since the 1980s. *Đổi Mới* has had an enormous impact on Hồ Khẩu, the household registration system introduced in 1954. Registration in the system involved gaining "access to rights, employment and services such as the

Women at a Community Level in Cambodia and Viet Nam (RAS/02/P09/HSF)" from ILO headquarters in Bangkok to Hanoi, Ho Chi Minh City, Vi Thanh and Phung Hiep in Hau Giang province. The project was funded by the United Nations Trust Fund for Human Security for a period of three years between May 2003 and April 2006.

10. See, e.g., Michel Foucault, *The Birth of Biopolitics: Lectures at the College De France, 1978–79*, trans. Graham Burchell (Basingstoke, Hampshire: Palgrave Macmillan, 2008).

11. Sara Ahmed, "Affective Economies", *Social Text*, Vol. 79 (2004), p. 117.

12. *Ibid.*, p. 119.

13. *Ibid.*

14. *Ibid.*, p. 128.

15. Leep Mathew Coen, "The Affective Production of Others: United States Policy Towards the Israeli-Palestinian Conflict", *Cooperation and Conflict*, Vol. 45 (2010), p. 331 (emphasis added).

distributions of rations and essential commodities."[16] The Vietnamese government used the system as a tool of regional planning which not only served to spatially enclose residents within Vietnamese provinces but also to police provincial borders in order to curtail massive southward migration following the partition of the country into North and South Vietnam in 1954. Travelling within Vietnam thereafter required governmental permission. The development of private enterprises in the reform period, however, "created a labour market which broke the tie between permanent residence and employment."[17] The relaxation of *Hộ Khẩu* has significantly increased mobility within and outside of Vietnam.

Indeed, as Anh *et al.* argue, "[t]he increasing commercialisation of labour with capital inputs has been of major significance in releasing the rural workforce and prompting them to leave rural areas."[18] "The growth in labour intensive garment, shoe and other factories"[19] provided greater incentives and opportunities to live and work in urban centres. Moreover, as Nguyen-vo has noted, the informal "hooking economy" that emerged in the wake of the scramble for profit-making business opportunities gave rise to a booming sex industry with a demand for sex workers. Entrepreneurs from the three sectors—state, private and/or foreign—"hook up" at *Bia Ôm* establishments, literally "hugging beer" venues, where business deals are agreed over food and sexual entertainment.[20] In this way, commercial sex became integral to the marketisation of the Vietnamese economy.[21]

Leaving behind high unemployment and poverty-ridden conditions of life, Vietnamese also move abroad to neighbouring and distant countries in search of better opportunities. Migrants may choose to travel via formal channels (for example labour export channels run by predominantly state-affiliated and private labour export companies), but subsequently end up in unsafe and exploitative working conditions.[22] Or they may opt to travel via unofficial, informal networks and

16. Tom Scott, Ngoc Ha Do, Van Buom Nguyen, Bich Diem Nguyen Thi and Thanh Ha Mai, "Report on a Rapid Assessment of the Situation of Migrant Children in Vietnam" (Hanoi, Vietnam: Save the Children UK, 2006), pp. 21–22.

17. *Ibid.*, p. 22.

18. Dang Nguyen Anh, Cecilia Tacoli and Hoang Xuan Thanh, "Migration in Vietnam: A Review of Information on Current Trends and Patterns and Their Policy Implications", Paper presented at the Regional Conference on Migration, Development and Pro Poor Policy Choices in Asia, Dhaka, Bangladesh, June 2003.

19. Scott *et al.*, *op. cit.*, p. 21.

20. Comparing life in Vietnam to life in the USA, Linh Dinh writes in the *Literary Review*: "A typical bia om has private rooms where a group of buddies can sit on a couch in front of a big screen TV to warble their favorite hits and oldies. Each man has a hostess to help him ease a tune along. A case of beer sits on the floor. […] There are also 'bida om' (billiards and a hug) and 'hot toc om' (a haircut and a hug). An 18-year-old girl in my neighborhood decided she wanted to work at a hot toc om. She assumed, innocently enough, that all she had to do was rub her breasts against a man's whiskers as she gave him a haircut. She was required to do more than that and was fired after four days. 'The place had six chairs. Three of these guys had their things out. One guy had two girls all over him. I was supposed to eat ice cream,' she giggled. 'And everyone was in the same room?' 'Yes'." Linh Dinh, "Eight Postcards from Vietnam", *Literary Review,* Vol. 45 (2002), pp. 812–822.

21. Thu-huong Nguyen-vo, *The Ironies of Freedom: Sex, Culture, and Neoliberal Governance in Vietnam*, Critical Dialogues in Southeast Asian Studies (Seattle and London: University of Washington Press, 2008), p. 24.

22. United Nations Population Fund (UNFPA), *State of World Population 2006, a Passage to Hope: Women and International Migration* (New York: UNFPA, 2006). Vietnamese legally migrating for work can subsequently end up in conditions of debt bondage. For example, the "Trafficking in Persons Report 2008" reported on 200 Vietnamese men and women recruited by Vietnamese state-run labour agencies for

recruitment channels to evade restrictive immigration policies and tight border controls. They may incur debt in order to finance these journeys or to pay agents and brokers but subsequently find themselves in relations of debt bondage.[23] Vietnamese women may wed foreign men in the hope of security but end up in the prostitution of their bodies or become domestic helpers in foreign countries.[24] They may have been made to believe they will obtain lucrative jobs only to find themselves with little or no pay, excessive working hours[25] and performing sex work. Experiences of exploitation "may not even be seen as such by the 'victim' who may see themselves as being nonetheless better off than if they had stayed at home."[26]

As the above illustrates, the journeys and destinations of Vietnamese migrants are often beset by immeasurable difficulties. Acts of smuggling and trafficking are difficult to distinguish. Differences are subtle, and the two may overlap. Unlike smuggling, however, which is considered "a criminal commercial transaction between two willing parties who go their separate ways once their business is complete," trafficking specifically targets

> the trafficked person as an object of criminal exploitation. The purpose from the beginning of the trafficking enterprise is to profit from the exploitation of the victim. It follows that fraud, force or coercion all play a major role in trafficking.[27]

The Vietnamese government has responded to the need to control increases in trafficking of women and children by framing it in the language of social evils and by linking it to the "downside" of *Đổi Mới*. The definition of social evil is vague, covering a variety and arbitrary kinds of practices including "premarital and extramarital sex, homosexuality, pornography, prostitution, drug and alcohol addiction, gambling, theft, abuse and violence as well as paintings (e.g. pin-up calendars), music videos and music referring to sex."[28] According to Rydstrom, as a category, social evils has been widely "associated with the kinds of practices condemned as being 'dirty' which, in turn, have been linked with assumptions about HIV and AIDS."[29] In this way, practising a social evil is interpreted as dirty and shameful.

---

work in apparel factories in Jordan who were allegedly "subjected to conditions of fraudulent recruitment, debt bondage, unlawful confiscation of travel documents, confinement, and manipulation of employment terms for the purpose of forced labor at their worksite." When workers began to strike and clashed with Jordanian police, they are said to have faced threats of retaliation by Vietnamese government officials and employment agency representatives. According to the "Trafficking in Persons Report," there were no reported efforts by the Vietnamese government to consider any of the repatriated workers as possible victims of trafficking. US Department of State, "Trafficking in Persons Report" (Washington, DC: USDS, 2008), pp. 261–262.

23. Marshall, *op. cit.*

24. For more information on the commodification of international marriages in Vietnam, see Hong-zen Wang and Shu-ming Chang, "The Commodification of International Marriages: Cross-Border Marriage Business in Taiwan and Viet Nam", *International Migration*, Vol. 40 (2002), pp. 93–116.

25. Marshall, *op. cit.*, p. 8.

26. *Ibid.* See also Nguyen-vo, *op. cit.*

27. US Department of State, "Distinctions between Human Smuggling and Human Trafficking 2006", available: <http://www.state.gov/m/ds/hstcenter/90434.htm> (accessed 14 October 2010).

28. Halle Rydstrom, "Sexual Desires and 'Social Evils': Young Women in Rural Vietnam", *Gender, Place and Culture*, Vol. 13 (2006), p. 284.

29. *Ibid.*

Thus, the Vietnamese government employed social evils as a governmental strategy that, drawing on an economy of shame, aimed to discourage morally reprehensible practices and encourage moral self-control.

Its nationalistic text posits social evils as a problem of morality affecting Vietnamese culture and national social order. As Derks argues, according to the Vietnamese government, social evils are the result of "the open-door policy, the change of economic management, the process of urbanization and the increasing exchanges with other countries, particularly with countries in the region."[30] In 1995, the government called for the "insertion of order and moral principles into cultural activities according to our cultural content" to "eliminate social evils."[31] Vietnam was "to build a 'progressive culture deeply colored with national characteristics' by cracking down on the dissemination of 'decadent, poisonous cultural products'."[32] In the scheme of national social evils, the source for "increasing drug dealing, prostitution, smuggling, and other criminal activities" is interpreted as a consequence of foreign influences and the concomitant corruption of traditional Vietnamese values.[33]

Rendering trafficking in women and children a social evil has led the Vietnamese government to intensify propaganda around traditional Vietnamese femininity. This has resulted in the stigmatisation of those women having experienced trafficking. Rydstrom has noted that, even today, appropriate female behaviour in Vietnam draws its guiding principles from Confucian precepts such as "men and women should remain physically distant" (*nam nu tho tho bat than*). Confucianism historically has "dictated that a Vietnamese woman should show good 'morality' by remaining a virgin until marriage and avoiding adultery, divorce, and abortion."[34] In the scheme of social evil, a trafficked woman may be considered to have risked trafficking by diverging from morally acceptable behaviour. The Vietnamese family unit plays a central role in this campaign, standing in as moral arbiter: "families may 'turn a blind eye' to the realities of the experiences of trafficked daughters or express shame towards daughters who have engaged in the 'social evil' of sex work, albeit against their will, in destination countries."[35] Yet Vietnamese cultural values including filial piety and self-sacrifice, central Confucian tenets, impose family obligations on girls, creating a desire to migrate, even if by unsafe and irregular methods or by needing to engage in "shameful" work in order to be able to support the family through home remittances.

Consider sex workers who engage in "shameful" work yet whose high earnings are seen as a way of making a living and pulling themselves and their families out of desperate conditions. For example, sex worker Minh recounts:

> My family was so desperate. Back then, we were poor to the extent that with plain rice, you'd count the bowls and never was there enough. I was in ninth grade. I was a good student. I had to quit after I took the

---

30. Derks, *op. cit.*, p. 46.

31. Nguyen-vo, *op. cit.*, p. 45.

32. *Ibid.*

33. Chris Dixon and Andrea Kilgour, "State, Capital, and Resistance to Globalisation in the Vietnamese Transitional Economy", *Environment and Planning A*, Vol. 34 (2002), p. 604.

34. Rydstrom, *op. cit.*, p. 284.

35. Ramona Vijeyarasa, "The State, the Family and Language of 'Social Evils': Re-Stigmatising Victims of Trafficking in Vietnam", *Culture, Health & Sexuality*, Vol. 12 (2010), p. 90.

> exam. Before I could go to the tenth grade, I had to quit to look for work. I hid what I did from my mom. The money I made I brought home to feed the little ones. Back then, school fees were a few dong for the little ones, and I brought home more than one hundred thousand dong in one day. Can you imagine?[36]

The value of self-sacrifice is evident even in celebrated Vietnamese poet Nguyễn Du's (1765–1820) now epic poem *The Kim Van Kieu* written 200 years earlier, at the turn of the eighteenth century. The poem tells the story of the life of Thúy Kiều, a beautiful and talented young woman who was compelled to sacrifice herself to save her family: "And now the girl must meet that capital account ... 'Desist!'—she cries, 'and in their place take me for bounty to be sold!"[37] She unwittingly sold herself as a prostitute to save her father and younger brother from prison. In the end, the welfare of the family is an important factor in the decision to migrate within and/or outside of Vietnam.[38] It is in this sense that the effect of the language of social evils has been argued to have led to the criminalisation of those otherwise considered, under the global standards of human trafficking, victims.[39]

From the mid-1990s onwards, however, in dealing with human trafficking, the Vietnamese government began drawing on the technical support and expertise of both national and international organisations.[40] In the end, the government's decision to invite international organisations to help manage the problem of trafficking in women and children in and from Vietnam is linked with its open-door policy to promote Vietnam as a serious player on the world stage. As such, it bowed to political pressures from the regional Association of Southeast Asian Nations (ASEAN) and other international organisations as well as to pressures arising from its bid for membership of the World Trade Organization (WTO).[41]

Governing the Risk of Trafficking through Self-responsibilisation

The mode of preventing trafficking in women and children introduced into Vietnam appeals to a different affective economy than does governing through *social evils*. According to the ILO IPEC programme to prevent trafficking in women and children analysed here, human trafficking is a labour issue. Accordingly, the aim is to cultivate an entrepreneurial spirit in women and children identified as at "high risk" of trafficking. These women and children are said to be "living in circumstances that render them vulnerable to trafficking."[42] In constituting subjects economic and self-responsible by offering training in market analyses, the identification of economic opportunities as well as skills development for

36. As quoted in Nguyen-vo, *op. cit.*, p. 117.

37. Nguyễn Du, *The Kim Van Kieu*, trans. Vladislav Zhukov (Canberra: Pandanus Books, 2004), p. 34.

38. Joanna Busza, "Sex Work and Migration: The Dangers of Oversimplification—a Case Study of Vietnamese Women in Cambodia", *Health and Human Rights*, Vol. 7 (2004), pp. 231–249.

39. Vijeyarasa, *op. cit.*

40. Derks, *op. cit.*, p. 46.

41. Interviews in Bangkok, September 2008, and Hanoi, October 2008. Vietnam became the WTO's 150th member on 11 January 2007.

42. ILO/IPEC, "Project Proposal: Prevention of Trafficking in Children and Women at a Community Level in Cambodia and Viet Nam" (Ras/02/P09/HSF), 2002, p. ii.

operating small businesses, the neoliberal programme aimed to instil a culture of entrepreneurialism rationalised as minimising the need to migrate for economic reasons, thereby reducing the risk of trafficking.

The ILO argued that the trafficking of women and children in Vietnam is "inevitably linked" to the significant movement of people across economies and markets within the Mekong Subregion in search of livelihood. Women and children who reside in communities "particularly vulnerable to trafficking" and who "live at or below the poverty line" are "likely" to have little or no access to basic services, and have "little or no chance of expanding their livelihood potentials."[43] They migrate and become "vulnerable to trafficking." The sites and forms of exploitation are said to vary considerably, including services provided to the commercial sex industry, street begging, labouring in the manufacturing sector, and domestic services.[44] Accordingly, the ILO aimed to create the conditions under which people are "empowered to take greater control over their lives."[45] While this involved raising awareness about trafficking and providing the credit and skills training to "at risk" women to set up businesses, crucially, it also involved cultivating an entrepreneurial spirit.[46]

Skills training and microfinance lending as tools to prevent trafficking in women and children were argued to constitute "training for life."[47] To encourage "new micro-enterprise activity," according to the ILO, individuals must be able to both manage credit and have the technical or vocational skills to develop the enterprise of their choice.[48] In the Cambodian leg of the same project, "Prek Ksay A Village, in Prey Veng Province, is now filled with healthy pigs, and is the envy of neighbouring villages."[49] This serves to emphasise the entrepreneurial spirit that was cultivated in the skills training exercises. Targeted women and girls are subjected to an economy of entrepreneurial spirit that is believed to help prevent trafficking.

Since the working practices of the social evils approach of Vietnamese state officials and institutions are markedly different from the neoliberal practices to "combat human trafficking" propagated by the ILO and other transnational organisations,[50] much of the latter's efforts in Vietnam have concentrated on authorising

43. *Ibid.*, p. 3.

44. *Ibid.*, p. i.

45. *Ibid.*, p. ii.

46. Ruth Bowen, Prom Tevy and Tran Minh Gioi, "Final Evaluation Report: Prevention of Trafficking in Children and Women at a Community Level in Cambodia and Vietnam" (Hanoi: ILO-IPEC Design, Evaluation and Documentation Section [DED], 2006), p. 2.

47. ILO/IPEC, "Project Proposal", *op. cit.*, p. 12.

48. *Ibid.*, p. 12.

49. *Ibid.*, p. 13.

50. At the turn of the millennium, Vietnam drew mainly on three expert intergovernmental organisations operating across the Greater Mekong Subregion (GMS) on the issue of human trafficking. Most influential in this respect has been the IOM, which has been active in Vietnam since the late 1980s. The IOM's promotion of the management of migration flows within the Mekong Subregion has been the precursor for more extensive collaboration between the five countries in the Subregion. Building on this, the United Nations Inter-Agency Project on Human Trafficking (UNIAP), established in 2000, sets out to facilitate a stronger and more coordinated response to trafficking in the GMS and beyond. It pools the expertise and efforts of several UN agencies including the IOM, ILO and the United Nations Office on Drugs and Crime (UNODC), and disseminates this through its regional office in Bangkok to country project offices in the capitals of Cambodia, China, Lao PDR, Burma, Thailand and Vietnam. By 2008, the UNIAP had managed to spin a web of collaboration on countering human trafficking anchored at key country nodal points, bringing together senior government officials

and disseminating expert knowledge about how to prevent the trafficking of women and children as well as taking minuscule steps in training Vietnamese officials in the management of the global battle against human trafficking. The encounter between governing through social evils and the neoliberal mode of preventing trafficking in women and children is in fact leading to the gradual hybridisation of the mode of preventing trafficking of women and children in and from Vietnam.

In effect, while the problem of "a growing market for clandestine migration services, including smuggling across borders, faking travel documents, and arranging marriages" is symptomatic of contemporary globalising times,[51] the solution to the problem of trafficking in women and children in Vietnam was seen to lie mainly with the women and children "at risk" and their government. They were to become self-responsible, entrepreneurial and alert or "enlightened" women who are immune to the lures of traffickers, and their government a better manager. For the Vietnamese government, this involved managing the designated population at risk of trafficking by learning to define the problem in neoliberal terms and "to devise technical solutions that can be implemented and assessed through modes of knowledge such as auditing, quality control, and safety standards."[52]

Following the development of haphazard policies and resolutions which formed part of a national policy to "address and prevent trafficking and prostitution of women and children" in the 1990s,[53] by 2003 a change could be registered in the governing ethos of the Vietnamese government towards a more realist representation of society reflecting emerging market, social and governing forces. For example, the "propatainment" movie *Bar Girls* was released as part of "a new wave of Vietnamese state-sanctioned cinema that mixes sensational story lines with the Communist Party's campaign against 'social evils'."[54] The movie taps into emotions relating to Vietnamese femininity and works towards instantiating accepted female behaviour. Set in the nightclubs and slums of Ho Chi Minh City, the movie follows to their dramatic end Hanh, a gentle character who hopes for a better life, and Hoa, a heroin-addicted rich girl working as a prostitute in nightclubs to satisfy her addiction.

In 2004, the Vietnamese government issued a plan to tackle trafficking in women and children. Although it continued to use the language of social evils and social cohesion, trafficking, it argued, is an "urgent and pressing problem, badly affecting the society, customs, tradition, social morals and Government laws, destroying family happiness, increasing the risks of HIV/AIDS transmission and resulting in

---

including police, border guards, women's organisations, NGO and IGO officials, of five GMS countries across the GMS. Simultaneously, between 2000 and 2008, the ILO together with the IPEC, was engaged in the region promoting the perspective that human trafficking is a labour issue.

51. Julia O'Connell Davidson, "Guest Editorial: Trafficking, Modern Slavery and the Human Security Agenda", *Human Security Journal*, Vol. 6 (2008), p. 9.

52. Christina Schwenkel and Ann Marie Leshkowich, "Guest Editor's Introduction: How Is Neoliberalism Good to Think Vietnam? How Is Vietnam Good to Think Neoliberalism?", *Positions*, Vol. 20 (2012), p. 387.

53. Derks, *op. cit.*, p. 46.

54. Kay Johnson, "Social Evil Sells", *Time*, 5 May 2003; Nguyen-vo, *op. cit.*, p. 215.

potential impacts on national and social security."[55] The Vietnamese Women's Union (VWU) was put in charge of the prevention of the trafficking in women and children. Under the Prime Minister's Decree 69 relating to marriage and family relations with "foreign elements," steps were taken to protect Vietnamese women from deceit or trafficked circumstances in brokered marriages including increased due diligence in issuing marriage certificates and ensuring that the marriage is voluntary. For example, the VWU began a programme in collaboration with the South Korean Women's Union to set up pre-marriage counselling centres and hotlines in key source areas of Vietnam. The VWU collaborated with the ILO in raising awareness of trafficking in women and children and in providing the skills training for women considered "at risk" to set up their own businesses. As these organisations began to work hand in hand to prevent human trafficking in one site, an image of Vietnamese femininity began to form, which incorporated both shame and entrepreneurial desire.

The Hybridisation of Vietnamese Femininity

In[56] Hau Giang province,[57] dedicated teams of women from the VWU organised a broad range of awareness-raising activities. The role of the VWU in alerting target populations to the dangers of trafficking and labour exploitation, and guiding individuals in their choice to migrate, is substantial. The Vietnamese organisation was considered ideally placed to oversee awareness-raising activities. Firstly, the VWU's intricate structure for community development work, with networks extending from national to village level, stretched deep into communities.[58] It claims a membership base of "nearly 13 million belonging to 10,472 local women's unions in communes and towns throughout the country." It is "divided into 4 levels, comprising the Central level, the Provincial and Municipal level (63 units), the District level (642 units), and the Commune level."[59] Secondly, the "propaganda"[60] or Information, Education, Communication (IEC) units of the VWU are experienced campaigners. Coupled with its extensive network, the VWU is able to mass mobilise.[61] Thirdly, as arbiter of Vietnamese femininity, the VWU bears significant moral

55. Deputy Prime Minister Pham Gia Khiem, "Decision of the Prime Minister. Approval of the National Plan of Action against Crime of Trafficking in Children and Women During the Period of 2004-2010", The Government of the Socialist Republic of Vietnam, document no. 130/2004/QD-TTg, 14 July 2004, available: <ftp://ftp2.allianceantitrafic.org/alliancea/001%20%20Vietnam/NationalPlanofActionVN.pdf> (accessed 25 March 2014).

56. The analysis in this section is based on field research conducted in multiple locations in Hau Giang province in October 2008.

57. Hau Giang province lies 240 kilometres south of Ho Chi Minh City in the centre of the Mekong Delta. The province is divided into five districts, including Phung Hiep, and one provincial town, Vi Thanh. The majority of Hau Giang residents belong to the mainstream Kinh ethnic group. Four-fifths of Hau Giang residents depend on rice farming to generate income. Less than 20% of the population is engaged in small-scale industries, trade or services. Christina Cacioppo, "Can Tho City, Hau Giang Province, and Tay Ninh Province in Southern Viet Nam. The Situation of Migration and Trafficking of Children and Women: A Rapid Assessment", ILO/IPEC, 2006.

58. VWU, "Basic Information on Vietnam Women's Union", 2014, available: <http://hoilhpn.org.vn/newsdetail.asp?CatId=66&NewsId=819&lang=EN> (accessed 5 February 2014).

59. *Ibid.*

60. Propaganda in Vietnamese does not carry the same negative connotations as in other places. Interview with VWU members of Vi Thanh Town in Hau Giang province, 7 October 2008.

61. Interview with VWU official in Hanoi, October 2008. See also VWU, "Basic Information", *op. cit.*

authority over the women targeted in the trafficking project.[62] Interestingly, the VWU operated under a hybrid logic of social evil and neoliberalism, as the article goes on to discuss. Finally, although a union, the VWU is a state organisation with links to the highest political office. Thus, the structure and facilities of the VWU allowed the message of human trafficking to trickle through various levels of Vietnamese society.

The VWU campaigned for *responsible and risk-free migration*. They carried out a wide range of awareness-raising activities. Under the guidance of the VWU, the IEC networks utilised traditional IEC and awareness approaches at mass level, including using multiple TV broadcasts, radio, columns in local newspapers, leaflets, posters, traditional cultural performances such as poetry and folk songs, competitions, morning assemblies under the flag, and communal loudspeakers.[63] The mass organisation also campaigned at the local level through family visits, children's forums in schools and small group discussions in communities.[64] The issue of human trafficking was integrated in school curricula.[65] The VWU was also trained by ILO staff in innovative approaches including programmes made to fit specific audiences. This was widely used in secondary schools in both target and non-target communes.[66] Through these large-scale campaigns and minuscule activities, the VWU teams attempted to imbue the neoliberal prevention programme throughout "at risk" communities.[67]

In its propagandistic efforts to promote responsible behaviour and risk-free migration, the VWU operated under a hybrid logic in which it collapsed the fault line between governance through social evils and neoliberal governance. Throwing the weight of its moral authority behind the campaign to prevent trafficking in women and children, the VWU disciplined "at risk" women through what Foucault referred to as "normalizing judgements."[68] The VWU promoted an image of a "healthy, knowledgeable, skilful, dynamic, innovative, cultured and kind-hearted Vietnamese woman"[69] against the "loose minded" and irresponsible woman that it presented as particularly "at risk of trafficking."[70] Indeed, it is the traditional role of the VWU to "raise women's awareness and encourage them to preserve and develop cultural traditions and

62. Interview with VWU officials in Vi Thang Town, Hau Giang province, October 2008. See also Nguyen-vo, *op. cit.*

63. The regular chatter of the governmental loudspeaker across rice paddies or in the busy centre of Hanoi is a traditional IEC technique, keeping people abreast of latest propaganda subjects. People hear but do they listen? Interview with VWU officials at VWU headquarters in Hanoi, October 2008. See also ILO/IPEC, "Project Proposal", *op. cit.*, p. ii.

64. Interviews with VWU officials in various locations at district and village level, Hau Giang province, October 2008.

65. Interviews with members of the Phung Hiep Commune Steering Committee, head teacher and pupils of a commune school, Hau Giang Province, October 2008.

66. Bowen *et al.*, *op. cit.*

67. Indeed, according to the evaluation report of the project, commune leaders believe that community awareness of the risks of exploitation facing migrants has improved. Local people have become more alert to recruiters and have changed their practices when they consider migrating to other provinces or abroad.

68. Michel Foucault, *Discipline and Punish: The Birth of the Prison* (Harmondsworth: Penguin, 1979).

69. VWU, "Goals of the Women's Movement in 2007–2012", 2009, available: <http://www.hoilhpn.org.vn/newsdetail.asp?CatId=78&NewsId=10103&lang=EN> (accessed 5 February 2014).

70. From a 2006 VWU leaflet distributed to local communities, made available to this researcher during a field visit in 2008.

morality."[71] As the VWU president said at the Eighth Congress in 1997, "we preserve the traditional role of women."[72] This is also emphasised in the Vietnamese government's "National Plan of Action" (NPA) against trafficking, where the role of the VWU as leader of the prevention programme is, among other things, to develop "cultural families, healthy communes, streets without social evils."[73]

The emphasis on "healthy communes" is also stressed in the VWU's widely distributed leaflet about trafficking in women and children. In a society that values social cohesion highly, the leaflet reminds us that it is not only individuals but also communities that are affected by trafficking. Accordingly, individuals bear a responsibility to themselves and their communities to be risk aware and to migrate safely. Similarly, communities are responsible for looking out for risks in their midst. This is a culture in which government agencies reward actions for social cohesion, such as the absence of prostitution in a family or dedicated commitment to VWU campaigns, with certificates of commendation that are proudly displayed.[74] In this respect, the role of the VWU, as set out in the NPA, involves "communication and education on laws and policies, tricky practices of traffickers in order to enhance the local people's awareness and vigilance."[75] Indeed, the campaign to prevent the trafficking of women and children through social evils is played out at the level of identity, tradition and culture.

The campaign to prevent the trafficking of women and children in Vietnam promoted by the ILO also promoted the tenets of *safe migration* within the country and across the border. As the ILO argues, it "aims to end trafficking, not migration."[76] The freedom to move, especially for the sake of livelihood, is a fundamental right that the ILO intends to protect "through programming that makes migration safer."[77] Such programming relates to the campaigning for risk-aware behaviour in the migration process carried out by the VWU, for which members of the organisation were trained. The desire to migrate, according to the ILO, becomes a risk factor when the conditions under which people can move freely are not established. For example, the risk of trafficking is high when "legal migration channels are closed, inaccessible, or unknown to the person seeking to move" and they seek out "irregular channels" which are "brokered by recruiters, illegal transporters, unscrupulous employers or other intermediaries."[78] While conditions to move freely remain inadequate,[79] "persons at risk" are to be made aware of "legal and protected migration channels." This reduces the likelihood (read risk) that "they are deceived by recruiters or trafficking brokers."[80] Thus, the ILO was seeking to "normalise" migration in Vietnam.

As the social evils campaign is gradually brought into and formative of the neoliberal regime preventing trafficking in Vietnam, it is transformed into a technical problem. In operating under the logics of social evil and neoliberalism, the VWU

71. ILO/IPEC, "Project Proposal", *op. cit.*, p. 32.

72. As quoted in Nguyen-vo, *op. cit.*, p. 137.

73. Deputy Prime Minister Pham Gia Khiem, *op. cit.*, p. 7.

74. Interview with WVU officials, Hau Giang Province, 10 October 2008.

75. Deputy Prime Minister Pham Gia Khiem, *op. cit.*, p. 4.

76. ILO/IPEC, "Meeting the Challenge: Proven Practices for Human Trafficking Prevention in the Greater Mekong Sub-Region", Mekong Sub-regional Project to Combat Trafficking in Children and Women (Bangkok: ILO/IPEC, 2008).

77. *Ibid.*

78. *Ibid.*, p. 13.

79. *Ibid.*

80. *Ibid.*, p. 20.

rendered governable the women and children targeted as "at risk" persons. Constituted as responsible and risk-aware subjects, the women and children were brought under the control of the global anti-trafficking regime oriented to contain and normalise abnormal migration. The solution to the problem of human trafficking was seen to lie with persons "at risk" themselves. Apart from campaigning to be responsible and risk-aware subjects, targeted populations were trained to cultivate the entrepreneurial spirit, "empowered to take greater control over their lives."[81] The affective constitution of entrepreneurial selves proceeded on the basis of a series of training "modules." "At-risk persons were to *train for life*. The kind of life for which they were trained was the life of an entrepreneur under the dictate of the logic of market.

The type of life skills required were determined "based on local market demand."[82] Vocational training programmes were provided by local training schools and employers. The main types of training offered were dressmaking, hairdressing/beauty, motor repair, animal raising and handicrafts. Under this scheme, for example, a new cottage industry of mat weaving was set up by the VWU in Hoa My commune of Hau Giang, selling to overseas markets they had identified through a similar enterprise in Can Tho city. The group of 30 original trainees had expanded to 60 through trainees transferring skills to others, including adult family members and children working in the home of the trainer.[83]

The "community-based model" to combat human trafficking at the level of communes also involved providing the alternative of receiving credit for household production. New economic opportunities were identified based on market analysis. The training involved included training in income generation, including in rural skills such as farming, animal husbandry and food processing. The provision of credit was carried out through the Bank for Social Policy which handed out loans based on approved business plans. Loans were provided to families with children in the target age range who were considered to be "at risk." The local poverty criteria were used to select and focus on "poor" or "near poor" families. An existing government loan source subsidised by the state as part of its poverty reduction strategy was used. Students were trained by the bank on bank loan regulations and received skills training in technical production skills and business skills. For instance, if a family planned to raise fish, training was provided by local agriculture department staff. Animal husbandry (e.g. cows, pigs, poultry), fish raising and small trade were common income-generating activities.[84] Finally, it included also training and services for "group formation assistance" and small business development and improving access to credit and markets. These activities were intended to increase economic security, which was reasoned as decreasing the pressure for women and children to leave.

"As a result of combined awareness raising, village mobilization, income generation interventions," according to the ILO, "target beneficiaries are now alert to traffickers and the number of 'blind' migrants—those that accept carelessly an offer to leave the village for employment opportunities elsewhere—had

81. ILO/IPEC, "Project Proposal", *op. cit.*, p. ii.
82. *Ibid.*, p. iii.
83. Bowen *et al.*, *op. cit.*, p. 27.
84. *Ibid.*

decreased."[85] Implicit in the bias towards the entrepreneurial woman in "combating human trafficking" is the epistemological grounding of the human subject in the market in which "rational" decision-making behaviour is endorsed. The constitution of self-governing selves does not, however, indicate a transfer of power from the Vietnamese state to the individual. Rather, these Vietnamese women and children are invested in a microphysical field of power-knowledge or governmentality in which they are governed primarily through the logics of risk and the market. This is significantly different from the governance of social evils in which the emphasis is put on an economy of shame and the constitution of moral subjects of femininity.

Gender and Vietnamese National Identity

The centrality of gender in governmental preoccupations is not new of course. Gender has served as an important governmental site for reinventing and strengthening national identity in Vietnam[86] as elsewhere.[87] For example, George Mosse has argued that symbols of masculinity and femininity were used to define and differentiate the ideals of the German and English middle classes in nineteenth-century Europe.[88] Similarly, Partha Chatterjee has examined the invocation of gender opposites in the Indian national struggle in the nineteenth century.[89] Concerning Vietnam, gender has repeatedly provided the governmental terrain on which governors have sought to intervene to steer the cultural norms of the Vietnamese people.[90] In the centuries-long struggle of the Vietnamese against the powerful neighbour China, Ashley Pettus has noted the way the Vietnamese woman functioned as a recurring point of distinction between indigenous Vietnamese customs and the Sino-Confucian state system.[91] A case in point is the famous folktale of the Trung sisters who spectacularly resisted Chinese overlords in the first century AD. Their spirits became "the object of popular cult worship in village temples and festivals throughout the country."[92] In this way, the iterative, performative nature of folklore helps to constitute and foster nationalistic feelings of belonging.

In the 1930s, the rise of the Indochinese Communist Party (ICP) within the anti-colonial factions saw an association between Vietnamese gender and the national cause.[93] The liberation of society from colonial and class oppression by Vietnamese Marxists involved the progressive change in the treatment of women and their legal status, including voting rights, freedom of marriage and divorce and equal pay for

85. ILO/IPEC, "Project Proposal", *op. cit.*, p. i.

86. See, e.g., Ashley Pettus, *Between Sacrifice and Desire: National Identity and the Governing of Femininity in Vietnam*, East Asia History, Politics, Sociology, Culture (London: Routledge, 2003).

87. For a general authoritative critique, see Nira Yuval-Davis, *Gender and Nation* (London, Thousand Oaks, CA, and New Delhi: Sage, 1997).

88. George Mosse, *Nationalism and Sexuality: Respectability and Abnormal Sexuality in Modern Europe* (New York: Howard Fertig, 1997).

89. Partha Chatterjee, *Nationalist Thought and the Colonial World: A Derivative Discourse* (Minneapolis, MN: University of Minnesota Press, 1993).

90. Nguyen-vo, *op. cit.*; Pettus, *op. cit.*

91. Pettus, *op. cit.*, p. 7.

92. *Ibid.*, p. 7.

93. *Ibid.*, p. 8.

equal labour. Yet, although the women's cause was included within the general communist struggle, the notion of female morality tied to traditional Confucian ideals was not given up. Pettus notes that communists were prepared to overrule the strictest traditions such as the "three submissions"—women owed obedience first to their father, then their husbands, then their eldest sons. However, they held on to softer patriarchal codes, commending female endurance, faithfulness, compassion and self-sacrifice for the national cause. During and after Ho Chi Minh's socialist revolution (1941–75), Vietnamese gender categories continued to be used to embody the values of the new socialist society. Pettus observes that Vietnamese women were also used to conjure an image of national progress. By representing women as the embodiment of a set of negative cultural characteristics such as greed, superstition and ignorance that could be overcome through re-education and re-socialisation, an image of development was engineered.[94]

In the recent transition from a socialist to a market economy, the Vietnamese government is again using Vietnamese gender identities to redefine the national idea. Vietnamese gender presents a subject through which the government and society are constituting traditions of the national self in the face of capitalist integration.[95] For example, in her compelling account of the commercialisation of sex in Vietnam's transition period (see below for more details about this), Nguyen-vo Thu-huong has noted the nationalistic rhetoric of Vietnamese men when discussing their pain on seeing Vietnamese women going for foreign clients. Indeed, Nguyen-vo has examined how these nationalistic feelings became attached to "the female body, to its mannerisms, its location in public spaces, and its markings."[96] Yet, while prostitution is countered by the Vietnamese government in the nationalistic policy of social evils, paradoxically, during this transitional period, sex had become a commodity which Vietnamese men use to "establish personal ties facilitating their access to the means of production and exchange."[97] This in turn created a clandestine market for Vietnamese female sex workers, which has been readily met both by the supply of women escaping rural settings and/or poverty and by trafficked women.

Emotions in relation to Vietnamese gender identities have played an important part in generating Vietnamese national identity. Whether it is the sensitivity of Vietnamese men seeing "busloads of Asian businessmen on sex tours in their city" and "young women who accompany foreigners in public in suggestive dress and heavy make-up"[98] or the sensitivity of the Vietnamese female sex worker who works to fulfil her traditional filial duty to support her poor family, as discussed above, Vietnamese gender has been the field around which emotions have circulated, aligning the Vietnamese with the Vietnamese and against the foreigner in the contemporary transition period. According to Ahmed, emotions circulate in concrete and specific ways, mediating "between the psychic and the social, between the individual and the collective." In her view, emotions work by "sticking figures together (adherence), a sticking that creates the very effect of a collective (coherence)."[99] Thus, social relations are created which delineate the body of the nation. It is in this

94. *Ibid.*, p. 9.
95. *Ibid.*, pp. 6–7.
96. Nguyen-vo, *op. cit.*, p. 48.
97. *Ibid.*, p. 3.
98. *Ibid.*, p. 48.
99. Ahmed, *op. cit.*, p. 110.

way that one might understand how the emotional investment of Vietnamese gender matters in the constitution of national identity. Here, the affective practices relating to social evil and to entrepreneurialism at play in regimes of Vietnamese gender in the governance of trafficking in women and children specifically presented a site in which to trace the uneven and contingent ways in which Vietnamese national identity emerges and matters in the current historical conjuncture. Indeed, the hybridisation of Vietnamese femininity in the interplay and convergence of the affective economies of shame and of entrepreneurialism demonstrated here suggests a complex identity emerging in which Vietnam is reconciling local ways with global governmentalities.

Conclusion

Until recently, the Vietnamese government has treated human trafficking as a "social evil" that is rationalised as one of the negative consequences of Vietnam's dramatic transition from a socialist to a market economy, urbanisation and increasing international involvement. This article examined how, in the prevention of trafficking in women and children in Vietnam, the "social evils" campaign converged with a global neoliberal governance logic. Specifically, it focused on one site where this can be seen playing out, namely in the attempt to prevent trafficking in women and children in Hau Giang province in the mid-2000s by the ILO and the VWU. The article drew particular attention to the affective economies at play in the discursive regimes of Vietnamese femininity deployed to prevent the trafficking of women and girls. While the "social evils" campaign cultivated an economy of shame in which young women and girls are discouraged from "shameful" immoral behavior said to put them in danger of trafficking, the neoliberal approach aimed at targeting women and girls "at risk" for self-responsibilisation exercises in which an entrepreneurial desire was cultivated. The article traced the way these affective economies converged in the hybridisation of Vietnamese femininity. The emerging Vietnamese gender categories in turn, the article suggested, can shed light towards understanding contemporary Vietnamese identity. The article thereby complemented a Foucauldian reading of governance with Ahmed's work on the cultural politics of emotions. Yet it must be said that this is a neoliberal intervention that is situated in a particular site and that is informed by cultural and historical particularities that continue to work to reconfirm but also reframe neoliberal technologies of acquisition of wealth, moral propriety and regimes of value.

About the Author

Nadine Voelkner is Assistant Professor in International Relations at the University of Groningen. Her current work revolves around understanding the medicalisation of security. She has published on forced migration, human security and health security as well as on critical security methods.

Index

Page numbers followed by 'n' refer to notes

For Product Safety Concerns and Information please contact our EU representative GPSR@taylorandfrancis.com Taylor & Francis Verlag GmbH, Kaufingerstraße 24, 80331 München, Germany

Batch number: 10726294

Printed by Printforce, the Netherlands